RUDYARD KIPLING

Something of Myself
and Other
Autobiographical
Writings

Rudyard Kipling's autobiography, *Something of Myself*, was his last work, but has not received the serious attention it deserves. Thomas Pinney's edition of the work, supplemented by other autobiographical pieces, is an attempt to change that. Professor Pinney has consulted the available source material relating to *Something of Myself*; constructed an outline of the book's composition; described the history of its publication; established a text and a set of variants; and given a critical account of the book's design and its main themes. His annotations to the work (and to the supplementary pieces) identify references and allusions, and provide a biographical context against which Kipling's selections, omissions, and distortions may be clearly seen. The extent to which Kipling's description of his life failed to match what actually happened in it is extraordinary.

Two of the additional items presented here (Kipling's Indian diary of 1885 and the illustrations he made for his autobiographical story, "Baa Baa, Black Sheep") are previously unpublished. Pinney shows how they, and other forms of autobiographical writing, reflect upon or complicate the narrative of *Something of Myself*. This very full edition will shed new light on Kipling as a man and writer, and will be of interest to readers of his work.

RUDYARD KIPLING

SOMETHING OF MYSELF

AND OTHER

AUTOBIOGRAPHICAL

WRITINGS

EDITED BY

THOMAS PINNEY

The right of the
University of Cambridge
to print and sell
all manner of books
was granted by
Henry VIII in 1534.
The University has printed
and published continuously
since 1584.

CAMBRIDGE UNIVERSITY PRESS

CAMBRIDGE

NEW YORK   PORT CHESTER

MELBOURNE   SYDNEY

Published by the Press Syndicate of the University of Cambridge
The Pitt Building, Trumpington Street, Cambridge CB2 1RP
40 West 20th Street, New York, NY 10011, USA
10 Stamford Road, Oakleigh, Melbourne 3166, Australia

First published 1990

Printed in Great Britain by
the University Press, Cambridge

British Library cataloguing in publication data

Kipling, Rudyard, 1865–1936
[Prose works. Selections] Something of myself
and other autobiographical writings.
I. Title   II. Pinney, Thomas
828'.808

Library of Congress cataloguing in publication data

Kipling, Rudyard, 1865–1936
Rudyard Kipling: something of myself and other
autobiographical writings / edited by Thomas Pinney.
p.   cm.
Bibliography
Includes index.
ISBN 0 521 35515 X
1. Kipling, Rudyard, 1865–1936 – Biography.   2. Authors,
English – 19th century – Biography.   3. Authors, English – 20th
century – Biography.   4. British – India – Biography.   I. Pinney,
Thomas.   II. Title.
PR4856.A37   1990
828'.809 – dc20   89-34311 CIP

ISBN 0 521 35515 X

CONTENTS

ABBREVIATIONS AND
SHORT TITLES

Carrington   Charles Carrington, *Rudyard Kipling: His Life and Work* (London, Macmillan, 1955).

CK diary   extracts from and summaries of Caroline Kipling's diaries, January 10, 1892–January 18, 1936, made by Charles Carrington.

CMG   *Civil and Military Gazette*, Lahore.

Harbord   R.E. Harbord (ed.), *The Readers' Guide to Rudyard Kipling's Work*, 8 vols. (privately printed, Canterbury, Bournemouth, 1961–72).

JLK   in the notes = John Lockwood Kipling (Rudyard's father).

Kipling Papers   papers of Rudyard Kipling and his family, the property of the National Trust, deposited in the University of Sussex Library.

RK   in the notes = Rudyard Kipling.

USC   in the notes = the United Services College, Westward Ho!, North Devon.

NOTE: references to Kipling's prose writings are, unless otherwise specified, to the Uniform Edition published by Macmillan; verse, unless otherwise specified, is cited from *Rudyard Kipling's Verse: Definitive Edition*, published by Hodder and Stoughton.

INTRODUCTION

The first reaction to Kipling's autobiography was summed up by one wit among the reviewers, who said that it was not in fact *Something of Myself* but *Hardly Anything of Myself*. He might have gone on to say that not only was it thin on the facts of Kipling's life, it often had them wrong as well. One would suppose that these two striking characteristics of the book, its incompleteness and its unreliability, would be fatal to its appeal as an autobiography, yet that is not so: the book is a highly characteristic example of a fully formed literary master's work – it is, in fact, Kipling's final work – and it has all the artistic interest inseparable from that fact. And, within the limits of its carefully determined reticence, it provides a fascinating view of a remarkable life.

With such a book, however, an editor has the opportunity to be particularly useful to the reader: he can correct details that have gone wrong; he can supplement passages that fail to provide a full account; and, most important, he can provide a background against which the selection, emphasis, lighting, and colors of Kipling's self-portrait can be better understood. I have tried to make myself useful in these ways in producing this edition.

Something of Myself was not Kipling's only autobiographical writing; much of his fiction has strong autobiographical elements in it – *Stalky & Co.*, for instance – and many of his articles, essays, and speeches are partly or largely autobiographical. From the large store of such material I have chosen three published titles and an unpublished diary to supplement the narrative of *Something of Myself*, items chosen with reasonable confidence that they can be called autobiographical. One of them, "Baa Baa, Black Sheep," is fiction, and therefore vulnerable to the argument that it cannot be trusted since it need pay no attention to the record. I admit the force of the argument but include the story anyway, on the grounds that it seems quite close to what we know about Kipling's experience from other sources.* I have not, however, chosen to use such an item as the first chapter of *The Light That Failed*. It is evidently drawn from Kipling's experiences at Southsea and with Flo Garrard. But those experiences seem already to have been reworked according to the needs of the book that Kipling is writing and thus to have become something other than parts of his life story. This is not an easy distinction to maintain, admittedly. If one attends to all the voices of Kipling's experience in his works, then hundreds of essays, speeches, poems, newspaper sketches, and stories clamor for attention as having something to add to "autobiography." It is necessary to draw some sort of line, even if the line cannot be drawn by neat theoretical rule. I have also been forced to exclude a number of eligible items simply for reasons of space: I particularly regret "Home," "Quo Fata Vocant," and "Souvenirs of France."

The four items chosen to supplement *Something of Myself* were all written within a decade of each other and all come from Kipling's early years. In many ways, then, they offer a contrast in tone and feeling to the swan song of *Something of Myself*. I have given something of the circumstances of these supplementary items in an introductory note to each of them and have annotated them on the same principles as those applied to the annotation of *Something of Myself*, explained below on pp. xxxiv–xxxv.

I

The first thing that a reader of *Something of Myself* needs to have in mind is an outline of Kipling's life. No full outline can be constructed from the book itself, yet without it one can form no very clear idea of Kipling's selections and ruthless omissions.

---

* For a skeptical discussion of "Baa Baa, Black Sheep" as autobiography, see C.E. Carrington, "'Baa, Baa, Black Sheep' – Fact or Fiction?" *Kipling Journal*, June 1972, pp. 7–19.

Rudyard Kipling was born in Bombay on December 30, 1865, the first-born child of his parents, who had gone out to India earlier that year. His father, John Lockwood Kipling, was the professor of architectural sculpture at the government-sponsored School of Art in Bombay; his mother, Alice Macdonald Kipling, was, like her husband, the child of a Methodist minister in England, and one of four sisters who are now remembered for their marriages to remarkable men or for their remarkable children or both. One sister married Sir Edward Poynter, a notable painter in his day, whose professional success was crowned when he was made president of the Royal Academy. Another sister married a prosperous iron-founder named Baldwin and became the mother of Stanley Baldwin, prime minister of England. A third sister married Sir Edward Burne-Jones, the great painter who sustained to the end of the nineteenth century the Pre-Raphaelite vision.

This cluster of distinguished aunts and uncles in England could do little to deflect the suffering that was Kipling's lot when, according to the strict and terrible rule of the English living in India, he was sent back to England to receive his education. The separation from his parents took place in 1871, when Kipling was not yet six. With his sister Alice (always called Trix), two years younger than he, Kipling was placed by his parents with a woman quite unknown to them who advertised her services as a foster parent to such children as Rudyard and Trix. Her name was Holloway, and she lived in Southsea, a district of Portsmouth. With her, the Kipling children spent five and a half years.

There is no evidence that Mrs. Holloway was anything but conscientious in the discharge of her stated duty to the children; unluckily, she and the young Rudyard were spiritual opposites, and for him these years were an almost unremitting experience of hell. Elements of his ordeal under Mrs. Holloway appear in *The Light That Failed*, and, more directly, in the story called "Baa Baa, Black Sheep." Before the appearance of *Something of Myself*, however, no one besides Kipling's wife and his sister knew that the sufferings of Dick Heldar and of Punch were drawn from the personal experience of their creator. The laconic pages of *Something of Myself* devoted to "the House of Desolation" are among the most vivid in the whole book: the experiences they evoke, ever since the book was published and revealed the story, have seemed to Kipling's biographers to make the crisis of his life, however that crisis may be interpreted. His relation to himself and others was, some have held, determined by the experience of these years: a mistrust of his own impulses, an unacknowledged sense of maternal betrayal, a desperate anxiety lest the things that he cherished be taken from him, have all been discovered in his life and work, and have all been traced to the years he suffered in the House of Desolation.

Early in 1878 Kipling was sent to an unpretentious public school called the United Services College at Westward Ho!, North Devon. The school had been founded by Indian Army officers not many years before to provide an education that they could afford for their sons; most of the pupils expected to enter the army, and those who did not were still likely to have India in view. The headmaster was a friend of the Kipling family named Cormell Price. If the Kipling–Holloway combination had been bad chemistry, the Kipling–Price combination worked beautifully. Kipling liked, admired, and re-spected Price; with his confidence in Price to sustain him, he man-aged to enjoy his school years. Perhaps not many famous English authors have done so, and that Kipling did is all the more testimony to the virtues of Cormell Price, for the school was without tradition, without money, without many amenities, and quite unable to attract students apart from the narrow clientele for which it had been invented.

While still a schoolboy, Kipling met and fell in love with a girl named Florence Violet Garrard. The attraction on his side was powerful and long-lasting; on her side, languid at best. Kipling regarded himself as engaged to her, but she seems never to have thought herself committed in any way. The relationship came to nothing, but it left its marks on Kipling. When, after nearly a decade of separation, he met Flo again by chance, he was at once over-whelmed by violent and confused emotion; he renewed his pursuit of her, and was again put off. However the long-term effects of this experience may be assessed, it was no light thing in Kipling's life. Nothing is said of the affair in *Something of Myself*.

From school Kipling went directly to India. His father had left

Bombay in 1875 to become head of the new School of Art in Lahore and curator of the Lahore Museum. He found a job for his son on the small English newspaper catering for the English establishment in the Punjab, the *Civil and Military Gazette*, published in Lahore. In his Indian years, which ran from the end of 1882 to the beginning of 1889, Kipling performed his apprenticeship to life and art. He saw the Empire at work in all of its directions and at all levels – from the viceroy high in the hills of Simla to the telegraph clerk in some remote *mofussil* station at the end of the line down on the plains. He paid special attention to the enlisted men of the army. He observed the routines, the amusements, the peccadilloes of the civil establishment. He did all this, and more, as a hard-working journalist, able to report a criminal trial, write a ponderous summary of affairs of state, paste up a front page, fill a vacant space with verse to measure, set type if needed, deal with outraged readers, and anything else that might be wanted on a paper of which he formed half the editorial staff. "Apprenticeship" is too mild a word. In *Something of Myself* Kipling calls his Indian years "Seven Years' Hard" – a term of penal servitude. And when one adds to the rigors of his job the burdens of Lahore's notorious heat, the constant threat of debilitating or fatal illness, the isolation of English life in India, and the meagerness of social opportunity, the phrase may not seem exaggerated.

Beginning about 1886, with the publication of *Departmental Ditties*, Kipling began to make a name for himself among the English community in India as an original and amusing writer, a better writer, in fact, than anyone who had ventured before to represent the English to themselves in that country. At the end of 1887 he was transferred to a larger and more prestigious paper, the *Pioneer* of Allahabad. Here he was given free rein to exercise his descriptive and narrative talents, and work poured out from his pen. It was in the little more than a year of his stay in Allahabad that he wrote and published *Soldiers Three*, *In Black and White*, *The Phantom 'Rickshaw*, *The Story of the Gadsbys*, *Wee Willie Winkie*, and the stories later gathered in *The Smith Administration*, *The City of Dreadful Night*, and *Letters of Marque*.

In Allahabad he met the third woman of importance in his life (after his mother and Flo Garrard), an American named Edmonia

Hill. She was the wife of an English scientist employed by the government, but the fact that she was married did not prevent Kipling from making Mrs. Hill his intimate confidante: to her he poured out his hopes, ambitions, plans, frustrations, defeats; to her he submitted his stories for judgment, and his emotional life for sympathy. For a time Kipling was a lodger in the Hills' house in Allahabad, and there he wrote a number of his Indian stories under her gaze and with her response as a stimulus to creation.

When Kipling determined, as was inevitable, to return to England and try his fortune in the literary markets of London, Mr. and Mrs. Hill agreed to accompany him. They would travel by way of China and Japan, then cross the United States. The trip began early in 1889; Kipling and the Hills parted in San Francisco, they to visit her parents in Pennsylvania and he to travel the west, writing descriptive letters to the *Pioneer*. He rejoined the Hills in Pennsylvania and then accompanied Mrs. Hill and her sister on the Atlantic voyage to London: Mr. Hill had already gone ahead on his return to India. When, at last, Mrs. Hill was to leave England for India, Kipling was desperately miserable. In a curiously perverse gesture, he engaged himself to Mrs. Hill's sister: if he could not have the true object of his affections, then a surrogate would have to do. The engagement quickly broke down, but that he could have entered into it at all throws a somewhat lurid light on Kipling and his emotional necessities. The episode would be echoed only a little later in the circumstances of his marriage.

For two full years – 1888–89 – two years of unbroken production and rising success, Kipling had worked, played, and dreamed in the presence of Edmonia Hill, or in the thought of her through every absence. If any woman could be called the muse of the young poet, she was that woman. Like Flo Garrard, she receives no mention whatever in *Something of Myself*.

Despite the confusion of his personal life, Kipling's professional life in London was a sensational triumph. He arrived there in obscurity late in 1889; within weeks his name was known everywhere. Thus began a marvellous decade, in which Kipling's output was matched only by the constant increase of his fame. He had already written with prodigal rapidity the Indian stories collected in the series running from *Soldiers Three* to *Wee Willie Winkie*; to these were now added *The Light That Failed, Life's Handicap, Many Inventions, The Jungle Book, The Seven Seas, "Captains Courageous," The Day's Work, Stalky & Co.*, and *Kim*.

Early in the course of these triumphs, Kipling had met a young American named Wolcott Balestier, a sometime author who was in London representing an American publisher of dubious repute. So greatly was Kipling taken by Balestier that he agreed not only to put his American publishing arrangements in Balestier's hands, he undertook a literary collaboration with him – a thing he had never done before and never did again* (the book that they produced, *The Naulahka: A Story of East and West*, 1892, has never stood high in the tale of Kipling's books, but it is full of curious interest). When Balestier died suddenly of typhoid at the end of 1891, while Kipling was on a round-the-world tour, Kipling broke off his plans, hastened back to London, procured a special license, and, little more than a month from Balestier's death, married his sister. One thinks irresistibly of his getting engaged to Mrs. Hill's sister as a response to Mrs. Hill's leaving him; now, Wolcott was gone, he would marry the sister. And he did.

By this point in the outline of Kipling's life, the reader will be able to guess that Wolcott Balestier, like Flo Garrard and Mrs. Hill, receives no mention at all in *Something of Myself*. Kipling's wife, Wolcott's sister, Caroline Balestier, fares hardly better. She is never mentioned by name in *Something of Myself*, and the name Balestier figures only once, casually and indirectly, in the book (p. 66). Of the origin and character of their courtship there is not one word. That history remains almost wholly unknown still.

Following his marriage Kipling settled in the United States, building a house near Brattleboro, Vermont, where the Balestier family was living. His daughters Josephine and Elsie were born there, and Kipling worked steadily and well during the four years of his Vermont residence. It came to an end in a distressing and humiliating way. Mrs. Kipling quarrelled with her brother Beatty Balestier; the quarrel inevitably drew Kipling in, and the upshot

* Except for his work with C.R.L. Fletcher on *A School History of England*, a much more restricted collaboration.

was a sharp encounter between the brothers-in-law, a threat of physical violence on Beatty's part, and a court case brought by Kipling in order to restrain Beatty. The hearing gave the papers a field day. Kipling, horrified by what had happened and by the resultant publicity, did not wait for the trial to come on; he left with his young family for England, never to return to the United States, with but one, fatal exception. Nothing of this violent and destructive turn in Kipling's life appears in *Something of Myself*.

Back in England, Kipling settled briefly on the coast of Devon near Torquay and then in the village of Rottingdean, on the Sussex coast. Here his son John was born in 1897. Early in 1899 Kipling took his family back across the Atlantic on a visit to New York. There, after a stormy winter crossing, first the children, then Kipling, fell ill in their New York hotel. Pneumonia developed, and for some days Kipling lay on the edge of death. As they had on the very different occasion of Kipling's family quarrel in 1896, the American papers had a field day with Kipling's illness and recovery. It was front-page news throughout the country, the object of an unwholesome excitement over the drama of a "great writer's" struggle with death. When Kipling at last pulled through, it was to be told that his beloved first-born, Josephine, had died of the illness that had spared him. The experience was so bitter that Kipling could never bring himself to revisit the United States, despite many invitations and many opportunities. He had evidently had some idea of reconciliation in making the trip in the first place; the disastrous outcome fixed in him a settled dislike for the United States, a dislike sometimes passing into contempt for the country's foolishness, sometimes warming into anger at its barbarities. Of this nightmare journey back to the country where he had once lived and worked in flourishing confidence there is no word in *Something of Myself*, save one passing reference to his illness in New York (p. 30). Josephine is not named, though her birth is noted (p. 68).

Kipling, whose restless life seemed to be that of a man who belonged to no particular country, nevertheless needed a place – or an idea that he could project upon a place – to which he could be loyal. The decisive end to his tentative affair with the United States was followed by a protracted and finally unsatisfactory affair with

South Africa. He went there first with his family early in 1898. He returned, after the catastrophe of his illness and Josephine's death, at the beginning of 1900, officially because the doctors told him that he could no longer spend winters in England after the damage done to his lungs by pneumonia. Unconsciously, he was looking for a new land to which he could transfer his affections and his hopes for redeeming action.

The Boer War had just begun, and Kipling plunged with excitement into the conflict of words, ideas, and visions that accompanied the fighting. He committed himself unreservedly to the side of his friends, Cecil Rhodes and Dr. Leander Starr Jameson, Rhodes's lieutenant. South Africa was to be a British dominion; the Dutch were to be subdued, then transformed; the limitless possibilities of the splendid country were to be realized by the unmatched abilities of the English colonist. And so on. It is at this point in his career that Kipling's political enthusiasms, and his political hatreds, begin to crowd into his work. He spent the winters of every year from 1900 through 1908 at the Woolsack, the attractive little house that Rhodes had built for him outside Cape Town, and he produced much work there. Most of these stories and poems are more overtly "imperialist" than anything that he did before or after, and not many of them have been regarded as among his best work. That they had passion behind them, however, cannot be doubted.

During these years, from the turn of the century down to the First World War, the love affair between Kipling and his public came to an end. He had grown all too audible as a political voice. He wrote insultingly about his political enemies, and they were surprisingly many. His art seemed to grow obscure and harsh as his political passions intensified. Kipling was caricatured by the press; worse, people began to grow bored by his criticizing and his exhorting both.

For Kipling himself, the South African episode ended in disillusion, leaving the taste of dust and ashes. The war against the Boers had been won; but the victory was then, as Kipling saw it, betrayed by the Liberals in England. Coming to power in a landslide electoral triumph in 1906, they proceeded rapidly and systematically to undo all that had been done before: the Boers were returned to political power; the great Imperialists, Milner and Jameson, were discredited or subverted; Rhodes's scheme of dominion was destroyed by visionless men who knew not what they did. In Kipling's imagination, the giants had been overcome by a swarm of mean-spirited dwarfs. Kipling left South Africa in 1908, never to return. It was all a disappointment from which he never fully recovered. His view of the world from this period on is marked by a tendency to see conspiracy and betrayal everywhere in public life. The experiences of the child in the House of Desolation were now repeated on a larger scene for the man.

In 1902 Kipling and his wife bought a house called "Bateman's" in East Sussex, near the village of Burwash. The house, built of stone in 1634 by a local iron master, was Kipling's residence for the rest of his days. He took up Sussex as another adopted country, enthusiastically informing himself of its history and antiquities, using its lore in stories and poems, and constructing a private mythology of Sussex values and Sussex meanings. Yet he was curiously aloof from the actual Sussex around him. He was personally remote from the villagers, and he accepted very few of the civic responsibilities that might have gone with his long residence and his status.

The First World War, when it came, was at first a sort of relief for Kipling. He had long prophesied it; Germany's rivalry with England had been an obsessive anxiety for Kipling since the Boer War, and a part of him at least was eager to see the question brought to trial. He urged his son John into the fray, using his influence to obtain a commission for the boy in the Irish Guards. John went out to France in 1915 – he was barely past his eighteenth birthday – and disappeared in one of the minor engagements associated with the Battle of Loos. Perhaps he was annihilated by a shell or buried in an explosion: no one knows. John's is one of the many thousand names on the pathetic memorial to the missing dead at Dud Corner, in northern France, a memorial that Kipling helped dedicate after the war, when he devoted himself to the work of the War Graves Commission. Nothing of this appears in *Something of Myself*. John is named when his birth is mentioned (p. 80); but the pathos of his father's remark on that birth – that it occurred "under what seemed every good omen" – would go undetected by a reader who knows only what Kipling chooses to tell in *Something of Myself*.

As the war dragged on, and the appalling tale of casualties mounted, Kipling came to see quite clearly what unrelieved horror modern war had become. If he had, once, thought too lightly of war's miseries and too highly of its glamor, that was all changed now: there was no glamor. But he never doubted that the Germans – the Huns, as he insisted on calling them always – had to be defeated and must be made to pay for their transgression. To the sense created in Kipling by the Boer War that power was used to conspire and betray was now added the sense that power could be in the hands of highly civilized barbarians: the Huns.

The settlement of Versailles was, of course, in Kipling's view another work of betrayal, mocking the sacrifices of the Allies. To the end of his life, Kipling's view of public affairs seemed to alternate between the equally ugly convictions that things were being run by venal traitors or by sub-human savages. It must be candidly acknowledged that this grim sense of things is strongly stamped upon *Something of Myself*. As a view of things from the vantage point of 1935, it was not wholly imaginary. But these unlovely ideas color all of Kipling's backward view when politics are his subject.

Late in 1915, only a few days before his son John was reported missing, Kipling was diagnosed as having "gastritis." This announced the onset of the illness that eventually killed him, and that gave him, in the next twenty years, an overflowing measure of disabling pain, anxiety, depression, and general wretchedness. The record of his wife's diary gives an account of suffering so frequent, so intense, and so baffling as to make one wonder how Kipling continued to function, as he somehow managed to do. "Sick and miserable"; "wretched with pain"; "constant spasms of pain"; "a dreadful night of pain"; such are the refrains that run through all these years in the diary account. Kipling was operated on in 1922, and he underwent innumerable examinations and treatments both before and after that date. Not until 1933 was a duodenal ulcer diagnosed; by that time, Kipling had only three more years to live. He would die from the hemorrhage the ulcer at last produced. This prolonged and intense suffering of course receives no mention in *Something of Myself*, though for the last twenty years of his life it must have been the chief fact in Kipling's daily awareness.

The narrative of *Something of Myself* scarcely proceeds beyond the move to Bateman's in 1902 and to the writing of such books as *Puck of Pook's Hill*, before the catastrophe of the war. Whether Kipling meant to carry it any further no one can say now; but if he had, given his studied avoidance of all merely personal revelation, he would not perhaps have had much to tell. Kipling's life after the war was, to all external view, reduced to his routine at Bateman's, varied by frequent trips to London on the work of the War Graves Commission, the Rhodes Trust, and other duties. He was also a regular traveller to the continent, mainly to France. France now became the last and least disappointing of Kipling's countries of the mind. He was constant in his praise of the French; he had real pleasure in being among them; and he rejoiced in the recognition they gave him both as an artist – "le grand Rutyar'" – and as a stout supporter of the French against the Germans. He continued to devote himself to writing and to developing his art. He died on January 18, 1936.

II

The occasion of Kipling's deciding to write *Something of Myself* can only be guessed at. He began it on August 1, 1935, at Bateman's, when he had scarcely six months to live. Perhaps a general sense of the approaching end is all one needs to suppose as a sufficient motive. Our evidence of the book's progress is almost wholly derived from his wife's diary, and is meager enough. When he began, Mrs. Kipling recorded that the autobiography was to deal with "his life from the point of view of his work" – an interesting statement of limitation at the outset. Kipling wrote steadily at the book for a fortnight, and then revised what he had done. He took the manuscript with him on a trip to Paris and Marienbad at the end of August, and after his return continued to work on it all through September. On October 1, an installment of the book was given to Kipling's secretary to be typed. Work continued in October, and he is reported as "revising" it on the 21st of that month. After continuing to work on the book through November, he broke off on December 2. He then resumed it in mid-month, when he is reported as revising the typescript (December 16). The last day on which he is reported as working on the autobiography is December 26, 1935, four days from his seventieth birthday. In January he died.

When Kipling died, then, he had been at work on *Something of Myself* for a period of not more than five months and a few days, and with many interruptions during that time. For a writer so fastidious as Kipling, who was more deeply committed to the arts of compression than to those of expansion, a narrative of such length composed in so short a time could be regarded only as, at best, a draft of his intentions. Yet what he left must have been distinct enough to persuade Mrs. Kipling, always fierce in the defense of her husband's reputation, that it was close enough to what he had meant to do. At any rate, on some unknown date in 1936 she began to prepare *Something of Myself* for publication. A contract for the book was signed on October 22, 1936. A typed copy of the manuscript was sent to Macmillan, the publisher, on November 26; Mrs. Kipling returned corrected proofs to Macmillan on December 21; and the book was published on February 16, 1937. Before publication, selections totalling about a third of the book ran serially in the *Morning Post*, the *New York Times*, the *Sydney Mail*, and the *Civil and Military Gazette* of Lahore in January and February 1937.

We learn a little about Mrs. Kipling's editorial practices from two sources: the correspondence, now in the British Library, between Kipling's agents, the firm of A.P. Watt, and the publisher, Macmillan; and the correspondence between Mrs. Kipling and H.A. Gwynne, the editor of the *Morning Post*, now in the Stewart Collection at Dalhousie University. Gwynne was an old friend of Kipling's, and it is evident that Mrs. Kipling relied on him especially in settling many editorial decisions. "No-one," she wrote to Gwynne on October 20, 1936, "loved him [Kipling] better or longer than you or has a more thorough understanding of him from the literary side." Gwynne did the work of making the extracts from the MS to be serialized, and in connection with this he had a chance to see and to discuss with Mrs. Kipling the actual text that Kipling had left behind.

From the Watt and Gwynne correspondences we learn that Mrs. Kipling corrected the proofs for the text of both the newspaper serialization and the book; that she supplied many corrections of detail, including some made after publication; that she sometimes altered or cut out passages; and that she selected the illustrations for the book. What we do not learn is the condition and character of the manuscript that she had to work from, nor whether she made any extensive cuts. If the manuscript survives, its whereabouts are unknown. The corrected proofs were returned to Mrs. Kipling, and it is more than likely that she then destroyed them. All that can be safely surmised is that she had the manuscript before her, and one or more typescript versions containing some correction and revision by Kipling himself.

The letters that passsed between Mrs. Kipling and Gwynne in October and November 1936, when she was working with him on the preparation of the text for newspaper serialization, contain some interesting evidence of her editorial practice. One of her guiding principles was to present Kipling in a way to avoid offense and controversy. Thus she writes on November 3, 1936:

> On page 5 [of the galley proofs for the *Morning Post*] I think I would like you to omit the words I have omitted and substitute those I have marked on the margin. I think the thing as it stands is too offensive, if it is not libellous, and I don't, above all things, want to have that kind of criticism of the Autobiography. I don't, in fact, want anything that people can ride off and dispute about.

Obviously, this rule would justify much omission; how often Mrs. Kipling may have applied it cannot now be known.

Another principle is stated in a letter of November 5, 1936, as she thanks Gwynne for his labor in cutting the text down for the purpose of serialization:

> It has been a terrific job for you, and for me something quite intolerable. This thinking back into the past is not an easy matter for me. I want to be wise and I want to remember everything that he said to me about the Autobiography, and I chiefly want to remember what he meant to change in another and later draft.

This, too, since it privileges merely prospective notions about the book – what Kipling might have done – would seem to authorize considerable changes; but, again, if such changes were made, we have no way to recognize them. Whatever was actually done, it is clear that in principle at least Mrs. Kipling in her role as editor did not feel bound to take her husband's words as she found them.

Mrs. Kipling had long experience of dealing with manuscripts and proofs, and there is every reason to think that in handling the details of copy she did a careful and capable job. She did not, however, appear to make much effort to check the factual details of her husband's narrative. As a result, the book as published contains a good many mistakes about times, places, and names. Once it had appeared, she began to receive notes of correction from various sources, and these – or some of these, at any rate – she undertook to incorporate into subsequent printings. There is only one edition of *Something of Myself*, but the differences in detail between the text of the first printing and the text printed in the Outward Bound and Sussex Editions in 1937 and 1938 – the last texts that Mrs. Kipling is likely to have had anything to do with – are quite considerable.

All of the changes that I have detected have been noted in this edition. Some are trivial, such as the correction of *Katzikopfs* to *Katzekopfs* (p. 7). Others are more substantial: Kipling's attribution of a poem to Wordsworth is corrected to Scott (p. 7); and his "friend Captain Bagley" is re-identified as "my friend Captain E.H. Bayly" (p. 86). In one case, Kipling's account of his meeting with Sir Edward Grey, the passage was found to be so incorrect that most of it was simply omitted in reprinting. It is highly probable that all of these changes in the published text were made only after Mrs. Kipling had seen and approved them. One may add that not every correction that she sent to the publisher was actually made. The statement that Kipling went to Canada in 1906 (p. 115) she corrected to 1907 in a note to the publisher in November 1936; at the same time, she changed Kipling's reference to the Duke of Northumberland (p. 125) to Earl Percy (MS, Dalhousie University). For some reason neither correction was made, and the mis-statements are to be found in all printings of the book.

III

We can never be sure, when we are speaking of the things "left out" of *Something of Myself*, whether they were left out by Kipling himself or were quietly omitted by Mrs. Kipling, the editor. Nor, even supposing that an omission in any given instance was Kipling's, can we be sure that he would not have supplied it in revision. We are dealing with a text at several removes from what may be imagined as its author's final intention: it had not been finished;* it had not been revised as Kipling surely would have revised it – that is, not once, but repeatedly and over a long time; and it had to pass through the hands of an editor, an editor who certainly had privileged information, but who had also the handicap of an intense personal interest in the story that Kipling had to tell.

The very structure of the book tells us pretty clearly, however, that Kipling's main object was to give special prominence to the first half of his life: childhood; India; early success; Vermont; South Africa; Bateman's – these are the organizing divisions of the narrative, which ranges beyond their limits only incidentally. Within those limits, as has already been said, Kipling (or the published book) omits almost everything in the way of personal crisis after the years of childhood: there is nothing of Flo Garrard, or of Mrs. Hill, of his courtship, of his illnesses and breakdowns, of his quarrels, or the afflicting deaths of friends, parents, children, to speak only of the merely factual omissions. The omission to describe his interior life is even more obvious. Yet the suffering of his childhood in the House of Desolation, and the labor of his Seven Years' Hard in India are both brought out clearly; these two parts of his life are made more prominent than any other, while the Kipling of the middle and late years hardly exists as a subject in the pages of *Something of Myself*. Kipling's self-presentation thus rather oddly confirms the distortion in the popular idea of his life and work: that the more interesting part of both was complete by the turn of the century, more or less.

The older Kipling, if not much of his story is told, is nonetheless

---

* It is arguable, however, that the book belongs to the class of "complete fragments," of which Coleridge's "Kubla Khan" and Macaulay's *History of England* are distinguished instances.

present everywhere in the book as a narrative voice, the personality that sees and judges. Some aspects of that personality are distinctly unattractive. It is often querulous, given to saying ill-tempered things about the English ("the inhabitants of that country never looked further than their annual seaside resorts"); or about radical politics ("pernicious varieties of safe sedition"); or about publishers ("one cannot get ahead of gentlemen of sound commercial instincts"). He can be unfairly contemptuous, as he is towards Emily Hobhouse, the self-sacrificing humanitarian, or stubbornly and sweepingly hostile, as he is towards the Irish ("their instincts of secrecy, plunder, and anonymous denunciation") or the Americans ("frank, brutal decivilisation"). About Americans he had to admit some concessions and qualifications. He had, after all, taken great interest in his life in the United States. At one point he speaks of his more than four years in Vermont as an "unreal life, indoors and out" (p. 78), a perplexing enough judgment, but perhaps indicating Kipling's recognition that not *everything* in his American experience could be subsumed under "frank, brutal decivilisation."

There are other unattractive things evident in *Something of Myself* that we must take as belonging to the personality expressed in the book. Anti-Semitism shows up in Kipling's remarks about "Israel" and its vocation to "abet disorder," and there is a distinct lack of charity in such incidental remarks as that on Oscar Wilde – "the suburban Toilet-Club school favoured by the late Mr. Oscar Wilde" (p. 128: and what does "Toilet-Club" mean?). Frequently Kipling writes as though the world were largely made up of knaves. An exemplary instance is his account of the turn-about that the *Civil and Military Gazette* made over the Ilbert Bill when Kipling was a very young and, he says, a very naive newspaperman. After strongly opposing the Bill for a time, the *CMG* changes its tune. Kipling wants to know why, but is put off with "none of your dam' business." When he goes that night to the Club, he is, to his bewildered astonishment, hissed by everyone at the table: "Your dam' rag has ratted over the Bill." Then, he says, he put two and two together: his proprietors had sold out for a price. "A few months later one of my two chief proprietors received the decoration that made him a Knight." And others were being paid for their betrayal too: "certain

smooth Civilians" who had "seen good in the Government measure" were somehow "shifted out of the heat to billets in Simla" (pp.
31–32).

It is impossible now to know anything about the "smooth Civilians," but Kipling's insinuation about his proprietors is false. James
Walker and George Allen, the two chief proprietors, did in fact
receive knighthoods, but not until long after the affair of the Ilbert
Bill in 1883 (Allen was knighted in 1897; Walker in 1903). Kipling
must have known that neither Allen nor Walker had been knighted
during his Indian years. He must also have known that the Ilbert
Bill, as finally passed, had been gutted: the provision that had raised
all the fuss among the English in India in the first place was given up,
after which there was nothing to object to. But Kipling says nothing
of this. He chooses instead to tell the story of the Ilbert Bill affair in
such a way as to make one of his proprietors, at least, seem certainly
to have bargained for honors at the cost of his principles. Since
Kipling's re-arrangement of the facts has the effect of "revealing" a
conspiracy, it must have satisfied a grim and somewhat perverse
wish on his part to discover such things. This is not, perhaps,
surprising in a man writing at the end of a life that had been devoted
to so many causes by then defeated or discredited, but it is not
attractive.

In matters merely personal he shows a comparable tendency to
prefer to see conspiracy or active malice at work when things go
wrong, rather than accident, or incompetence, or any of the abun-
dant other reasons for disappointment in an imperfect world. So, in
the comic episode of *The Times* and its publishing the bogus Kipling
poem called "The Old Volunteer," Kipling is unable to take it as the
sort of innocent prank that literary jokesters are always trying to pull
off: to put over a fake in the name of a famous author on the editors of
a prestigious paper. It is hard to see that any more insidious motive
was at work behind "The Old Volunteer." Yet Kipling is determined to see it as a work of malice, and, moreover, of Jewish malice:
so he combines paranoia with anti-Semitism in this instance.

These signs of hostility and mistrust are expressed in another way:
his combative defensiveness of his private life. His private life was
emphatically *his* private life, not to be known by or shared in by

anyone who had not been invited. This is certainly a reasonable and dignified position. But any effort to step over the line that he drew around himself always provoked a furious agitation and deep distress in Kipling, as though not an indecorum merely but a real aggression were threatened against him. His outburst against the reporters of Boston, briefly alluded to on p. 67, is an instance: and that goes back to the very early days of his fame. It is not to be expected that in writing an autobiography – even one restricted, as the sub-title says, to "My Friends Known and Unknown" – he could overcome something so deeply laid in his character.

Indeed, a part of the method of *Something of Myself* is not just concealment and omission but repeated reminders to the reader that only certain kinds of things are to be talked of. The notification begins with the title – only *Something* of myself is in question* – and is continued in most of the chapter titles: not his domestic life but "The Very-Own House"; not the inner history of his books, but "Working-Tools." The most striking and oblique of these titles are "The Interregnum" and "The Committee of Ways and Means." The first of these covers the little more than two years between Kipling's return to England at the end of 1889 and his marriage at the beginning of 1892. These were the years of exciting and rapid fulfillment, when all the energies and abilities laboriously developed during the Seven Years' Hard in India were suddenly released on an international public. Most men, in looking back on such a period and trying to find a name for it, would surely invent something positive. Not Kipling; it was merely an "interregnum." But between whose reigns? That of Caroline, his wife, at one end, clearly enough; but whose was the first? his mother's? Mrs. Hill's? his Indian employers'? However we answer that question, we are left with Kipling's judgment that the brilliant years of his first fame were not a fruition, or a harvest, or a conquest, but only a time without a ruler and without a dynastic name.

An even more extravagant reduction and concealment of things is

* According to Lord Birkenhead, the title was given to the book by Lord Webb-Johnson after RK's death; Birkenhead also states that Webb-Johnson "edited" the book (*Rudyard Kipling*, New York, 1978, p. 353). I have no evidence on these points beyond Birkenhead's statement.

accomplished by the phrase "The Committee of Ways and Means." This, it develops, is Kipling's image for his marriage, and it arises from the young husband and wife's coping with their experience on honeymoon in Japan, when their bank fails and they are left stranded and nearly penniless in a far country. As a metaphor for marriage in its sense of a partnership against the world, it is by no means a bad one. But what a message of invincible reticence Kipling sends to his readers in such a figure!

One can hardly overlook the distortions, the reticences, the bad-tempered parts of *Something of Myself*, since they lie so obviously in the way of the reader. They have their value as contributing to the portrait of Kipling, but they are not what make the book worth reading. It is time now to turn to some of the things that do. One of the first is the descriptive mastery that was always Kipling's and is found in this, his last work, in fully matured form. Scenes, gestures, impressions are rendered in a way that combines the utmost vivid-ness with the utmost economy; the book is so rich in moments of this sort that one can choose only by a *sortes kiplingianae*. Open the book to p. 61, and there discover General Booth of the Salvation Army, glimpsed on the pier of the remotest southern port of New Zealand:

> I saw him walking backward in the dusk over the uneven wharf, his cloak blown upwards, tulip-fashion, over his grey head, while he beat a tambourine in the face of the singing, weeping, praying crowd who had come to see him off.

Open again to p. 94, to the description of the wide country north of Bloemfontein, in the Orange Free State, where Kipling saw, for the first and only time, a live battle take place, in "a vacant world full of sunshine and distances, where now and again a single bullet sang to himself."

> Then to the left, almost under us, a small piece of hanging woodland filled and fumed with our shrapnel much as a man's moustache fills with cigarette-smoke. It was most impressive and lasted for quite twenty minutes. Then silence; then a movement of men and horses from our side up the slope, and the hangar our guns had been hammering spat steady fire at them. More Boer ponies on more skylines; a last flurry of pom-poms on the right and a little frieze of far-off meek-tailed ponies, already out of rifle range.

The selection and ordering of detail, and its transformation by a variety of surprising images, all work to create a richly complex vignette with what seems, deceptively, the most casual, impressionistic ease.

Open to p. 117, and there find Kipling at the other end of the world, in Stockholm, to receive the Nobel Prize; the Swedish king had died while Kipling and his wife were on their way to Stockholm, and they arrived to find the court in mourning:

> Winter darkness in those latitudes falls at three o'clock, and it was snowing. One half of the vast acreage of the Palace sat in darkness, for there lay the dead King's body. We were conveyed along interminable corridors looking out into black quadrangles, where snow whitened the cloaks of the sentries, the breeches of old-time cannon, and the shot-piles alongside of them. Presently, we reached a living world of more corridors and suites all lighted up, but wrapped in that Court hush which is like no other silence on earth.

Unsympathetic readers may perhaps jib at the last phrase, seeing in it something of Kipling's notorious "knowingness," but it is not out of place from a man whose fame has doubtless taken him into more than one palace and who is about to receive the Nobel Prize; and even if it were, it would be only a small deduction from a passage so controlled and yet so brilliant.

Each of the passages that I have just quoted renders something seen in different parts of the world. They point to another of Kipling's outstanding qualities, fully at work in *Something of Myself*: the quick and sympathetic perception of local life. His move to Sussex in 1902, for example, showed how he could respond to novelty. Sussex opened up an English world he had not known before, and, as *Something of Myself* shows, he studied its types with affectionate curiosity: the poacher "by heredity and instinct," and his wife, who would "range through a past that accepted magic, witchcraft and love-philtres"; the "smuggling, sheep-stealing stock" who lived in the village, and who were, most of them, "artists and craftsmen, either in stone or timber, or wood-cutting, or drain-laying or – which is a gift – the aesthetic disposition of dirt."

He had been equally quick, earlier, to take the feel and flavor of his neighbors in Vermont, who lived in a country whose roads were "sketched in dirt" and whose farm houses were, often, "reduced to a stone-chimney stack or mere green dimples still held by an undefeated lilac-bush." His view of decaying rural New England mingled clear judgment and sympathy:

> It would be hard to exaggerate the loneliness and sterility of life on the farms. . . . What might have become characters, powers and attributes perverted themselves in that desolation as cankered trees throw out branches akimbo, and strange faiths and cruelties, born of solitude to the edge of insanity, flourished like lichen on sick bark. *(p. 70)*

One can only regret that Kipling never ventured to write those stories about New England that he once hoped to do.

One of the strongest and most impressive elements in Kipling's view of life, wherever he found it, was his sense of how the present is bound up with the past. Sometimes this is based on obvious mementos, as in Lahore, where

> The dead of all times were about us – in the vast forgotten Moslem cemeteries round the Station, where one's horse's hoof of a morning might break through to the corpse below; skulls and bones tumbled out of our mud garden walls, and were turned up among the flowers by the Rains. *(p. 27)*

Sometimes the perception is more fanciful, as when he writes of the Sussex workmen who came to dig a well for him that they were "two dark and mysterious Primitives" who had come "out of the woods that know everything and tell nothing." At its best, this perception of the past in the present, and of the present in the past, raises scenes and characters in *Something of Myself* to a new level of seriousness and dignity without falsification. In describing a story that he wrote for *Puck of Pook's Hill* but later discarded, Kipling suggests how past and present mingled for him:

> I went off at score – not on Parnesius, but a story told in a fog by a petty Baltic pirate, who had brought his galley to Pevensey and, off Beachy Head – where in the War we heard merchant-ships being torpedoed – had passed the Roman fleet abandoning Britain to her doom. *(p. 109)*

The imagined Baltic pirate reminds us that the Roman retreat from Britain opened the way for the German invasions that followed, just as the allusions to merchant ships being torpedoed remind us that the Germans had only yesterday been repelled from those same shores: scenes 1,500 years apart become versions of each other.

It is appropriate that Kipling devotes by far the most extended discussion of his literary work in *Something of Myself* to the two collections of stories about the English past, *Puck of Pook's Hill* and *Rewards and Fairies*. In these, despite the fact that they are historical fictions, his most personal experience is to be found: the stories belong, many of them, to the small patch of England that he had elected to live in; they are told to his own children, who, he hoped, would inherit not only the place that he had made for them but the special understanding and sympathy that he had for it; a number of them are stories of artists of different kinds and hence fables of his own experience; and they express the living connection between past and present that is, I think, at one of the deepest levels of his imagination.

In his presentation of himself as an artist, Kipling does not talk about the imagination. He emphasizes instead the element of craftsmanship, and the link between the artist in literature and the artist in all sorts of crafts: stone cutters, masons (he was, we remember, a reverent Mason from an early time), hedgers and ditchers, horsedealers, ship captains, soldiers, and anything else demanding a secure knowledge of how to do something. He did this not in any spirit of self-deprecation but out of a real pride in the sense of craft and commitment. The line he drew between those who were the real thing and those who only played at it was unyielding: as he wrote of his hard-earned status as a newspaperman in India, "the difference . . . between me and the vulgar herd who 'write for papers' was, as I saw it, the gulf that divides the beneficed clergyman from ladies and gentlemen who contribute pumpkins and dahlias to Harvest Festival decorations" (p. 42). Like a good craftsman, he paid special attention to his materials: "I made my own experiments in the weights, colours, perfumes, and attributes of words in relation to other words, either as read aloud so that they may hold the ear, or, scattered over the page, draw the eye" (pp. 43–44).

At another level, Kipling chose to speak of himself as the servant of a "Daemon" in his art: the Daemon was something apart from him, a "not-self" who used Kipling as the channel of an invention and expression that Kipling himself was powerless to account for. This is the ancient Socratic notion of the artist, who may be the instrument of power but who is without knowledge. Kipling would not have objected to the somewhat condescending view of the artist that the idea implies. He appears to have been unaffectedly modest in the face of his gifts at the same time that he was genuinely proud of his participation in a craft. The two attitudes are not contradictory but complementary.*

We come closest to Kipling's intimate idea of himself as an artist, I think, in his identification of himself with Browning's Fra Lippo Lippi, an association that runs like a *leitmotif* through the earlier part of *Something of Myself*. If Kipling could not say, as Fra Lippo does, "I was a baby when my mother died / And father died and left me in the street," his case was close enough; and in Mrs. Holloway he had an equivalent to "Old Aunt Lapaccia," under whose hard tutelage Fra Lippo learned to read the signs of the world:

> Why, soul and sense of him grow sharp alike,
> He learns the look of things and none the less
> For admonition.

At school Kipling discovered the Browning of *Men and Women*, the collection in which "Fra Lippo Lippi" first appeared; and in describing the experience of that discovery at the end of his life in *Something of Myself*, he again claims kinship with Fra Lippo Lippi: "a not too remote – I dare to think – ancestor of mine" (p. 22). The opening lines of the poem stand at the head of the third chapter of *Something of Myself*, the "Seven Years' Hard" of the Indian experience. The scene in Browning's poem is of the discovery by the town guard of the unclerical Fra Lippo returning to the Medici Palace late at night after a revel in the city:

---

* In RK's late story, "Proofs of Holy Writ," Shakespeare, preparing to translate Isaiah for the King James Version, announces that "I wait on my Demon!" But he is shown throughout the story as a shrewd master of his craft.

> I am poor Brother Lippo by your leave.
> You need not clap your torches to my face.

Kipling did not have to explain himself for his unseemly conduct, but, like Fra Lippo, he wants to explain the hard conditions of his apprenticeship and to justify his art by an appeal to his experience. The *apologia* of the priest would be a parallel to that of the journalist.

It is remarkable that Kipling identifies himself in each of the three formative phases of his life – childhood, school years, and Indian apprenticeship – with Fra Lippo. And so, when he has proven his abilities in India and has the pages of *The Week's News* opened to him without restriction, he describes his response in the boast of Fra Lippo:

> 'Twas ask and have,
> Choose, for more's ready!

Fra Lippo, as Browning presents him, was the founder of artistic realism, intent on portraying the world and the flesh and the devil in all their variety and color, to the scandal of his churchly employers: "give us no more of body than shows soul," they say. But Fra Lippo cannot be restrained from painting all that he sees, not out of a wish to scandalize but from a conviction of the good of the world: "it means intensely and means good" is his defense of whatever it may be that he renders. It is doubtful that Kipling, even the young Kipling, would have given an unqualified Yes to the peculiarly optimistic tenets of Fra Lippo's realism. But he shared many of the assumptions that lay beneath the dominant realistic practice of the high Victorian age. And he quotes with approval, in *Something of Myself*, the aesthetic credo of "Fra Lippo Lippi":

> If you get simple beauty and naught else,
> You get about the best thing God invents.

It is in the figure of the artist especially, rather than in the idea of art, that Kipling saw his closest relation to Fra Lippo: both were keen observers, sharpened by personal suffering; both delighted in the variety of the world; both were exhilarated by the act of offending against official notions of decorum; both took the most intense pleasure in the exercise of their art; both knew they possessed a talent far beyond the ordinary, and that it should not lie buried. Kipling could hardly have put it more modestly when he hoped to be recognized as among the remote kindred of Fra Lippo Lippi: he was close kin – and from the upper branch of the family.

Kipling's subject in *Something of Myself* was his "working life" only. What idea did he have of that as a whole? The only explicit venture that he makes towards answering this question is curiously passive. "It seems to me," he announces in the opening sentence, "that every card in my working life has been dealt me in such a manner that I had but to play it as it came" (p. 3). His part, then, was only to know the rules of the game being played; and if he had good cards, then that was to be ascribed, with tranquil piety, to "Allah the Dispenser of Events."

Games, and the idea of playing, are, in fact, quite prominent among the figures that run through Kipling's work. The polo match in "The Maltese Cat" is a perfectly serious version of working life; the maneuverings between boys and masters in *Stalky & Co.* make up an elaborate game; the picaresque experiences of Kim are all an apprenticeship that will qualify him to take part in the game of Imperial politics – the "great game." One could name many other such versions of game-playing to be found in the stories and poems. Card-playing, however, is not very frequent, nor does it provide for Kipling the sort of game that can be elaborated into a figure of the moral life. That he should choose it to represent his own working life is no doubt a determined understatement, intended to make clear at once that there was to be no boasting, no self-congratulation, in his version of his own accomplishments. In this respect, it fits readily with Kipling's dependence upon his Daemon, who, like good luck in a card game, cannot be compelled but only waited for. The figure of the cards recurs in *Something of Myself*, but it is not really insisted upon. His years of obscure toil in the provincial remoteness of the Punjab were evidence, Kipling says, of "how discreetly the cards were being dealt me" (p. 41): only thus, he thinks, could he have learned his trade with so little risk of being hurt or spoiled. When fame does come, he is already used to the game: "I took, as a matter of course, the fantastic cards that Fate was pleased to deal me" (p. 47). Kipling's final use of the figure occurs after he describes how he discovered the rich layers of history that surrounded him in Sussex. Evidences of Phoenicians, Romans, Armada times, ghosts, shadows, and all the "Old things of our Valley" converged to produce the stories of *Puck of Pook's Hill* and *Rewards and Fairies*: "You see how patiently the cards were stacked and dealt into my hands?" (p. 109).

The mild notion of "fate" implicit in the card-playing figure is perhaps no more than would arise from any perception of pattern in one's life: the pattern is not so much created by one's efforts as discovered afterwards. The idea is given a new twist in a passage towards the end of the book, when Kipling makes a rare excursion into his dream life. He has been writing, disapprovingly, of the temptation to dive after "psychical experiences," and then, in spite of his disapproval, offers one of his own, a dream about his being at some inexplicable ceremony and of someone's coming to speak to him. Six weeks later, in actuality, Kipling finds himself at a ceremony in Westminster Abbey to honor the war dead, and there recognizes the images of his dream made real. "But how, and why, had I been shown an unreleased roll of my life-film?" (p. 126).

How seriously should we take that metaphor? Are our lives already on film? Are they scenarios already written, cast, acted out, and stored? Life, then, is solely and simply the process of developing the images already laid up in the film? Kipling, of course, affirms nothing; yet his choosing to tell this story at all is strongly suggestive. He touches lightly on the mysteries of perception in a few other places in *Something of Myself*, as when, early in the book, he wonders how he could have associated the name "Cumnor" with "sorrow and darkness and a raven that 'flapped its wings'" without knowing the poem that expressed these things (p. 7):

> But how and where I first heard the lines that cast the shadow is beyond me – unless it be that the brain holds everything that passes within reach of the senses, and it is only ourselves who do not know this.

The thought is not pursued.

Kipling's attraction towards the "occult," to the imaginative persuasion that we are surrounded by mystery and that the overwhelming truth of one's life is already determined but hidden, to be revealed only in tantalizing glimpses, is written out in so many forms and in so many stories that it would be impossible even to enumerate the evidence here. In T.S. Eliot's words, "Kipling knew something of the things which are underneath, and of the things which are beyond the frontier." I make the point only to draw attention to what might be called the final reticence in *Something of Myself*: Kipling's unwillingness to acknowledge and to develop for his "friends known and unknown" what must have been the chief form of religious experience that he knew. Without the evidence of his other work, such hints and light breaths of suggestion as occur in *Something of Myself* would certainly not seem to ask to be taken seriously.

Biographers can, no doubt, go wrong in their work: they can be kept in ignorance of essential facts; they can get the emphasis wrong; they can misread, misinterpret, misjudge. It is arguable, however, that no autobiographer can go wrong: every mistake, distortion, suppression, or invention has its expressive value and contributes to the self-definition of the autobiographer. The truth of autobiography is whatever the subject chooses to tell, and if he tells much that did not happen and does not tell much that did, we are not therefore misinformed. To get the full expressiveness of this indirect sort of revelation, however, it is obviously necessary to know something of what did or did not happen and might or might not have been put in. Since we have at least some such knowledge about Kipling, his autobiography has both direct and indirect evidence for the reconstruction of the man in the mind of the reader. It is also the work of a master of his craft.

IV

In annotating this edition of *Something of Myself* I have tried to identify names, places, and events, to ascertain dates, to provide information about Kipling's writings, and to call attention, at appropriate places, to material omissions in the narrative. I have also tried, with incomplete success, to identify the sources of Kipling's quotations, but I have not made any attempt to comment on his richly allusive style. When he writes that "My telegrams were given priority by sweating R.E. sergeants" (p. 88) or that the cow-keeper's son "was on terms of terrifying familiarity with the herd-bull, whom he would slap on the nose to make him walk disposedly" (p. 119), the temptation is strong to refer the reader to *II Henry IV* and to Sir James Melville's *Memoirs*. But to do this on every occasion would be to swell the notes intolerably. I have therefore refrained, and leave to the reader the pleasure of tracing the rich current of allusion that flows strongly just below the surface of Kipling's prose.

I have pleasure in acknowledging my dependence, as an editor of *Something of Myself*, upon the work of my predecessor, the late Roger Lancelyn Green, whose notes on the book in R.E. Harbord's *Readers' Guide to Kipling*, VII (1972), 3359–415, have materially simplified my task; in some cases, as in the identification of Kipling's childhood reading, Mr. Green has solved puzzles to which he alone has had the key. I would also like to thank a knot of friends from the Kipling Society, who have helped me in this as in my other work on Kipling: Lisa Lewis, Margaret Newsom, John Shearman, and George Webb.

The text of this edition is that of the first printing of *Something of Myself*, London, Macmillan, 1937. The book was reprinted several times during 1937, allowing opportunity for the correction of such mistakes as had been noticed by Mrs. Kipling and by others (see above, p. xxi). In 1937 it was added as the final volume to the Outward Bound Edition in the United States (Scribners, 1897–1937); in 1938, to the Sussex Edition in England (Macmillan, 1937–38). There does not seem to be any alteration of the text after the date of the Sussex Edition, but the number of changes between then and the first printing is considerable. No complete collation of the various printings has been made, but I have called attention in the notes to such changes as I have detected by an incomplete comparison.

Kipling's diary is reproduced by kind permission of the National Trust and the Houghton Library; and the illustrations to "Baa Baa, Black Sheep" by courtesy of the Berg Collection, New York Public Library.

SOMETHING

OF

MYSELF

*For My
Friends
Known
and
Unknown*

CHAPTER I

A Very Young Person
1865–1878

> Give me the first six years of a child's
> life and you can have the rest.[1]

Looking back from this my seventieth year, it seems to me that every card in my working life has been dealt me in such a manner that I had but to play it as it came. Therefore, ascribing all good fortune to Allah the Dispenser of Events, I begin:—

My first impression is of daybreak, light and colour and golden and purple fruits at the level of my shoulder. This would be the memory of early morning walks to the Bombay fruit market with my *ayah*[2] and later with my sister[3] in her perambulator, and of our returns with our purchases piled high on the bows of it. Our *ayah* was a Portuguese Roman Catholic who would pray—I beside her—at a wayside Cross. Meeta,[4] my Hindu bearer, would sometimes go into little Hindu temples where, being below the age of caste, I held his hand and looked at the dimly-seen, friendly Gods.

Our evening walks were by the sea in the shadow of palm-groves which, I think, were called the Mahim Woods. When the wind blew the great nuts would tumble, and we fled—my *ayah*, and my sister in her perambulator—to the safety of the open. I have always felt the menacing darkness of tropical eventides, as I have loved the voices of night-winds through palm or banana leaves, and the song of the tree-frogs.

3

There were far-going Arab dhows on the pearly waters, and gaily dressed Parsees wading out to worship the sunset. Of their creed I knew nothing, nor did I know that near our little house on the Bombay Esplanade were the Towers of Silence, where their Dead are exposed to the waiting vultures on the rim of the towers, who scuffle and spread wings when they see the bearers of the Dead below. I did not understand my Mother's distress when she found 'a child's hand' in our garden, and said I was not to ask questions about it. I wanted to see that child's hand. But my *ayah* told me.

In the afternoon heats before we took our sleep, she or Meeta would tell us stories and Indian nursery songs all unforgotten, and we were sent into the dining-room after we had been dressed, with the caution 'Speak English now to Papa and Mamma.' So one spoke 'English,' haltingly translated out of the vernacular idiom that one thought and dreamed in.[5] The Mother sang wonderful songs at a black piano and would go out to Big Dinners. Once she came back, very quickly, and told me, still awake, that 'the big Lord Sahib' had been killed and there was to be no Big Dinner. This was Lord Mayo,[6] assassinated by a native. Meeta explained afterwards that he had been 'hit with a knife.' Meeta unconsciously saved me from any night terrors or dread of the dark. Our *ayah*, with a servant's curious mixture of deep affection and shallow device, had told me that a stuffed leopard's head on the nursery wall was there to see that I went to sleep. But Meeta spoke of it scornfully as 'the head of an animal,' and I took it off my mind as a fetish, good or bad, for it was only some unspecified 'animal.'

Far across green spaces round the house was a marvellous place filled with smells of paints and oils, and lumps of clay with which I played. That was the atelier of my Father's School of Art,[7] and a Mr. 'Terry Sahib'[8] his assistant, to whom my small sister was devoted, was our great friend. Once, on the way there alone, I passed the edge of a huge ravine a foot deep, where a winged monster as big as myself attacked me, and I fled and wept. My Father drew for me a picture of the tragedy with a rhyme beneath:—

> There was a small boy in Bombay
> Who once from a hen ran away.

4

When they said: 'You're a baby,'
He replied: 'Well, I may be:
But I don't like these hens of Bombay.'[9]

This consoled me. I have thought well of hens ever since.

Then those days of strong light and darkness passed, and there was a time in a ship[10] with an immense semi-circle blocking all vision on each side of her. (She must have been the old paddlewheel P. & O. *Ripon*.[11]) There was a train across a desert (the Suez Canal was not yet opened) and a halt in it, and a small girl wrapped in a shawl on the seat opposite me, whose face stands out still.[12] There was next a dark land, and a darker room full of cold, in one wall of which a white woman made naked fire, and I cried aloud with dread, for I had never before seen a grate.

Then came a new small house[13] smelling of aridity and emptiness, and a parting in the dawn with Father and Mother, who said that I must learn quickly to read and write so that they might send me letters and books.

I lived in that house for close on six years.[14] It belonged to a woman who took in children whose parents were in India. She was married to an old Navy Captain, who had been a midshipman at Navarino,[15] and had afterwards been entangled in a harpoon-line while whale-fishing, and dragged down till he miraculously freed himself. But the line had scarred his ankle for life—a dry, black scar, which I used to look at with horrified interest.

The house itself stood in the extreme suburbs of Southsea, next to a Portsmouth unchanged in most particulars since Trafalgar—the Portsmouth of Sir Walter Besant's *By Celia's Arbour*.[16] The timber for a Navy that was only experimenting with iron-clads such as the *Inflexible* lay in great booms in the harbour. The little training-brigs kept their walks opposite Southsea Castle, and Portsmouth Hard[17] was as it had always been. Outside these things lay the desolation of Hayling Island, Lumps Fort, and the isolated hamlet of Milton. I would go for long walks with the Captain, and once he took me to see a ship called the *Alert* (or *Discovery*)[18] returned from Arctic explorations, her decks filled with old sledges and lumber, and her spare rudder being cut up for souvenirs. A sailor gave me a piece, but I lost it. Then the old Captain died,[19] and I was sorry, for he was the only person in that house as far as I can remember who ever threw me a kind word.

It was an establishment run with the full vigour of the Evangelical as revealed to the Woman. I had never heard of Hell, so I was introduced to it in all its terrors—I and whatever luckless little slavey might be in the house, whom severe rationing had led to steal food. Once I saw the Woman beat such a girl who picked up the kitchen poker and threatened retaliation. Myself I was regularly beaten. The Woman had an only son[20] of twelve or thirteen as religious as she. I was a real joy to him, for when his mother had finished with me for the day he (we slept in the same room) took me on and roasted the other side.

If you cross-examine a child of seven or eight on his day's doings (specially when he wants to go to sleep) he will contradict himself very satisfactorily. If each contradiction be set down as a lie and retailed at breakfast, life is not easy. I have known a certain amount of bullying, but this was calculated torture—religious as well as scientific. Yet it made me give attention to the lies I soon found it necessary to tell: and this, I presume, is the foundation of literary effort.

But my ignorance was my salvation. I was made to read without explanation, under the usual fear of punishment. And on a day that I remember it came to me that 'reading' was not 'the Cat lay on the Mat,' but a means to everything that would make me happy. So I read all that came within my reach. As soon as my pleasure in this was known, deprivation from reading was added to my punishments. I then read by stealth and the more earnestly.

There were not many books in that house, but Father and Mother as soon as they heard I could read sent me priceless volumes. One I have still, a bound copy of *Aunt Judy's Magazine* of the early 'seventies, in which appeared Mrs. Ewing's *Six to Sixteen*.[21] I owe more in circuitous ways to that tale than I can tell. I knew it, as I know it still, almost by heart. Here was a history of real people and real things. It was better than Knatchbull-Hugesson's *Tales at Tea-time*,[22] better even than *The Old Shikarri*[23] with its steel engravings of charging pigs and angry tigers. On another plane was an old magazine[24] with Wordsworth's 'I climbed the dark brow of the mighty Helvellyn.'[25] I knew nothing of its meaning but the words moved and pleased. So did other extracts from the poems of 'A. Tennyson.'

A visitor, too, gave me a little purple book of severely moral tendency called *The Hope of the Katzikopfs*[26] — about a bad boy made virtuous, but it contained verses that began, 'Farewell Rewards and Fairies,' and ended with an injunction 'To pray for the "noddle" of William Churne of Staffordshire.' This bore fruit afterwards.[27]

And somehow or other I came across a tale about a lion-hunter in South Africa who fell among lions who were all Freemasons, and with them entered into a confederacy against some wicked baboons.[28] I think that, too, lay dormant until the *Jungle Books* began to be born.

There comes to my mind here a memory of two books of verse about child-life which I have tried in vain to identify. One—blue and fat[29]—described 'nine white wolves' coming 'over the wold' and stirred me to the deeps; and also certain savages who 'thought the name of England was something that could not burn.'[30]

The other book—brown and fat[31]—was full of lovely tales in strange metres. A girl was turned into a water-rat 'as a matter of course'; an Urchin cured an old man of gout by means of a cool cabbage-leaf, and somehow 'forty wicked Goblins' were mixed up in the plot; and a 'Darling' got out on the house-leads with a broom and tried to sweep stars off the skies. It must have been an unusual book for that age, but I have never been able to recover it, any more than I have a song that a nursemaid sang at low-tide in the face of the sunset on Littlehampton Sands when I was less than six. But the impression of wonder, excitement and terror and the red bars of failing light is as clear as ever.

Among the servants in the House of Desolation was one from Cumnor, which name I associated with sorrow and darkness and a raven that 'flapped its wings.' Years later I identified the lines: 'And thrice the Raven flapped her wing Around the towers of Cumnor Hall.'[32] But how and where I first heard the lines that cast the shadow is beyond me—unless it be that the brain holds everything that passes within reach of the senses, and it is only ourselves who do not know this.

When my Father sent me a *Robinson Crusoe*[33] with steel engravings I set up in business alone as a trader with savages (the wreck parts of the tale never much interested me), in a mildewy basement room where I stood my solitary confinements. My apparatus was a coconut shell strung on a red cord, a tin trunk, and a piece of packing-case which kept off any other world. Thus fenced about, everything inside the fence was quite real, but mixed with the smell of damp cupboards. If the bit of board fell, I had to begin the magic all over again. I have learned since from children who play much alone that this rule of 'beginning again in a pretend game' is not uncommon. The magic, you see, lies in the ring or fence that you take refuge in.

Once I remember being taken to a town called Oxford and a street called Holywell, where I was shown an Ancient of Days who, I was told, was the Provost of Oriel;[34] wherefore I never understood, but conceived him to be some sort of idol. And twice or thrice we went, all of us, to pay a day-long visit to an old gentleman in a house in the country near Havant.[35] Here everything was wonderful and unlike my world, and he had an old lady sister who was kind, and I played in hot, sweet-smelling meadows and ate all sorts of things.

After such a visit I was once put through the third degree by the Woman and her son, who asked me if I had told the old gentleman that I was much fonder of him than was the Woman's son. It must have been the tail-end of some sordid intrigue or other—the old gentleman being of kin to that unhappy pair—but it was beyond my comprehension. My sole concern had been a friendly pony in the paddock. My dazed attempts to clear myself were not accepted and, once again, the pleasure that I was seen to have taken was balanced by punishments and humiliation—above all humiliation. That alternation was quite regular. I can but admire the infernal laborious ingenuity of it all. *Exempli gratia.* Coming out of church once I smiled. The Devil-Boy demanded why. I said I didn't know, which was child's truth. He replied that I *must* know. People didn't laugh for nothing. Heaven knows what explanation I put forward; but it was duly reported to the Woman as a 'lie.' Result, afternoon upstairs with the Collect to learn. I learned most of the Collects that way and a great deal of the Bible. The son after three or four years went into a Bank and was generally too tired on his return to torture me, unless things had gone wrong with him. I learned to know what was coming from his step into the house.

But, for a month each year I possessed a paradise which I verily believe saved me. Each December I stayed with my Aunt Georgy, my mother's sister, wife of Sir Edward Burne-Jones, at The Grange, North End Road.[36] At first I must have been escorted there, but later I went alone, and arriving at the house would reach up to the open-work iron bell-pull on the wonderful gate that let me into all felicity. When I had a house of my own, and The Grange was emptied of meaning, I begged for and was given that bell-pull for my entrance, in the hope that other children might also feel happy when they rang it.[37]

At The Grange I had love and affection as much as the greediest, and I was not very greedy, could desire. There were most wonderful smells of paints and turpentine whiffing down from the big studio on the first floor where my Uncle worked; there was the society of my two cousins,[38] and a sloping mulberry tree which we used to climb for our plots and conferences. There was a rocking-horse in the nursery and a table that, tilted up on two chairs, made a toboggan-slide of the best. There were pictures finished or half finished of lovely colours; and in the rooms chairs and cupboards such as the world had not yet seen, for William Morris[39] (our Deputy 'Uncle Topsy') was just beginning to fabricate these things. There was an incessant come and go of young people and grown-ups all willing to play with us—except an elderly person called 'Browning,'[40] who took no proper interest in the skirmishes which happened to be raging on his entry. Best of all, immeasurably, was the beloved Aunt herself reading us *The Pirate*[41] or *The Arabian Nights* of evenings, when one lay out on the big sofas sucking toffee, and calling our cousins 'Ho, Son,' or 'Daughter of my Uncle' or 'O True Believer.'

Often the Uncle, who had a 'golden voice,' would assist in our evening play, though mostly he worked at black and white in the middle of our riots. He was never idle. We made a draped chair in the hall serve for the seat of 'Norna of the Fitful Head'[42] and

9

addressed her questions till the Uncle got inside the rugs and gave us answers which thrilled us with delightful shivers, in a voice deeper than all the boots in the world. And once he descended in broad daylight with a tube of 'Mummy Brown' in his hand, saying that he had discovered it was made of dead Pharaohs and we must bury it accordingly. So we all went out and helped—according to the rites of Mizraim and Memphis, I hope—and—to this day I could drive a spade within a foot of where that tube lies.

At bedtime one hastened along the passages, where unfinished cartoons lay against the walls. The Uncle often painted in their eyes first, leaving the rest in charcoal—a most effective presentation. Hence our speed to our own top-landing, where we could hang over the stairs and listen to the loveliest sound in the world—deep-voiced men laughing together over dinner.

It was a jumble of delights and emotions culminating in being allowed to blow the big organ in the studio for the beloved Aunt, while the Uncle worked, or 'Uncle Topsy' came in full of some business of picture-frames or stained glass or general denunciations. Then it was hard to keep the little lead weight on its string below the chalk mark, and if the organ ran out in squeals the beloved Aunt would be sorry. Never, *never* angry!

As a rule Morris took no notice of anything outside what was in his mind at the moment. But I remember one amazing exception. My cousin Margaret and I, then about eight, were in the nursery eating pork-dripping on brown bread, which is a dish for the Gods, when we heard 'Uncle Topsy' in the hall calling, as he usually did, for 'Ned' or 'Georgie.' The matter was outside our world. So we were the more impressed when, not finding the grown-ups, he came in and said he would tell us a story. We settled ourselves under the table which we used for a toboggan-slide and he, gravely as ever, climbed on to our big rocking-horse. There, slowly surging back and forth while the poor beast creaked, he told us a tale full of fascinating horrors, about a man who was condemned to dream bad dreams. One of them took the shape of a cow's tail waving from a heap of dried fish. He went away as abruptly as he had come. Long afterwards, when I was old enough to know a maker's pains, it dawned on me that we must have heard the Saga of Burnt Njal,[43] which was then interesting him. In default of grown-ups, and pressed by need to pass the story between his teeth and clarify it, he had used us.

But on a certain day—one tried to fend off the thought of it—the delicious dream would end, and one would return to the House of Desolation, and for the next two or three mornings there cry on waking up. Hence more punishments and cross-examinations.

Often and often afterwards, the beloved Aunt would ask me why I had never told any one how I was being treated. Children tell little more than animals, for what comes to them they accept as eternally established. Also, badly-treated children have a clear notion of what they are likely to get if they betray the secrets of a prison-house before they are clear of it.

In justice to the Woman I can say that I was adequately fed. (I remember a gift to her of some red 'fruit' called 'tomatoes' which, after long consideration, she boiled with sugar; and they were very beastly. The tinned meat of those days was Australian beef with a crumbly fat, and string-boiled mutton, hard to get down.) Nor was my life an unsuitable preparation for my future, in that it demanded constant wariness, the habit of observation, and attendance on moods and tempers; the noting of discrepancies between speech and action; a certain reserve of demeanour; and automatic suspicion of sudden favours. Brother Lippo Lippi, in his own harder case, as a boy discovered:—

> Why, soul and sense of him grow sharp alike,
> He learns the look of things and none the less
> For admonition.[44]

So it was with me.

My troubles settled themselves in a few years. My eyes went wrong, and I could not well see to read. For which reason I read the more and in bad lights. My work at the terrible little day-school[45] where I had been sent suffered in consequence, and my monthly reports showed it. The loss of 'reading-time' was the worst of my 'home' punishments for bad school-work. One report was so bad that I threw it away and said that I had never received it. But this is a hard world for the amateur liar. My web of deceit was swiftly exposed—the Son spared time after banking-hours to help in the auto-da-fé—and I was well beaten and sent to school through the streets of Southsea with the placard 'Liar' between my shoulders.[46] In the long run these things, and many more of the like, drained me of any capacity for real, personal hate for the rest of my days. So close must any life-filling passion lie to its opposite. 'Who having known the Diamond will concern himself with glass?'[47]

Some sort of nervous break-down followed, for I imagined I saw shadows and things that were not there, and they worried me more than the Woman. The beloved Aunt must have heard of it, and a man came down to see me as to my eyes and reported that I was half-blind. This, too, was supposed to be 'showing-off,' and I was segregated from my sister—another punishment—as a sort of moral leper. Then—I do not remember that I had any warning—the Mother returned from India.[48] She told me afterwards that when she first came up to my room to kiss me goodnight, I flung up an arm to guard off the cuff that I had been trained to expect.

I was taken at once from the House of Desolation, and for months ran wild in a little farm-house on the edge of Epping Forest,[49] where I was not encouraged to refer to my guilty past. Except for my spectacles, which were uncommon in those days, I was completely happy with my Mother and the local society, which included for me a gipsy of the name of Saville, who told me tales of selling horses to the ignorant; the farmer's wife; her niece Patty who turned a kind blind eye on our raids into the dairy; the postman; and the farm-boys. The farmer did not approve of my teaching one of his cows to stand and be milked in the field. My Mother drew the line at my return to meals red-booted from assisting at the slaughter of swine, or reeking after the exploration of attractive muck-heaps. These were the only restrictions I recall.

A cousin,[50] afterwards to be a Prime Minister, would come down on visits. The farmer said that we did each other 'no good.' Yet the worst I can remember was our self-sacrificing war against a wasps' nest on a muddy islet in a most muddy pond. Our only weapons were switches of broom, but we defeated the enemy unscathed. The trouble at home centred round an enormous currant roly-poly—a 'spotted dog' a foot long. We took it away to sustain us in action and we heard a great deal about it from Patty in the evening.

Then we went to London and stayed for some weeks in a tiny lodging-house in the semi-rural Brompton Road,[51] kept by an ivory-faced, lordly-whiskered ex-butler and his patient wife. Here, for the first time, it happened that the night got into my head. I rose up and wandered about that still house till daybreak, when I slipped out into the little brick-walled garden and saw the dawn break. All would have been well but for Pluto, a pet toad brought back from Epping Forest, who lived mostly in one of my pockets. It struck me that he might be thirsty, and I stole into my Mother's room and would have given him drink from a water-jug. But it slipped and broke and very much was said. The ex-butler could not understand why I had stayed awake all night. I did not know then that such night-wakings would be laid upon me through my life; or that my fortunate hour would be on the turn of sunrise, with a sou'-west breeze afoot.

The sorely tried Mother got my sister and me season-tickets for the old South Kensington Museum[52] which was only across the road. (No need in those days to caution us against the traffic.) Very shortly we two, on account of our regular attendance (for the weather had turned wet), owned that place and one policeman in special. When we came with any grown-ups he saluted us magnificently. From the big Buddha with the little door in his back, to the towering dull-gilt ancient coaches and carven chariots in long dark corridors—even the places marked 'private' where fresh treasures were always being unpacked—we roved at will, and divided the treasures child-fashion.[53] There were instruments of music inlaid with lapis, beryl and ivories; glorious gold-fretted spinets and clavichords; the bowels of the great Glastonbury clock; mechanical models; steel- and silver-butted pistols, daggers and arquebusses— the labels alone were an education; a collection of precious stones and rings—we quarrelled over those—and a big bluish book which was the manuscript of one of Dickens' novels. That man seemed to me to have written very carelessly; leaving out lots which he had to squeeze in between the lines afterwards.

These experiences were a soaking in colour and design with, above all, the proper Museum smell; and it stayed with me. By the end of that long holiday I understood that my Mother had written verses, that my Father 'wrote things' also;[54] that books and pictures were among the most important affairs in the world; that I could read as much as I chose and ask the meaning of things from any one I met. I had found out, too, that one could take pen and set down what one thought, and that nobody accused one of 'showing off' by so doing. I read a good deal; *Sidonia the Sorceress*;[55] Emerson's poems; and Bret Harte's stories; and I learned all sorts of verses for the pleasure of repeating them to myself in bed.

CHAPTER II

The School before its Time
1878–1882

Then came school at the far end of England.[1] The Head of it was a lean, slow-spoken, bearded Arab-complexioned man whom till then I had known as one of my Deputy-Uncles at The Grange—Cormell Price, otherwise 'Uncle Crom.'[2] My Mother, on her return to India, confided my sister and me to the care of three dear ladies[3] who lived off the far end of Kensington High Street over against Addison Road, in a house filled with books, peace, kindliness, patience and what to-day would be called 'culture.' But it was natural atmosphere.

One of the ladies wrote novels on her knee, by the fireside, sitting just outside the edge of conversation, beneath two clay pipes tied with black ribbon, which once Carlyle had smoked. All the people one was taken to see either wrote or painted pictures or, as in the case of a Mr. and Miss de Morgan,[4] ornamented tiles. They let me play with their queer, sticky paints. Somewhere in the background were people called Jean Ingelow[5] and Christina Rossetti,[6] but I was never lucky enough to see those good spirits. And there was a choice in the walls of bookshelves of anything one liked from *Firmilian*[7] to *The Moonstone* and *The Woman in White*[8] and, somehow, all Wellington's Indian Despatches, which fascinated me.[9]

These treasures were realised by me in the course of the next few years. Meantime (Spring of '78[10]), after my experience at Southsea, the prospect of school did not attract. The United Services College was in the nature of a company promoted by poor officers and the like for the cheap education of their sons, and set up at Westward Ho! near Bideford. It was largely a caste-school—some seventy-five per cent of us had been born outside England and hoped to follow their fathers in the Army. It was but four or five years old when I joined, and had been made up under Cormell Price's hand by drafts from Haileybury, whose pattern it followed, and, I think, a percentage of 'hard cases' from other schools. Even by the standards of those days, it was primitive in its appointments, and our food would now raise a mutiny in Dartmoor. I remember no time, after home-tips had been spent, when we would not eat dry bread if we could steal it from the trays in the basement before tea. Yet the sick-house was permanently empty except for lawful accidents; I remember not one death of a boy; and only one epidemic—of chicken-pox. Then the Head called us together and condoled with us in such fashion that we expected immediate break-up and began to cheer. But he said that, perhaps, the best thing would be to take no notice of the incident, and that he would 'work us lightly' for the rest of the term. He did and it checked the epidemic.

Naturally, Westward Ho! was brutal enough, but, setting aside the foul speech that a boy ought to learn early and put behind him by his seventeenth year, it was clean with a cleanliness that I have never heard of in any other school. I remember no cases of even suspected perversion, and am inclined to the theory that if masters did not suspect them, and show that they suspected, there would not be quite so many elsewhere. Talking things over with Cormell Price afterwards, he confessed that his one prophylactic against certain unclean microbes was to 'send us to bed dead tired.' Hence the wideness of our bounds, and his deaf ear towards our incessant riots and wars between the Houses.

At the end of my first term, which was horrible,[11] my parents could not reach England for the Easter holidays, and I had to stay up with a few big boys reading for Army Exams. and a batch of youngsters whose people were very far away. I expected the worst, but when we survivors were left in the echoing form-rooms after the others had driven cheering to the station, life suddenly became a new thing (thanks to Cormell Price). The big remote seniors turned into tolerant elder brothers, and let us small fry rove far out of bounds; shared their delicacies with us at tea; and even took an interest in our hobbies. We had no special work to do and enjoyed ourselves hugely. On the return of the school 'all smiles stopped together,'[12] which was right and proper. For compensation I was given a holiday when my Father came home, and with him went to the Paris Exhibition of '78, where he was in charge of Indian Exhibits.[13] He allowed me, at twelve years old, the full freedom of that spacious and friendly city, and the run of the Exhibition grounds and buildings. It was an education in itself; and set my life-long love for France. Also, he saw to it that I should learn to read French at least for my own amusement, and gave me Jules Verne[14] to begin with. French as an accomplishment was not well-seen at English schools in my time, and knowledge of it connoted leanings towards immorality. For myself:—

> I hold it truth with him who sung
> Unpublished melodies,
> Who wakes in Paris, being young,
> O' summer, wakes in Paradise.[15]

For those who may be still interested in such matters, I wrote of this part of my life in some *Souvenirs of France*,[16] which are very close to the facts of that time.

My first year and a half was not pleasant. The most persistent bullying comes not less from the bigger boys, who merely kick and pass on, than from young devils of fourteen acting in concert against one butt. Luckily for me I was physically some years in advance of my age, and swimming in the big open sea baths, or off the Pebble Ridge, was the one accomplishment that brought me any credit. I played footer (Rugby Union), but here again my sight hampered me. I was not even in the Second Fifteen.

After my strength came suddenly to me about my fourteenth year, there was no more bullying; and either my natural sloth or past experience did not tempt me to bully in my turn. I had by then found me two friends with whom, by a carefully arranged system of mutual aids, I went up the school on co-operative principles.

How we—the originals of Stalky, M'Turk, and Beetle[17]—first came together I do not remember, but our Triple Alliance was well established before we were thirteen.[18] We had been oppressed by a large toughish boy who raided our poor little lockers. We took him on in a long, mixed rough-and-tumble, just this side of the real thing. At the end we were all-out (we worked by pressure and clinging, much as bees 'ball' a Queen) and he never troubled us again.[19]

Turkey possessed an invincible detachment—far beyond mere insolence—towards all the world: and a tongue, when he used it, dipped in some Irish-blue acid. Moreover, he spoke, sincerely, of the masters as 'ushers,' which was not without charm. His general attitude was that of Ireland in English affairs at that time.

For executive capacity, the organisation of raids, reprisals, and retreats, we depended on Stalky, our Commander-in-Chief and Chief of his own Staff. He came of a household with a stern head, and, I fancy, had training in the holidays. Turkey never told us much about his belongings. He turned up, usually a day or two late, by the Irish packet, aloof, inscrutable, and contradictious. On him lay the burden of decorating our study, for he served a strange God called Ruskin.[20] We fought among ourselves 'regular an' faithful as man an' wife,' but any debt which we owed elsewhere was faithfully paid by all three of us.

Our 'socialisation of educational opportunities'[21] took us unscathed up the school, till the original of Little Hartopp,[22] asking one question too many, disclosed that I did not know what a co-sine was and compared me to 'brute beasts.' I taught Turkey all he ever knew of French, and he tried to make Stalky and me comprehend a little Latin. There is much to be said for this system, if you want a boy to learn anything, because he will remember what he gets from an equal where his master's words are forgotten. Similarly, when it was necessary to Stalky that I should get into the Choir, he taught me how to quaver 'I know a maiden fair to see' by punching me in the kidneys all up and down the cricket-field. (But some small trouble over a solitaire marble pushed from beneath the hem of a robe down the choir-steps into the tiled aisle ended that venture.)

I think it was his infernal impersonality that swayed us all in our wars and peace. He saw not only us but himself from the outside, and in later life, as we met in India and elsewhere, the gift persisted. At long last, when with an equipment of doubtful Ford cars and a collection of most-mixed troops, he put up a monumental bluff against the Bolsheviks somewhere in Armenia (it is written in his *Adventures of Dunsterforce*[23]) and was as nearly as possible destroyed, he wrote to the authorities responsible. I asked him what happened. 'They told me they had no more use for my services,' said he. Naturally I condoled. 'Wrong as usual,' said the ex-Head of Number Five study. 'If any officer under *me* had written what I did to the War Office, I'd have had him broke in two-twos.' That fairly sums up the man—and the boy who commanded us. I think I was a buffer state between his drivings and his tongue-lootings and his campaigns in which we were powers; and the acrid, devastating Turkey who, as I have written, 'lived and loved to destroy illusions'[24] yet reached always after beauty. They took up room on tables that I wanted for writing; they broke into my reveries; they mocked my Gods; they stole, pawned or sold my outlying or neglected possessions; and—I could not have gone on a week without them or they without me.

But my revenge was ample. I have said I was physically precocious. In my last term I had been thrusting an unlovely chin at C——[25] in form. At last he blew up, protested he could no longer abide the sight, and ordered me to shave. I carried this word to my House-master.[26] He, who had long looked on me as a cultivated sink of iniquities, brooded over this confirmation of his suspicions, and gave me a written order on a Bideford barber for a razor, etc. I kindly invited my friends to come and help, and lamented for three miles the burden of compulsory shaving. There were no *ripostes*. There was no ribaldry. But why Stalky and Turkey did not cut their throats experimenting with the apparatus I do not understand.

We will now return to the savage life in which all these prodigious events 'transpired.'

We smoked, of course, but the penalties of discovery were heavy because the Prefects, who were all of the 'Army Class' up for the Sandhurst or Woolwich Preliminary,[27] were allowed under restrictions to smoke pipes. If any of the rank and file were caught smoking, they came up before the Prefects, not on moral grounds, but for usurping the privileges of the Ruling Caste. The classic phrase was: 'You esteem yourself to be a Prefect, do you? *All* right. Come to my study at six, please.' This seemed to work better than religious lectures and even expulsions which some establishments used to deal out for this dread sin.

Oddly enough 'fagging' did not exist, though the name 'fag' was regularly used as a term of contempt and sign of subordination against the Lower School. If one needed a 'varlet' to clean things in a study or run errands, that was a matter for private bargaining in our only currency—food. Sometimes such service gave protection, in the sense that it was distinct cheek to oppress an accredited 'varlet.' I never served thus, owing to my untidiness; but our study entertained one sporadically, and to him we three expounded all housewifely duties. But, as a rule, Turkey would tidy up like the old maid to whom we always compared him.

Games were compulsory unless written excuse were furnished by competent authority. The penalty for wilful shirking was three cuts with a ground ash from the Prefect of Games. One of the most difficult things to explain to some people is that a boy of seventeen or eighteen can thus beat a boy barely a year his junior, and on the heels of the punishment go for a walk with him; neither party bearing malice or pride.

So too in the War of '14 to '18 young gentlemen found it hard to understand that the Adjutant who poured vitriol on their heads at Parade, but was polite and friendly at Mess, was not sucking up to them to make amends for previous rudeness.

Except in the case of two House-masters I do not recall being lectured or preached at on morals or virtue. It is not always expedient to excite a growing youth's religious emotions, because one set of nerves seems to communicate with others, and Heaven knows what mines a 'pi-jaw'[28] may touch off. But there were no doors to our bare windy dormitories, nor any sort of lock on the form-rooms. Our masters, with one exception who lived outside, were unmarried. The school buildings, originally cheap lodging-houses, made one straight bar against a hillside, and the boys circulated up and down in front of it. A penal battalion could not have been more perfectly policed, though that we did not realise. Mercifully we knew little outside the immediate burden of the day and the necessity for getting into the Army. I think, then, that when we worked we worked harder than most schools.

My House-master was deeply conscientious and cumbered about with many cares for his charges. What he accomplished thereby I know not. His errors sprang from pure and excessive goodness. Me and my companions he always darkly and deeply suspected. Realising this, we little beasts made him sweat, which he did on slight provocation.

My main interest as I grew older was C——, my English and Classics Master, a rowing-man of splendid physique, and a scholar who lived in secret hope of translating Theocritus worthily. He had a violent temper, no disadvantage in handling boys used to direct speech, and a gift of schoolmaster's 'sarcasm' which must have been a relief to him and was certainly a treasure-trove to me. Also he was a good and House-proud House-master. Under him I came to feel that words could be used as weapons, for he did me the honour to talk at me plentifully; and our year-in year-out form-room bickerings gave us both something to play with. One learns more from a good scholar in a rage than from a score of lucid and laborious drudges; and to be made the butt of one's companions in full form is no bad preparation for later experiences. I think this 'approach' is now discouraged for fear of hurting the soul of youth, but in essence it is no more than rattling tins or firing squibs under a colt's nose. I remember nothing save satisfaction or envy when C—— broke his precious ointments over my head.

I tried to give a pale rendering of his style when heated in a 'Stalky' tale, 'Regulus,' but I wish I could have presented him as he blazed forth once on the great Cleopatra Ode—the 27th of the Third Book.[29] I had detonated him by a very vile construe of the first few lines. Having slain me, he charged over my corpse and delivered an interpretation of the rest of the Ode unequalled for power and insight. He held even the Army Class breathless.

There must be still masters of the same sincerity; and gramophone records of such good men, on the brink of profanity, struggling with a Latin form, would be more helpful to education than bushels of printed books. C—— taught me to loathe Horace for two years; to forget him for twenty, and then to love him for the rest of my days and through many sleepless nights.

After my second year at school, the tide of writing set in. In my holidays the three ladies listened—it was all I wanted—to anything I had to say. I drew on their books, from *The City of Dreadful Night*[30] which shook me to my unformed core, Mrs. Gatty's *Parables from Nature*[31] which I imitated and thought I was original, and scores of others. There were few atrocities of form or metre that I did not perpetrate and I enjoyed them all.

I discovered, also, that personal and well-pointed limericks on my companions worked well, and I and a red-nosed boy of uncertain temper exploited the idea—not without dust and heat; next, that the metre of *Hiawatha*[32] saved one all bother about rhyme: and that there had been a man called Dante who, living in a small Italian town at general issue with his neighbours, had invented for most of them lively torments in a nine-ringed Hell, where he exhibited them to after-ages. C—— said, 'He must have made himself infernally unpopular.' I combined my authorities.

I bought a fat, American cloth-bound note-book, and set to work on an *Inferno*, into which I put, under appropriate torture, all my friends and most of the masters. This was really remunerative because one could chant his future doom to a victim walking below the windows of the study which I with my two companions now possessed. Then, 'as rare things will,'[33] my book vanished, and I lost interest in the *Hiawatha* metre.

Tennyson and *Aurora Leigh*[34] came in the way of nature to me in the holidays, and C—— in form once literally threw *Men and Women*[35] at my head. Here I found 'The Bishop orders his Tomb,' 'Love among the Ruins' and 'Fra Lippo Lippi,' a not too remote—I dare to think—ancestor of mine.

Swinburne's poems I must have come across first at the Aunt's. He did not strike my very young mind as 'anything in particular' till I read *Atalanta in Calydon*,[36] and one verse of verses which exactly set the time for my side-stroke when I bathed in the big rollers off the Ridge. As thus:—

> Who shall *seek* thee and *bring*
> And re*store* thee thy *day*, (*Half roll*)
> When the *dove* dipt her *wing*
> And the *oars* won their *way*
> Where the narrowing Symplegades whitened the straits of Propontis
> with spray? (*Carry on with the impetus*)

If you can time the last line of it to end with a long roller crashing on your head, the cadence is complete. I even forgave Bret Harte, to whom I owed many things, for taking that metre in vain in his 'Heathen Chinee.'[37] But I never forgave C—— for bringing the fact to my notice.

Not till years later—talking things over with my 'Uncle Crom'— did I realise that injustices of this sort were not without intention.[38] 'You needed a tight hand in those days,' he drawled. 'C—— gave it to you.' 'He did,' said I, 'and so did H——,'[39] the married master whom the school thoroughly feared.

'I remember *that*,' Crom answered. 'Yes, that was me too.' This had been an affair of an Essay—'A Day in the Holidays,' or something of that nature. C—— had set it but the papers were to be marked by H——. My essay was of variegated but constant vileness, modelled, I fancy, on holiday readings of a journal called *The Pink 'Un*.[40] Even I had never done anything worse. Normally H——'s markings would have been sent in to C—— without comment. On this occasion, however (I was in Latin form at the time), H—— entered and asked for the floor. C—— yielded it to him with a grin. H—— then told me off before my delighted companions in his best style, which was acid and contumelious. He wound up by a few general remarks about dying as a 'scurrilous journalist.' (I think now that H—— too may have read *The Pink 'Un*.) The tone, matter, and setting of his discourse were as brutal as they were meant to be— brutal as the necessary wrench on the curb that fetches up a too-flippant colt. C—— added a rider or two after H—— had left.

(But it pleased Allah to afflict H—— in after years. I met him in charge of a 'mixed' College in New Zealand,[41] where he taught a class of young ladies Latinity. 'And when they make false quantities, like *you* used to, they make—eyes at me!' I thought of my chill mornings at Greek Testament under his ready hand, and pitied him from the bottom of my soul.)

Yes—I must have been 'nursed' with care by Crom and under his orders. Hence, when he saw I was irretrievably committed to the ink-pot, his order that I should edit the School Paper[42] and have the run of his Library Study. Hence, I presume, C——'s similar permission, granted and withdrawn as the fortunes of our private war varied. Hence the Head's idea that I should learn Russian[43] with him (I got as far as some of the cardinal numbers) and, later *précis*-writing. This latter meant severe compression of dry-as-dust material, no essential fact to be omitted. The whole was sweetened with reminiscences of the men of Crom's youth, and throughout the low, soft drawl and the smoke of his perpetual Vevey[44] he shed light on the handling of words. Heaven forgive me! I thought these privileges were due to my transcendent personal merits.

Many of us loved the Head for what he had done for us, but I owed him more than all of them put together; and I think I loved him even more than they did. There came a day when he told me that a fortnight after the close of the summer holidays of '82, I would go to India to work on a paper in Lahore, where my parents lived, and would get one hundred silver rupees a month! At term-end he most unjustly devised a prize poem—subject 'The Battle of Assaye' which, there being no competitor, I won in what I conceived was the metre of my latest 'infection'—Joaquin Miller.[45] And when I took the prize-book, Trevelyan's *Competition Wallah*,[46] Crom Price said that if I went on I might be heard of again.

I spent my last few days before sailing with the beloved Aunt in the little cottage that the Burne-Jones' had bought for a holiday house at Rottingdean.[47] There I looked across the village green and the horse-pond at a house called 'The Elms' behind a flint wall, and at a church opposite; and—had I known it—at 'The bodies of those to be In the Houses of Death and of Birth.'[48]

CHAPTER III

Seven Years' Hard

I am poor Brother Lippo by your leave.
You need not clap your torches to my face.
Fra Lippo Lippi[1]

So, at sixteen years and nine months,[2] but looking four or five years older, and adorned with real whiskers which the scandalised Mother abolished within one hour of beholding, I found myself at Bombay where I was born, moving among sights and smells that made me deliver in the vernacular sentences whose meaning I knew not. Other Indian-born boys have told me how the same thing happened to them.

There were yet three or four days' rail to Lahore, where my people lived. After these, my English years fell away, nor ever, I think, came back in full strength.

That was a joyous home-coming. For—consider!—I had returned to a Father and Mother of whom I had seen but little since my sixth year. I might have found my Mother 'the sort of woman *I* don't care for,' as in one terrible case that I know; and my Father intolerable. But the Mother proved more delightful than all my imaginings or memories. My father was not only a mine of knowledge and help, but a humorous, tolerant, and expert fellow-crafts-man. I had my own room in the house; my servant, handed over to me by my father's servant, whose son he was, with the solemnity of a marriage-contract; my own horse, cart, and groom; my own office-

25

hours and direct responsibilities; and—oh joy!—my own office-box, just like my Father's, which he took daily to the Lahore School of Art and Museum.[3] I do not remember the smallest friction in any detail of our lives. We delighted more in each other's society than in that of strangers; and when my sister came out,[4] a little later, our cup was filled to the brim. Not only were we happy, but we knew it.

But the work was heavy. I represented fifty per cent of the 'editorial staff' of the one daily paper of the Punjab[5]—a small sister of the great *Pioneer* at Allahabad under the same proprietorship.[6] And a daily paper comes out every day even though fifty per cent of the staff have fever.

My Chief[7] took me in hand, and for three years or so I loathed him. He had to break me in, and I knew nothing. What he suffered on my account I cannot tell; but the little that I ever acquired of accuracy, the habit of trying at least to verify references, and some knack of sticking to desk-work, I owed wholly to Stephen Wheeler.

I never worked less than ten hours and seldom more than fifteen per diem; and as our paper came out in the evening did not see the midday sun except on Sundays. I had fever too, regular and persistent, to which I added for a while chronic dysentery. Yet I discovered that a man can work with a temperature of 104, even though next day he has to ask the office who wrote the article. Our native Foreman, on the News side, Mian Rukn Din, a Muhammedan gentleman of kind heart and infinite patience, whom I never saw unequal to a situation, was my loyal friend throughout. From the modern point of view I suppose the life was not fit for a dog, but my world was filled with boys, but a few years older than I, who lived utterly alone, and died from typhoid mostly at the regulation age of twenty-two. As regarding ourselves at home, if there were any dying to be done, we four were together. The rest was in the day's work, with love to sweeten all things.

Books, plays, pictures, and amusements, outside what games the cold weather allowed, there were none. Transport was limited to horses and such railways as existed. This meant that one's normal radius of travel would be about six miles in any direction, and—one did not meet new white faces at every six miles. Death was always our near companion. When there was an outbreak of eleven cases of

typhoid in our white community of seventy, and professional nurses
had not been invented, the men sat up with the men and the women
with the women. We lost four of our invalids and thought we had
done well. Otherwise, men and women dropped where they stood.
Hence our custom of looking up any one who did not appear at our
daily gatherings.

The dead of all times were about us—in the vast forgotten
Moslem cemeteries round the Station, where one's horse's hoof of a
morning might break through to the corpse below; skulls and bones
tumbled out of our mud garden walls, and were turned up among
the flowers by the Rains; and at every point were tombs of the dead.
Our chief picnic rendezvous and some of our public offices had been
memorials to desired dead women; and Fort Lahore, where Runjit
Singh's wives lay, was a mausoleum of ghosts.[8]

This was the setting in which my world revolved. Its centre for
me—a member at seventeen—was the Punjab Club, where bache-
lors, for the most part, gathered to eat meals of no merit among men
whose merits they knew well. My Chief was married and came there
seldom, so it was mine to be told every evening of the faults of that
day's issue in very simple language. Our native compositors 'followed copy' without knowing one word of English. Hence glorious
and sometimes obscene misprints. Our proof-readers (sometimes we
had a brace of them) drank, which was expected; but systematic and
prolonged D.T. on their part gave me more than my share of their
work. And in that Club and elsewhere I met none except picked men
at their definite work—Civilians, Army, Education, Canals, Forestry, Engineering, Irrigation, Railways, Doctors, and Lawyers—
samples of each branch and each talking his own shop. It follows
then that that 'show of technical knowledge' for which I was blamed
later came to me from the horse's mouth, even to boredom.

So soon as my paper could trust me a little, and I had behaved
well at routine work, I was sent out, first for local reportings; then to
race-meetings which included curious nights in the lottery-tent. (I
saw one go up in flame once, when a heated owner hove an oil-lamp
at the handicapper on the night the owner was coming up for
election at the Club. That was the first and last time I had seen every
available black ball expended and members begging for more.)

Later I described openings of big bridges and such-like, which meant a night or two with the engineers; floods on railways—more nights in the wet with wretched heads of repair gangs; village festivals and consequent outbreaks of cholera or small-pox; communal riots under the shadow of the Mosque of Wazir Khan, where the patient waiting troops lay in timber-yards or side-alleys till the order came to go in and hit the crowds on the feet with the gun-butt[9] (killing in Civil Administration was then reckoned confession of failure), and the growling, flaring, creed-drunk city would be brought to hand without effusion of blood, or the appearance of any agitated Viceroy; visits of Viceroys to neighbouring Princes on the edge of the great Indian Desert, where a man might have to wash his raw hands and face in soda-water; reviews of Armies expecting to move against Russia next week; receptions of an Afghan Potentate, with whom the Indian Government wished to stand well (this included a walk into the Khyber, where I was shot at, but without malice, by a rapparee who disapproved of his ruler's foreign policy); murder and divorce trials, and (a really filthy job) an inquiry into the percentage of lepers among the butchers who supplied beef and mutton to the European community of Lahore.[10] (Here I first learned that crude statements of crude facts are not well seen by responsible official authorities.) It was Squeers' method of instruction,[11] but how could I fail to be equipped with more than all I might need? I was saturated with it, and if I tripped over detail, the Club attended to me.

My first bribe was offered to me at the age of nineteen when I was in a Native State[12] where, naturally, one concern of the Administration was to get more guns of honour added to the Ruler's official salute when he visited British India, and even a roving correspondent's good word might be useful. Hence in the basket of fruits (*dali* is its name) laid at my tent door each morning, a five-hundred-rupee note and a Cashmere shawl. As the sender was of high caste I returned the gift at the hands of the camp-sweeper, who was not. Upon this my servant, responsible to his father, and mine, for my well-being, said without emotion: 'Till we get home you eat and drink from my hands.' This I did.

On return to work I found my Chief had fever, and I was in sole charge. Among his editorial correspondence was a letter from this Native State setting forth the record during a few days' visit of 'your reporter, a person called Kipling'; who had broken, it seemed, the Decalogue in every detail from rape to theft. I wrote back that as Acting-Editor I had received the complaints and would investigate, but they must expect me to be biassed because I was the person complained of.

I visited the State more than once later, and there was not a cloud on our relations. I had dealt with the insult *more Asiatico*—which *they* understood; the ball had been returned *more Asiatico*—which *I* understood; and the incident had been closed.

My second bribe came when I worked under Stephen Wheeler's successor, Kay Robinson,[13] brother of Phil Robinson[14] who wrote *In My Indian Garden*. With him, thanks to his predecessor having licked me into some shape, my relations were genial. It was the old matter of gun-salutes again; the old machinery of the basket of fruit and shawls and money for us both, but this time left impudently on the office verandah. Kay and I wasted a happy half-hour pricking *Timeo Danaos et dona ferentes*'[15] into the currency notes, mourned that we could not take the shawls, and let the matter go.

My third and most interesting bribe was when reporting a divorce case in Eurasian society. An immense brown woman penned me in a corner and offered 'if I would but keep her name out of it' to give me most intimate details, which she began at once to do. I demanded her name before bargaining. 'Oah! I am the Respondent. Thatt is why I ask you.' It is hard to report some dramas without Ophelias if not Hamlets. But I was repaid for her anger when Counsel asked her if she had ever expressed a desire to dance on her husband's grave. Till then she had denied everything. 'Yess,' she hissed, 'and I jolly-damn-well *would* too.'

A soldier of my acquaintance had been sentenced to life-imprisonment for a murder which, on evidence not before the court, seemed to me rather justified. I saw him later in Lahore gaol at work on some complicated arrangement of nibs with different coloured inks, stuck into a sort of loom which, drawn over paper, gave the ruling for the blank forms of financial statements. It seemed wickedly monotonous. But the spirit of man is undefeatable. 'If I made a mistake of an eighth of an inch in spacing these lines, I'd throw out *all* the accounts of the Upper Punjab,' said he.

As to our reading public, they were at the least as well educated as fifty per cent of our 'staff'; and by force of their lives could not be stampeded or much 'thrilled.' Double headlines we had never heard of, nor special type, and I fear that the amount of 'white' in the newspapers to-day would have struck us as common cheating. Yet the stuff we dealt in would have furnished modern journals of enterprise with almost daily sensations.

My legitimate office-work was sub-editing, which meant eternal cutting-down of unwieldy contributions—such as discourses on abstruse questions of Revenue and Assessment from a great and wise Civilian who wrote the vilest hand that even our compositors ever saw; literary articles about Milton. (And how was I to know that the writer was a relative of one of our proprietors, who thought our paper existed to air his theories?) Here Crom Price's training in *précis*-work helped me to get swiftly at what meat there might be in the disorderly messes. There were newspaper exchanges from Egypt to Hong-Kong to be skimmed nearly every morning and, once a week, the English papers on which one drew in time of need; local correspondence from out-stations to vet for possible libels in their innocent allusions; 'spoofing'-letters from subalterns to be guarded against (twice I was trapped here); always, of course, the filing of cables, and woe betide an error then! I took them down from the telephone—a primitive and mysterious power whose native operator broke every word into monosyllables. One cut-and-come-again affliction was an accursed Muscovite paper, the *Novoie Vremya*, written in French, which, for weeks and weeks, published the war diaries of Alikhanoff, a Russian General then harrying the Central Russian Khanates.[16] He gave the name of every camp he halted at, and regularly reported that his troops warmed themselves at fires of *sax-aul*,[17] which I suppose is perhaps sage-brush. A week after I had translated the last of the series every remembrance of it passed from my normal memory.

Ten or twelve years later, I fell sick in New York[18] and passed through a long delirium which, by ill-chance, I remembered when I returned to life. At one stage of it I led an enormous force of cavalry mounted on red horses with brand-new leather saddles, under the glare of a green moon, across steppes so vast that they revealed the very curve of earth. We would halt at one of the camps named by Alikhanoff in his diary (I would see the name of it heaving up over the edge of the planet), where we warmed ourselves at fires of *sax-aul*, and where, scorched on one side and frozen on the other, I sat till my infernal squadrons went on again to the next fore-known halt; and so through the list.

In 1885[19] a Liberal Government had come into power at Home and was acting on liberal 'principle,' which so far as I have observed ends not seldom in bloodshed. Just then, it was a matter of principle that Native Judges should try white women.[20] Native in this case meant overwhelmingly Hindu; and the Hindu's idea of women is not lofty. No one had asked for any such measure—least of all the Judiciary concerned. But principle is principle, though the streets swim. The European community were much annoyed. They went to the extremity of revolt—that is to say even the officials of the Service and their wives very often would not attend the functions and levées of the then Viceroy,[21] a circular and bewildered recluse of religious tendencies. A pleasant English gentleman called C. P. Ilbert had been imported to father and god-father the Bill. I think he, too, was a little bewildered. Our paper, like most of the European Press, began with stern disapproval of the measure, and, I fancy, published much comment and correspondence which would now be called 'disloyal.'

One evening, while putting the paper to bed, I looked as usual over the leader. It was the sort of false-balanced, semi-judicial stuff that some English journals wrote about the Indian White Paper[22] from 1932 to '34, and like them it furnished a barely disguised exposition of the Government's high ideals. In after-life one got to know that touch better, but it astonished me at the time, and I asked my Chief what it all meant. He replied, as I should have done in his place: 'None of your dam' business,' and, being married, went to his home. I repaired to the Club which, remember, was the whole of my outside world.

As I entered the long, shabby dining-room where we all sat at one table, everyone hissed. I was innocent enough to ask: 'What's the joke? Who are they hissing?' 'You,' said the man at my side. 'Your dam' rag has ratted over the Bill.'[23]

It is not pleasant to sit still when one is twenty[24] while all your universe hisses you. Then uprose a Captain, our Adjutant of Volunteers, and said: 'Stop that! The boy's only doing what he's paid to do.' The demonstration tailed off, but I had seen a great light. The Adjutant was entirely correct. I was a hireling, paid to do what I was paid to do, and—I did not relish the idea. Someone said kindly: 'You damned young ass! Don't you know that your paper has the Government printing-contract?' I *did* know it, but I had never before put two and two together.

A few months later one of my two chief proprietors received the decoration that made him a Knight.[25] Then I began to take much interest in certain smooth Civilians, who had seen good in the Government measure and had somehow been shifted out of the heat to billets in Simla. I followed under shrewd guidance, often native, the many pretty ways by which a Government can put veiled pressure on its employees in a land where every circumstance *and* relation of a man's life is public property. So, when the great and epoch-making India Bill turned up fifty years later, I felt as one retreading the tortuous by-ways of his youth. One recognised the very phrases and assurances of the old days still doing good work, and waited, as in a dream, for the very slightly altered formulas in which those who were parting with their convictions excused themselves. Thus: 'I may act as a brake, you know. At any rate I'm keeping a more extreme man out of the game.' 'There's no sense running counter to the inevitable,'—and all the other Devil-provided camouflage for the sinner-who-faces-both-ways.

In '85[26] I was made a Freemason by dispensation (Lodge Hope and Perseverance 782 E.C.), being under age, because the Lodge hoped for a good Secretary. They did not get him, but I helped, and got the Father to advise, in decorating the bare walls of the Masonic Hall with hangings after the prescription of Solomon's Temple. Here I met Muslims, Hindus, Sikhs, members of the Araya and Brahmo Samaj,[27] and a Jew tyler,[28] who was priest and butcher to his little community in the city. So yet another world opened to me which I needed.[29]

My Mother and Sister would go up to the Hills for the hot weather, and in due course my Father too. My own holiday came when I could be spared. Thus I often lived alone in the big house, where I commanded by choice native food, as less revolting than meat-cookery, and so added indigestion to my more intimate possessions.

In those months—mid-April to mid-October—one took up one's bed and walked about with it from room to room, seeking for less heated air; or slept on the flat roof with the waterman to throw half-skinfuls of water on one's parched carcase. This brought on fever but saved heat-stroke.

Often the night got into my head as it had done in the boarding-house in the Brompton Road, and I would wander till dawn in all manner of odd places—liquor-shops, gambling and opium-dens, which are not a bit mysterious, wayside entertainments such as puppet-shows, native dances; or in and about the narrow gullies under the Mosque of Wazir Khan for the sheer sake of looking. Sometimes, the Police would challenge, but I knew most of their officers, and many folk in some quarters knew me for the son of my Father, which in the East more than anywhere else is useful. Otherwise, the word 'Newspaper' sufficed; though I did not supply my paper with many accounts of these prowls.[30] One would come home, just as the light broke, in some night-hawk of a hired carriage which stank of hookah-fumes, jasmine-flowers, and sandalwood; and if the driver were moved to talk, he told one a good deal. Much of real Indian life goes on in the hot weather nights. That is why the native staff of the offices are not much use next morning. All native offices aestivate from May at least till September. Files and correspondence are then as a matter of course pitched unopened into corners, to be written up or faked when the weather gets cooler. But the English who go Home on leave, having imposed the set hours of a northern working day upon the children of children, are surprised that India does not work as they do. This is one of the reasons why autonomous India will be interesting.

And there were 'wet' nights too at the Club or one Mess, when a table-full of boys, half-crazed with discomfort, but with just sense enough to stick to beer and bones which seldom betray, tried to rejoice and somehow succeeded. I remember one night when we ate tinned haggis with cholera in the cantonments 'to see what would happen,' and another when a savage stallion in harness was presented with a very hot leg of roast mutton, as he snapped. Theoretically this is a cure for biting, but it only made him more of a cannibal.

I got to meet the soldiery of those days in visits to Fort Lahore and, in a less degree, at Mian Mir Cantonments.[31] My first and best beloved Battalion was the 2nd Fifth Fusiliers,[32] with whom I dined in awed silence a few weeks after I came out. When they left I took up with their successors, the 30th East Lancashire,[33] another North-country regiment; and, last, with the 31st East Surrey[34] — a London recruited confederacy of skilful dog-stealers, some of them my good and loyal friends. There were ghostly dinners too with Subalterns in charge of the Infantry Detachment at Fort Lahore, where, all among marble-inlaid, empty apartments of dead Queens, or under the domes of old tombs, meals began with the regulation thirty grains of quinine in the sherry, and ended—as Allah pleased!

I am, by the way, one of the few civilians who have turned out a Quarter-Guard of Her Majesty's troops.[35] It was on a chill winter morn, about 2 A.M. at the Fort, and though I suppose I had been given the countersign on my departure from the Mess, I forgot it ere I reached the Main Guard, and when challenged announced myself spaciously as 'Visiting Rounds.' When the men had clattered out I asked the Sergeant if he had ever seen a finer collection of scoundrels. That cost me beer by the gallon, but it was worth it.

Having no position to consider, and my trade enforcing it, I could move at will in the fourth dimension. I came to realise the bare horrors of the private's life, and the unnecessary torments he endured on account of the Christian doctrine which lays down that 'the wages of sin is death.' It was counted impious that bazaar prostitutes should be inspected; or that the men should be taught elementary precautions in their dealings with them. This official virtue cost our Army in India nine thousand expensive white men a year always laid up from venereal disease. Visits to Lock Hospitals[36] made me desire, as earnestly as I do to-day, that I might have six hundred priests—Bishops of the Establishment for choice—to handle for six months precisely as the soldiers of my youth were handled.

Heaven knows the men died fast enough from typhoid, which seemed to have something to do with water, but we were not sure; or from cholera, which was manifestly a breath of the Devil that could kill all on one side of a barrack-room and spare the others; from seasonal fever; or from what was described as 'blood-poisoning.'

Lord Roberts,[37] at that time Commander-in-Chief in India, who knew my people, was interested in the men, and—I had by then written one or two stories about soldiers—the proudest moment of my young life was when I rode up Simla Mall beside him on his usual explosive red Arab, while he asked me what the men thought about their accommodation, entertainment-rooms and the like. I told him, and he thanked me as gravely as though I had been a full Colonel.[38]

My month's leave at Simla,[39] or whatever Hill Station my people went to, was pure joy—every golden hour counted. It began in heat and discomfort, by rail and road. It ended in the cool evening, with a wood fire in one's bedroom, and next morn—thirty more of them ahead!—the early cup of tea, the Mother who brought it in, and the long talks of us all together again. One had leisure to work, too, at whatever play-work was in one's head, and that was usually full.

Simla was another new world. There the Hierarchy lived, and one saw and heard the machinery of administration stripped bare. There were the Heads of the Viceregal and Military staffs and their Aides-de-Camp; and playing whist with Great Ones, who gave him special news, was the Correspondent of our big Sister Paper the *Pioneer*, then a power in the land.[40]

The dates, but not the pictures, of those holidays are blurred. At one time our little world was full of the aftermaths of Theosophy as taught by Madame Blavatsky[41] to her devotees. My Father knew the lady and, with her, would discuss wholly secular subjects; she being, he told me, one of the most interesting and unscrupulous impostors he had ever met. This, with his experience, was a high compliment. I was not so fortunate, but came across queer, bewildered, old people, who lived in an atmosphere of 'manifestations' running about their houses. But the earliest days of Theosophy devastated the *Pioneer*, whose Editor[42] became a devout believer, and used the paper for propaganda to an extent which got on the nerves not only of the public but of a proof-reader, who at the last moment salted an impassioned leader on the subject with, in brackets: '*What do you bet this is a dam' lie?*' The Editor was most untheosophically angry!

On one of my Simla leaves—I had been ill with dysentery again—I was sent off for rest along the Himalaya-Tibet road in the company of an invalid officer and his wife.[43] My equipment was my servant—he from whose hands I had fed in the Native State before-mentioned; Dorothea Darbishoff, *alias* Dolly Bobs, a temperamental she-pony; and four baggage-coolies who were recruited and changed at each stage. I knew the edge of the great Hills both from Simla and Dalhousie, but had never marched any distance into them. They were to me a revelation of 'all might, majesty, dominion, and power, henceforth and for ever,'[44] in colour, form, and substance indescribable. A little of what I realised then came back to me in *Kim*.

On the day I turned back for Simla—my companions were going further—my servant embroiled himself with a new quartette of coolies and managed to cut the eye of one of them. I was a few score miles from the nearest white man, and did not wish to be haled before any little Hill Rajah, knowing as I did that the coolies would unitedly swear that I had directed the outrage. I therefore paid blood-money, and strategically withdrew—on foot for the most part because Dolly Bobs objected to every sight and most of the smells of the landscape. I had to keep the coolies who, like the politicians, would not stay put, in front of me on the six-foot-wide track, and, as is ever the case when one is in difficulties, it set in to rain. My urgent business was to make my first three days' march in one—a matter of thirty odd miles. My coolies wanted to shy off to their village and spend their ill-gotten silver. On me developed[45] the heart-breaking job of shepherding a retreat. I do not think my mileage that day could have been much less than forty miles of sheer up-hill and down-dale slogging. But it did me great good, and enabled me to put away bottles of strong Army beer at the wet evening's end in the resthouse. On our last day, a thunderstorm, which had been at work a few thousand feet below us, rose to the level of the ridge we were crossing and exploded in our midst. We were all flung on our faces, and when I was able to see again I observed the half of a well-grown pine, as neatly split lengthwise as a match by a penknife, in the act of hirpling[46] down the steep hillside by itself. The thunder drowned everything, so that it seemed to be posturing in dumb show, and when it began to hop—horrible vertical hops—the effect was of pure D.T. My coolies, however, who had had the tale of my misdeeds from their predecessors, argued that if the local Gods missed such a sitting shot as I had given them, I could not be altogether unlucky.

It was on this trip that I saw a happy family of four bears out for a walk together, all talking at the tops of their voices; and also—the sun on his wings, a thousand feet below me—I stared long at a wheeling eagle, himself thousands of feet above the map-like valley he was quartering.

On my return I handed my servant over to his father, who dealt faithfully with him for having imperilled my Father's son. But what I did *not* tell him was that my servant, a Punjabi Muslim, had in his first panic embraced the feet of the injured hill-coolie, a heathen, and begged him to 'show mercy.' A servant, precisely because he is a servant, has his *izzat*—his honour—or, as the Chinese say, his 'face.' Save that, and he is yours. One should never rate one's man before others; nor, if he knows that you know the implication of the words that you are using to him, should you ever use certain words and phrases. But to a young man raw from England, or to an old one in whose service one has grown grey, anything is permitted. In the first case: 'He is a youngster. He slangs as his girl has taught him,' and the man keeps his countenance even though his master's worst words are inflected woman-fashion. In the second case, the aged servitor and deputy-conscience says: 'It is naught. We were young men together. Ah! you should have heard him *then*!'

The reward for this very small consideration is service of a kind that one accepted as a matter of course—till one was without it. My man would go monthly to the local Bank and draw my pay in coined rupees, which he would carry home raw in his waist-band, as the whole bazaar knew, and decant into an old wardrobe, whence I would draw for my needs till there remained no more.

Yet, it was necessary to his professional honour that he should present me monthly a list of petty disbursements on my personal behalf—such as oil for the buggy-lamps, bootlaces, thread for darning my socks, buttons replaced and the like—all written out in bazaar-English by the letter-writer at the corner of the road. The total rose, of course, with my pay, and on each rupee of this bill my man took the commission of the East, say one-sixteenth or perhaps one-tenth of each rupee.

For the rest, till I was in my twenty-fourth year,[47] I no more dreamed of dressing myself than I did of shutting an inner door or—I was going to say turning a key in a lock. But we had no locks. I gave myself indeed the trouble of stepping into the garments that were held out to me after my bath, and out of them as I was assisted to do. And—luxury of which I dream still—I was shaved before I was awake!

One must set these things against the taste of fever in one's mouth, and the buzz of quinine in one's ears; the temper frayed by heat to breaking-point but for sanity's sake held back from the break; the descending darkness of intolerable dusks; and the less supportable dawns of fierce, stale heat through half of the year.

When my people were at the Hills and I was alone, my Father's butler took command. One peril of solitary life is going to seed in details of living. As our numbers at the Club shrank between April and mid-September, men grew careless, till at last our conscience-stricken Secretary, himself an offender, would fetch us up with a jerk, and forbid us dining in little more than singlet and riding-breeches.

This temptation was stronger in one's own house, though one knew if one broke the ritual of dressing for the last meal one was parting with a sheet-anchor. (Young gentlemen of larger views to-day consider this 'dress-for-dinner' business as an affectation ranking with 'the old school tie.' I would give some months' pay for the privilege of enlightening them.) Here the butler would take charge. 'For the honour of the house there must be a dinner. It is long since the Sahib has bidden friends to eat.' I would protest like a fretful child. He would reply: 'Except for the names of the Sahibs to be invited all things are on *my* head.' So one dug up four or five companions in discomfort; the pitiful, scorched marigold blooms would appear on the table and, to a full accompaniment of glass, silver, and napery, the ritual would be worked through, and the butler's honour satisfied for a while.

At the Club, sudden causeless hates flared up between friends and died down like straw fires; old grievances were recalled and brooded over aloud; the complaint-book bristled with accusations and inventions. All of which came to nothing when the first Rains fell, and after a three days' siege of creeping and crawling things, whose bodies stopped our billiards and almost put out the lamps they sizzled in, life picked up in the blessed cool.

But it was a strange life. Once, suddenly, in the Club ante-room a man asked a neighbour to pass him the newspaper. 'Get it yourself,' was the hot-weather answer. The man rose but on his way to the table dropped and writhed in the first grip of cholera. He was carried to his quarters, the Doctor came, and for three days he went through all the stages of the disease even to the characteristic baring of discoloured gums. Then he returned to life and, on being condoled with, said: 'I remember getting up to get the paper, but after that, give you my word, I don't remember a thing till I heard Lawrie[48] say that I was coming out of it.' I have heard since that oblivion is sometimes vouchsafed.

Though I was spared the worst horrors, thanks to the pressure of work, a capacity for being able to read, and the pleasure of writing what my head was filled with, I felt each succeeding hot weather more and more, and cowered in my soul as it returned.

This is fit place for a 'pivot' experience to be set side by side with the affair of the Adjutant of Volunteers at the Club. It happened one hot-weather evening, in '86 or thereabouts, when I felt that I had come to the edge of all endurance. As I entered my empty house in the dusk there was no more in me except the horror of a great darkness, that I must have been fighting for some days. I came through that darkness alive, but how I do not know. Late at night I picked up a book by Walter Besant which was called *All in a Garden Fair*.[49] It dealt with a young man who desired to write; who came to realise the possibilities of common things seen, and who eventually succeeded in his desire. What its merits may be from today's 'literary' standpoint I do not know. But I *do* know that that book was my salvation in sore personal need, and with the reading and re-reading it became to me a revelation, a hope and strength. I was certainly, I argued, as well equipped as the hero and—and—after all, there was no need for me to stay here for ever. I could go away and measure myself against the doorsills of London as soon as I had money. Therefore I would begin to save money, for I perceived there was absolutely no reason outside myself why I should not do exactly what to me seemed good. For proof of my revelation I did, sporadically but sincerely, try to save money, and I built up in my head— always with the book to fall back upon—a dream of the future that sustained me. To Walter Besant singly and solely do I owe this—as I told him when we met, and he laughed, rolled in his chair, and seemed pleased.[50]

In the joyous reign of Kay Robinson, my second Chief, our paper changed its shape and type.[51] This took up for a week or so all hours of the twenty-four and cost me a break-down due to lack of sleep. But we two were proud of the results. One new feature was a daily 'turnover'—same as the little pink *Globe* at Home—of one column and a quarter. Naturally, the 'office' had to supply most of them and once more I was forced to 'write short.'[52]

All the queer outside world would drop into our workshop sooner or later—say a Captain just cashiered for horrible drunkenness, who reported his fall with a wry, appealing face, and then— disappeared. Or a man old enough to be my father, on the edge of tears because he had been overpassed for Honours in the *Gazette*. Or three troopers of the Ninth Lancers, one of whom was an old schoolmate of mine who became a General with an expedition of his own in West Africa in the Great War.[53] The other two also were gentlemen-rankers who rose to high commands. One met men going up and down the ladder in every shape of misery and success.

There was a night at the Club when some silly idiot found a half-dead viper and brought it to dinner in a pickle-bottle. One man of the company kept messing about with the furious little beast on the table-cloth till he had to be warned to take his hands away. A few weeks after, some of us realised it would have been better had he accomplished what had been in his foreboding mind that night.

But the cold weather brought ample amends. The family were together again and—except for my Mother's ukase against her men bringing bound volumes of the *Illustrated London News* to meals (a survival of hot-weather savagery)—all was bliss. So, in the cold weather of '85 we four made up a Christmas annual called *Quartette*,[54] which pleased us a great deal and attracted a certain amount of attention. (Later, much later, it became a 'collector's piece' in the U.S. book-market, and to that extent smudged the happy memories of its birth.) In '85 I began a series of tales in the *Civil and Military Gazette* which were called *Plain Tales from the Hills*.[55] They came in when and as padding was needed. In '86 also I published a collection of newspaper verses on Anglo-Indian life, called *Departmental Ditties*, which, dealing with things known and suffered by many people, were well received. I had been allowed, further, to send stuff that we, editorially, had no use for, to far-off Calcutta papers, such as the *Indigo Planters' Gazette*,[56] and elsewhere. These things were making for me the beginnings of a name even unto Bengal.

But mark how discreetly the cards were being dealt me. Up till '87 my performances had been veiled in the decent obscurity of the far end of an outlying province, among a specialised community who did not interest any but themselves. I was like a young horse entered for small, up-country events where I could get used to noise and crowds, fall about till I found my feet, and learn to keep my head with the hoofs drumming behind me. Better than all, the pace of my office-work was 'too good to inquire,'[57] and its nature—that I should realise all sorts and conditions of men and make others realise them—gave me no time to 'realise' myself.

Here was my modest notion of my own position at the end of my five years' Viceroyalty on the little *Civil and Military Gazette*. I was still fifty per cent of the editorial staff, though for a while I rose to have a man under me.[58] But—just are the Gods!—that varlet was 'literary' and must needs write Elia-like 'turnovers'[59] instead of sticking to the legitimate! Any fool, I knew to my sorrow, could write. My job was to sub-edit him or her into some sort of shape. Any other fool could review; (I myself on urgent call have reviewed the later works of a writer called Browning,[60] and what my Father said

41

about *that* was unpublishable). Reporting was a minor 'feature,' although we did not use that word. I myself *qua* reporter could turn in stuff one day and *qua* sub-editor knock it remorselessly into cocked hats the next. The difference, then, between me and the vulgar herd who 'write for papers' was, as I saw it, the gulf that divides the beneficed clergyman from ladies and gentlemen who contribute pumpkins and dahlias to Harvest Festival decorations. To say that I magnified my office is to understate. But this may have saved me from magnifying myself beyond decency.

In '87[61] orders came for me to serve on the *Pioneer*, our big sister-paper at Allahabad, hundreds of miles to the southward, where I should be one of four at least and a new boy at a big school.

But the North-West Provinces, as they were then, being largely Hindu, were strange 'air and water' to me. My life had lain among Muslims, and a man leans one way or other according to his first service. The large, well-appointed Club, where Poker had just driven out Whist and men gambled seriously, was full of large-bore officials, and of a respectability all new. The Fort where troops were quartered had its points; but one bastion jutted out into a most holy river.[62] Therefore, partially burned corpses made such a habit of stranding just below the Subalterns' quarters that a special expert was entertained to pole them off and onward. In Fort Lahore we dealt in nothing worse than ghosts.

Moreover, the *Pioneer* lived under the eye of its chief proprietor,[63] who spent several months of each year in his bungalow over the way. It is true that I owed him my chance in life, but when one has been second in command of even a third-class cruiser, one does not care to have one's Admiral permanently moored at a cable's length. His love for his paper, which his single genius and ability had largely created, led him sometimes to 'give the boys a hand.' On those hectic days (for he added and subtracted to the last minute) we were relieved when the issue caught the down-country mail.

But he was patient with me, as were the others, and through him again I got a wider field for 'outside stuff.' There was to be a weekly edition of the *Pioneer* for Home consumption. Would I edit it, additional to ordinary work? Would I not?[64] There would be fiction—syndicated serial-matter bought by the running foot from agencies at Home. That would fill one whole big page. The 'sight of means to do ill deeds'[65] had the usual effect. Why buy Bret Harte,[66] I asked, when I was prepared to supply home-grown fiction on the hoof? And I did.

My editing of the *Weekly* may have been a shade casual—it was but a re-hash of news and views after all. My head was full of, to me, infinitely more important material. Henceforth no mere twelve-hundred Plain Tales jammed into rigid frames, but three- or five-thousand-word cartoons once a week. So did young Lippo Lippi, whose child I was, look on the blank walls of his monastery when he was bidden decorate them! ' 'Twas ask and have, Choose for more's ready,'[67] with a vengeance.

I fancy my change of surroundings and outlook precipitated the rush. At the beginning of it I had an experience which, in my innocence, I mistook for the genuine motions of my Daemon.[68] I must have been loaded more heavily than I realised with 'Gyp,'[69] for there came to me in scenes as stereoscopically clear as those in the crystal an Anglo-Indian *Autour du Mariage*. My pen took charge and I, greatly admiring, watched it write for me far into the nights. The result I christened *The Story of the Gadsbys*,[70] and when it first appeared in England I was complimented on my 'knowledge of the world.' After my indecent immaturity came to light, I heard less of these gifts. Yet, as the Father said loyally: 'It wasn't *all* so dam' bad, Ruddy.'

At any rate it went into the *Weekly*, together with soldier tales, Indian tales, and tales of the opposite sex. There was one of this last which, because of a doubt, I handed up to the Mother, who abolished it and wrote me: *Never you do that again*. But I did and managed to pull off, not unhandily, a tale called 'A Wayside Comedy,'[71] where I worked hard for a certain 'economy of implication,' and in one phrase of less than a dozen words believed I had succeeded. More than forty years later a Frenchman, browsing about some of my old work, quoted this phrase as the *clou* of the tale and the key to its method.[72] It was a belated 'workshop compliment' that I appreciated. Thus, then, I made my own experiments in the weights, colours, perfumes, and attributes of words in relation to other words, either as read aloud so that they may hold the ear, or, scattered over the page, draw the eye. There is no line of my verse or prose which has not been mouthed till the tongue has made all smooth, and memory, after many recitals, has mechanically skipped the grosser superfluities.

These things occupied and contented me, but—outside of them— I felt that I did not quite fit the *Pioneer*'s scheme of things and that my superiors were of the same opinion. My work on the *Weekly* was not legitimate journalism. My flippancy in handling what I was trusted with was not well seen by the Government or the departmental officialism, on which the *Pioneer* rightly depended for advance and private news, gathered in at Simla or Calcutta by our most important Chief Correspondent.[73] I fancy my owners thought me safer on the road than in my chair; for they sent me out to look at Native State mines, mills, factories and the like.[74] Here I think they were entirely justified. My proprietor at Allahabad had his own game to play (it brought him his well-deserved knighthood in due course[75]) and, to some extent, my vagaries might have embarrassed him. One, I know, did. The *Pioneer* editorially, but cautiously as a terrier drawing up to a porcupine, had hinted that some of Lord Roberts' military appointments at that time verged on nepotism. It was a regretful and well-balanced allocution. My rhymed comment (and why my Chief passed it I know not!) said just the same thing, but not quite so augustly. All I remember of it are the last two flagrant lines:

> And if the *Pioneer* is wrath
> Oh Lord, what *must* you be![76]

I don't think Lord Roberts was pleased with it, but I know he was not half so annoyed as my chief proprietor.

On my side I was ripe for change and, thanks always to *All in a Garden Fair*, had a notion now of where I was heading. My absorption in the *Pioneer Weekly* stories, which I wanted to finish, had put my plans to the back of my head, but when I came out of that furious spell of work towards the end of '88 I rearranged myself. I wanted money for the future. I counted my assets. They came to one book of verse; one ditto prose; and—thanks to the *Pioneer*'s permission—a set of six small paper-backed railway bookstall volumes[77] embodying most of my tales in the *Weekly*—copyright of which the *Pioneer* might well have claimed. The man who then controlled the Indian railway bookstalls[78] came of an imaginative race, used to taking chances. I sold him the six paper-backed books for £200 and a small royalty.[79] *Plain Tales from the Hills* I sold for £50, and I forget how much the same publisher gave me for *Departmental Ditties*.[80] (This was the first and last time I ever dealt direct with publishers.)

Fortified with this wealth, and six months' pay in lieu of notice, I left India for England[81] by way of the Far East and the United States, after six and a half years of hard work and a reasonable amount of sickness. My God-speed came from the managing director,[82] a gentleman of sound commercial instincts, who had never concealed his belief that I was grossly overpaid, and who, when he paid me my last wages, said: 'Take it from me, you'll never be worth more than four hundred rupees a month to anyone.' Common pride bids me tell that at that time I was drawing seven hundred a month.

Accounts were squared between us curiously soon. When my notoriety fell upon me, there was a demand for my old proofs, signed and unsigned stuff not included in my books, and a general turning out of refuse-bins for private publication and sale.[83] This upset my hopes of editing my books decently and responsibly, and wrought general confusion. But I was told later that the *Pioneer* had made as much out of its share in this remnant-traffic as it had paid me in wages since I first landed. (Which shows how one cannot get ahead of gentlemen of sound commercial instincts.)

Yet a man must needs love anything that he has worked and suffered under. When, at long last, the *Pioneer*—India's greatest and most important paper which used to pay twenty-seven per cent to its shareholders—fell on evil days and, after being bedevilled and bewitched, was sold to a syndicate, and I received a notification beginning: 'We think you may be interested to know that,' etc., I felt curiously alone and unsponsored.[84] But my first mistress and most true love, the little *Civil and Military Gazette*, weathered the storm.[85] Even if I wrote them, these lines are true:—

> Try as he will, no man breaks wholly loose
> From his first love, no matter who she be.
> Oh, was there ever sailor free to choose,
> That didn't settle somewhere near the sea?

45

Parsons in pulpits, tax-payers in pews,
   Kings on your thrones, you know as well as me,
We've only one virginity to lose,
   And where we lost it there our hearts will be![86]

And, besides, there is, or was, a tablet in my old Lahore office asserting that here I 'worked.'[87] And Allah knows that is true also!

CHAPTER IV

The Interregnum

The youth who daily further from the East
Must travel . . .   *Wordsworth*[1]

And, in the autumn of '89,[2] I stepped into a sort of waking dream
when I took, as a matter of course, the fantastic cards that Fate was
pleased to deal me.

The ancient landmarks of my boyhood still stood. There were the
beloved Aunt and Uncle, the little house of the Three Old Ladies,
and in one corner of it the quiet figure by the fireplace composedly
writing her next novel on her knee. It was at the quietest of tea-
parties, in this circle, that I first met Mary Kingsley,[3] the bravest
woman of all my knowledge. We talked a good deal over the cups,
and more while walking home afterwards—she of West African
cannibals and the like. At last, the world forgetting, I said: 'Come up
to my rooms and we'll talk it out there.' She agreed, as a man would,
then suddenly remembering said: 'Oh, I forgot I was a woman.
'Fraid I mustn't.' So I realised that my world was all to explore
again.

A few—a very few—people in it had died, but no one expected to
do so for another twenty years. White women stood and waited on
one behind one's chair. It was all whirlingly outside my
comprehension.

But my small stock-in-trade of books had become known in

certain quarters; and there was an evident demand for my stuff. I do not recall that I stirred a hand to help myself. Things happened to me. I went, by invitation, to Mowbray Morris[4] the editor of *Macmillan's Magazine*, who asked me how old I was and, when I told him I hoped to be twenty-four at the end of the year, said: 'Good God!' He took from me an Indian tale and some verses,[5] which latter he wisely edited a little. They were both published in the same number of the *Magazine*—one signed by my name and the other 'Yussuf.' All of this confirmed the feeling (which has come back at intervals through my life), 'Lord ha' mercy on me, this is none of I.'[6]

Then more tales were asked for, and the editor of the *St. James's Gazette*[7] wanted stray articles, signed and unsigned. My 'turnover' training on the *Civil and Military* made this easy for me, and somehow I felt easier with a daily paper under my right elbow.

About this time was an interview in a weekly paper,[8] where I felt myself rather on the wrong side of the counter and that I ought to be questioning my questioner. Shortly after, that same weekly made me a proposition which I could not see my way to accept, and then announced that I was 'feeling my oats,' of which, it was careful to point out, it had given me my first sieveful. Since, at that time, I was overwhelmed, not to say scared, by the amazing luck that had come to me, the pronouncement gave me confidence. If that was how I struck the external world—good! For naturally I considered the whole universe was acutely interested in me only—just as a man who strays into a skirmish is persuaded he is the pivot of the action.

Meantime, I had found me quarters in Villiers Street, Strand,[9] which forty-six years ago was primitive and passionate in its habits and population. My rooms were small, not over-clean or well-kept, but from my desk I could look out of my window through the fanlight of Gatti's Music-Hall entrance, across the street, almost on to its stage. The Charing Cross trains rumbled through my dreams on one side, the boom of the Strand on the other, while, before my windows, Father Thames under the Shot Tower walked up and down with his traffic.

At the outset I had so muddled and mismanaged my affairs that, for a while, I found myself with some money owing me for work done, but no funds in hand. People who asked for money, however justifiably, have it remembered against them. The beloved Aunt, or any one of the Three Old Ladies, would have given to me without question; but that seemed too like confessing failure at the outset. My rent was paid; I had my dress-suit; I had nothing to pawn save a collection of unmarked shirts picked up in all the ports; so I made shift to manage on what small cash I had in pocket.

My rooms were above an establishment of Harris the Sausage King, who, for tuppence, gave as much sausage and mash as would carry one from breakfast to dinner when one dined with nice people who did not eat sausage for a living. Another tuppence found me a filling supper. The excellent tobacco of those days was, unless you sank to threepenny 'Shag' or soared to sixpenny 'Turkish,' tuppence the half-ounce: and fourpence, which included a pewter of beer or porter, was the price of admission to Gatti's.

It was here, in the company of an elderly but upright barmaid from a pub near by, that I listened to the observed and compelling songs of the Lion and Mammoth Comiques,[10] and the shriller strains—but equally 'observed'—of the Bessies and Bellas, whom I could hear arguing beneath my window with their cab-drivers, as they sped from Hall to Hall. One lady sometimes delighted us with *viva-voce* versions of—'what 'as just 'appened to me outside 'ere, if you'll believe it.' Then she would plunge into brilliant improvisations. Oh, we believed! Many of us had, perhaps, taken part in the tail of that argument at the doors, ere she stormed in.

Those monologues I could never hope to rival, but the smoke, the roar, and the good-fellowship of relaxed humanity at Gatti's 'set' the scheme for a certain sort of song. The Private Soldier in India I thought I knew fairly well. His English brother (in the Guards mostly) sat and sang at my elbow any night I chose; and, for Greek chorus, I had the comments of my barmaid—deeply and dispassionately versed in all knowledge of evil as she had watched it across the zinc she was always swabbing off. (Hence, some years later, verses called 'Mary, pity Women,'[11] based on what she told me about 'a friend o' mine 'oo was mistook in 'er man.') The outcome was the first of some verses called *Barrack-Room Ballads*[12] which I showed to Henley[13] of the *Scots*, later *National Observer*, who wanted more; and I became for a while one of the happy company who used to gather in

49

a little restaurant off Leicester Square[14] and regulate all literature till all hours of the morning.

I had the greatest admiration for Henley's verse and prose and, if such things be merchandise in the next world, will cheerfully sell a large proportion of what I have written for a single meditation—illumination—inspiration or what you please—that he wrote on the *Arabian Nights* in a tiny book of Essays and Reviews.[15]

As regards his free verse I—plus some Chianti—once put forward the old notion that free verse was like fishing with barbless hooks. Henley replied volcanically. It was, said he, 'the cadences that did it.' That was true; but he alone, to my mind, could handle them aright, being a Master Craftsman who had paid for his apprenticeship.

Henley's demerits were, of course, explained to the world by loving friends after his death. I had the fortune to know him only as kind, generous, and a jewel of an editor, with the gift of fetching the very best out of his cattle, with words that would astonish oxen. He had, further, an organic loathing of Mr. Gladstone[16] and all Liberalism. A Government Commission of Enquiry was sitting in those days on some unusually blatant traffic in murder among the Irish Land Leaguers; and had whitewashed the whole crowd.[17] Whereupon, I wrote some impolite verses called 'Cleared!' which at first *The Times* seemed ready to take but on second thoughts declined. I was recommended to carry them to a monthly review of sorts edited by a Mr. Frank Harris,[18] whom I discovered to be the one human being that I could on no terms get on with. He, too, shied at the verses, which I referred to Henley, who, having no sense of political decency, published them in his *Observer* and—after a cautious interval—*The Times* quoted them in full.[19] This was rather like some of my experiences in India, and gave me yet more confidence.

To my great pride I was elected a Member of the Savile[20]—'the little Savile' then in Piccadilly—and, on my introduction, dined with no less than Hardy[21] and Walter Besant. My debts to the latter grew at once, and you may remember that I owed him much indeed. He had his own views on publishers, and was founding, or had just founded, the Authors' Society.[22] He advised me to entrust my business to an agent and sent me to his own—A. P. Watt,[23] whose

son was about my own age. The father took hold of my affairs at once
and most sagely; and on his death his son succeeded. In the course of
forty odd years I do not recall any difference between us that three
minutes' talk could not clear up. This, also, I owed to Besant.

Nor did his goodness halt there. He would sit behind his big,
frosted beard and twinkling spectacles, and deal me out wisdom
concerning this new incomprehensible world. One heard very good
talk at the Savile. Much of it was the careless give-and-take of the
atelier when the models are off their stands, and one throws bread-
pellets at one's betters, and makes hay of all schools save one's own.
But Besant saw deeper. He advised me to 'keep out of the dog-fight.'
He said that if I were 'in with one lot' I would have to be out with
another; and that, at last, 'things would get like a girls' school where
they stick out their tongues at each other when they pass.' That was
true too. One heard men vastly one's seniors wasting energy and
good oaths in recounting 'intrigues' against them, and of men who
had 'their knife into' their work, or whom they themselves wished to
'knife.' (This reminded me somehow of the elderly officials who
opened their hearts in my old office when they were disappointed
over anticipated Honours.) It seemed best to stand clear of it all. For
that reason, I have never directly or indirectly criticised any fellow-
craftsman's output, or encouraged any man or woman to do so; nor
have I approached any persons that they might be led to comment
on my output. My acquaintance with my contemporaries has from
first to last been very limited.

At 'the little Savile' I remember much kindness and toleration.
There was Gosse,[24] of course, sensitive as a cat to all atmospheres, but
utterly fearless when it came to questions of good workmanship;
Hardy's grave and bitter humour; Andrew Lang,[25] as detached to
all appearances as a cloud but—one learned to know—never kinder
in your behalf than when he seemed least concerned with you;
Eustace Balfour,[26] a large, lovable man, and one of the best of
talkers, who died too soon: Herbert Stephen,[27] very wise and very
funny when he chose: Rider Haggard,[28] to whom I took at once, he
being of the stamp adored by children and trusted by men at sight;
and he could tell tales, mainly against himself, that broke up the
tables: Saintsbury,[29] a solid rock of learning and geniality whom I

revered all my days; profoundly a scholar and versed in the art of good living. There was a breakfast with him and Walter Pollock[30] of the *Saturday Review* in the Albany, when he produced some specially devilish Oriental delicacy which we cooked by the light of our united ignorances. It was splendid! Why those two men took the trouble to notice me, I never knew; but I learned to rely on Saintsbury's judgment in the weightier matters of the Laws of Literature. At his latter end he gave me inestimable help in a little piece of work called 'Proofs of Holy Writ,'[31] which without his books could never have been handled. I found him at Bath, compiling with erudition equal to his earnestness the Cellar-book of the Queen's Doll's House.[32] He produced a bottle of real Tokay, which I tasted, and lost my number badly by saying that it reminded me of some medicinal wine. It is true he merely called me a blasphemer of the worst, but what he thought I do not care to think![33]

There were scores of other good men at the Savile, but the tones and the faces of those I have named come back clearest.

My home life—it was a far cry from Piccadilly to Villiers Street— was otherwise, through the months of amazement which followed my return to England. That period was all, as I have said, a dream, in which it seemed that I could push down walls, walk through ramparts and stride across rivers. Yet I was so ignorant, I never guessed when the great fogs fell that trains could take me to light and sunshine a few miles outside London. Once I faced the reflection of my own face in the jet-black mirror of the window-panes for five days. When the fog thinned, I looked out and saw a man standing opposite the pub where the barmaid lived. Of a sudden his breast turned dull red like a robin's, and he crumpled, having cut his throat. In a few minutes—seconds it seemed—a hand-ambulance arrived and took up the body. A pot-boy with a bucket of steaming water sluiced the blood off into the gutter, and what little crowd had collected went its way.

One got to know that ambulance[34] (it lived somewhere at the back of St. Clement Danes) as well as the Police of the E. Division, and even as far as Piccadilly Circus where, any time after 10.30 P.M., the forces might be found at issue with 'real ladies.' And through all this shifting, shouting brotheldom the pious British householder and his family bored their way back from the theatres, eyes-front and fixed, as though not seeing.

Among my guests in chambers was a Lion Comique from Gatti's[35]—an artist with sound views on art. According to him, 'it was all right to keep on knockin' 'em' ('puttin' it across' came later) 'but, outside o' *that*, a man wants something to lay *hold* of. I'd ha' got it, I think, but for this dam' whisky. But, take it from me, life's all a bloomin' kick-up.'[36] Certainly my life was; but, to some extent, my Indian training served to ballast me.

I was plentifully assured, *viva voce* and in the Press cuttings— which is a drug that I do not recommend to the young—that 'nothing since Dickens' compared with my 'meteoric rise to fame,' etc. (But I was more or less inoculated, if not immune, to the coarser sorts of print.) And there was my portrait to be painted for the Royal Academy[37] as a notoriety. (But I had a Muhammedan's objection to having my face taken, as likely to draw the Evil Eye. So I was not too puffed up.) And there were letters and letters of all sorts of tendencies. (But if I answered them all I might as well be back at my old table.) And there were proposals from 'certain people of importance,'[38] insistent and unscrupulous as horse-copers, telling me how 'the ball was at my feet' and that I had only to kick it—by repeating the notes I had already struck and trailing characters I had already 'created' through impossible scenes—to achieve all sorts of desirable things. But I had seen men as well as horses foundered in my lost world behind me. One thing only stood fast through this welter. I was making money—much more than four hundred rupees a month—and when my Bank-book told me I had one thousand whole pounds saved, the Strand was hardly wide enough for my triumph. I had intended a book 'to take advantage of the market.' This I had just sense enough to countermand.[39] What I most needed was that my people should come over and see what had overtaken their son. This they did on a flying visit,[40] and then my 'kick-up' had some worth.

As always, they seemed to suggest nothing and interfere nowhere. But they were there—my Father with his sage Yorkshire outlook and wisdom; my Mother, all Celt and three-parts fire—both so entirely comprehending that except in trivial matters we had hardly need of words.

I think I can with truth say that those two made for me the only public for whom then I had any regard whatever till their deaths, in my forty-fifth year. Their arrival simplified things, and 'set' in my head a notion that had been rising at the back of it. It seemed easy enough to 'knock 'em'—but to what end beyond the heat of the exercise? (That both my grandfathers had been Wesleyan Ministers[41] did not strike me till I was, familiarly, reminded of it.) I had been at work on the rough of a set of verses called later 'The English Flag'[42] and had boggled at a line which had to be a key-line but persisted in going 'soft.' As was the custom between us, I asked into the air: 'What am I trying to get *at?*' Instantly the Mother, with her quick flutter of the hands: 'You're *trying* to say: "What do they know of England who only England know."' The Father confirmed. The rest of the rhetoric came away easily; for it was only pictures seen, as it were, from the deck of a long fourteen-footer,[43] a craft that will almost sail herself.

In the talks that followed, I exposed my notion of trying to tell to the English something of the world outside England—not directly but by implication.

They understood. Long before the end the Mother, summarising, said: '*I* see. "Unto them did he discover His swan's nest among the reeds."[44] Thank you for telling us, dear.' That settled that; and when Lord Tennyson (whom alas! I never had the good fortune to meet) expressed his approval of the verses[45] when they appeared, I took it for a lucky sign. Most men properly broke to a trade pick up some sort of workshop facility which gives them an advantage over their untrained fellows. My office-work had taught me to think out a notion in detail, pack it away in my head, and work on it by snatches in any surroundings. The lurch and surge of the old horse-drawn buses made a luxurious cradle for such ruminations. Bit by bit, my original notion grew into a vast, vague conspectus—Army and Navy Stores List if you like—of the whole sweep and meaning of things and effort and origins throughout the Empire. I visualised it, as I do most ideas, in the shape of a semi-circle of buildings and temples projecting into a sea—of dreams. At any rate, after I had got it straight in my head, I felt there need be no more 'knockin' 'em' in the abstract.

Likewise, in my wanderings beyond Villiers Street, I had met several men and an occasional woman, whom I by no means loved. They were overly soft-spoken or blatant, and dealt in pernicious varieties of safe sedition. For the most part they seemed to be purveyors of luxuries to the 'Aristocracy,' whose destruction by painful means they loudly professed to desire. They derided my poor little Gods of the East, and asserted that the British in India spent violent lives 'oppressing' the Native. (This in a land where white girls of sixteen, at twelve or fourteen pounds per annum, hauled thirty and forty pounds weight of bath-water at a time up four flights of stairs!)

The more subtle among them had plans, which they told me, for 'snatching away England's arms when she isn't looking—just like a naughty child—so that when she wants to fight she'll find she can't.' (We have come far on that road since.) Meantime, their aim was peaceful, intellectual penetration and the formation of what to-day would be called 'cells' in unventilated corners. Collaborating with these gentry was a mixed crowd of wide-minded, wide-mouthed Liberals, who darkened counsel with pious but disintegrating catchwords, and took care to live very well indeed.[46] Somewhere, playing up to them, were various journals, not at all badly written, with a most enviable genius for perverting or mistaking anything that did not suit their bilious doctrine. The general situation, as I saw it, promised an alluring 'dog-fight,' in which I had no need to take aggressive part because, as soon as the first bloom had faded off my work, my normal output seemed to have the gift of *arriding*[47] *per se* the very people I most disliked. And I had the additional luck not to be taken seriously for some time. People talked, quite reasonably, of rockets and sticks; and that genius, J. K. S.,[48] brother to Herbert Stephen, dealt with Haggard and me in some stanzas which I would have given much to have written myself. They breathed a prayer for better days when:—

> The world shall cease to wonder
> At the genius of an Ass,

55

> And a boy's eccentric blunder
> Shall not bring success to pass:

> When there stands a muzzled stripling,
> Mute, beside a muzzled bore:
> When the Rudyards cease from Kipling
> And the Haggards Ride no more.

It ran joyously through all the papers. It still hangs faintly in the air and, as I used to warn Haggard, may continue as an aroma when all but our two queer names are forgotten.

Several perfectly good reviewers also helped me by demonstrating how I had arrived at my effects by a series of happy accidents. One kind man even went to some trouble, including a good dinner, to discover personally whether I had 'ever read much.' I could not do less than confirm his worst suspicions, for I had been 'taken on' in that way at the Punjab Club, till my examiner found out that I was pulling his leg, and chased me all round the compound. (The greatest reverence is due to the young. They have, when irritated, little of their own.)

But in all this jam of work done or devising, demands, distractions, excitements, and promiscuous confusions, my health cracked again.[49] I had broken down twice in India from straight overwork, plus fever and dysentery, but this time the staleness and depression came after a bout of real influenza, when all my Indian microbes joined hands and sang for a month in the darkness of Villiers Street.

So I took ship to Italy, and there chanced to meet Lord Dufferin,[50] our Ambassador, who had been Viceroy of India and had known my people. Also, I had written some verses called 'The Song of the Women'[51] about Lady Dufferin's maternity work for women in India, which both she and he liked. He was kindness itself, and made me his guest at his Villa near Naples where, one evening between lights, he talked—at first to me directly, then sliding into a reverie—of his work in India, Canada, and the world at large. I had seen administrative machinery from beneath, all stripped and overheated. This was the first time I had listened to one who had handled it from above. And unlike the generality of Viceroys, Lord Dufferin *knew*. Of all his revelations and reminiscences, the sentence that stays with me is: 'And so, you see, there can be no room' (or was it 'allowance'?) 'for good intentions in one's work.'

Italy, however, was not enough. My need was to get clean away and re-sort myself. Cruises were then unknown; but my dependence was Cook.[52] For the great J. M. himself—the man with the iron mouth and domed brow—had been one of my Father's guests at Lahore when he was trying to induce the Indian Government to let him take over the annual pilgrimage to Mecca as a business proposition. Had he succeeded some lives, and perhaps a war or two, might have been saved. His home offices took friendly interest in my plans and steamer connections.

I sailed first to Cape Town in a gigantic three-thousand-ton liner called *The Moor*,[53] not knowing I was in the hands of Fate. Aboard her, I met a Navy Captain[54] going to a new Command at Simons Town. At Madeira he desired to lay in wine for his two-year commission. I assisted him through a variegated day and fluctuating evening, which laid the foundations of life-long friendship.

Cape Town in '91 was a sleepy, unkempt little place, where the stoeps of some of the older Dutch houses still jutted over the pavement. Occasional cows strolled up the main streets, which were full of coloured people of the sort that my *ayah* had pointed out to me were curly-haired (*hubshees*) who slept in such posture as made it easy for the devils to enter their bodies. But there were also many Malays who were Muslims of a sort and had their own Mosques, and whose flamboyantly-attired women sold flowers on the curb, and took in washing. The dry, spiced smell of the land and the smack of the clean sunshine were health-restoring. My Navy Captain introduced me to the Naval society of Simons Town, where the south-easter blows five days a week, and the Admiral of the Cape Station lived in splendour, with at least a brace of live turtles harnessed to the end of a little wooden jetty, swimming about till due to be taken up for turtle soup. The Navy Club there and the tales of the junior officers delighted me beyond words. There I witnessed one of the most comprehensive 'rags' I had ever seen. It rose out of a polite suggestion to a newly-appointed Lieutenant-Commander that the fore-topmast of his tiny gunboat 'wanted staying forward.' It went on till all the furniture was completely rearranged all over the room. (How was I to guess that in a few years I should know Simons Town like the inside of my own pocket, and should give much of my life and love to the glorious land around it.)

We parted, my Captain and I, after a farewell picnic, among white, blowing sand where natives were blasting and where, of a sudden, a wrathful baboon came down the rock-face and halted waist-deep in a bed of arum-lilies. 'We'll meet again,' said my Captain, 'and if ever you want a cruise, let me know.'

A day or so before my departure for Australia, I lunched at an Adderley Street restaurant next to three men. One of them, I was told, was Cecil Rhodes,[55] who had made the staple of our passengers' talk on *The Moor* coming out. It never occurred to me to speak to him; and I have often wondered why. . . .

Her name was *The Doric*.[56] She was almost empty, and she spent twenty-four consecutive days and nights trying, all but successfully, to fill her boats at one roll and empty them down the saloon skylight the next. Sea and sky were equally grey and naked on that weary run to Melbourne.[57] Then I found myself in a new land with new smells and among people who insisted a little too much that they also were new. But there are no such things as new people in this very old world.

The leading paper offered me the most distinguished honour of describing the Melbourne Cup, but I had reported races before and knew it was not in my line. I was more interested in the middle-aged men who had spent their lives making or managing the land. They were direct of speech among each other, and talked a political slang new to me. One learned, as one always does, more from what they said to each other or took for granted in their talk, than one could have got at from a hundred questions. And on a warm night I attended a Labour Congress, where Labour debated whether some much-needed life-boats should be allowed to be ordered from England, or whether the order should be postponed till life-boats could be built in Australia under Labour direction at Labour prices.

Hereafter my memories of Australian travel are mixed up with trains transferring me, at unholy hours, from one too-exclusive State gauge to another; of enormous skies and primitive refreshment rooms, where I drank hot tea and ate mutton, while now and then a hot wind, like the *loo* of the Punjab, boomed out of the emptiness. A hard land, it seemed to me, and made harder for themselves by the action of its inhabitants, who—it may have been the climate—always seemed a bit on edge.

I went also to Sydney,[58] which was populated by leisured multitudes all in their shirt-sleeves and all picnicking all the day. They volunteered that they were new and young, but would do wonderful things some day, which promise they more than kept. Then to Hobart, in Tasmania, to pay my respects to Sir Edward Grey, who had been Governor at Cape Town in the days of the Mutiny, and on his own responsibility had diverted to India troop-ships filled with troops intended for some native war that had flared up behind him in the colony. He was very old, very wise and foreseeing, with the gentleness that accompanies a certain sort of strength.[59]

Then came New Zealand by steamer (one was always taking small and rickety coast-wise craft across those big seas), and at Wellington I was met, precisely where warned to expect him, by 'Pelorus Jack,' the big, white-marked shark,[60] who held it his duty to escort shipping up the harbour. He enjoyed a special protection of the Legislature proclaiming him sacred, but, years later, some animal shot and wounded him and he was no more seen. Wellington opened another world of kindly people, more homogeneous, it struck me, than the Australian, large, long-eyelashed, and extraordinarily good-looking. Maybe I was prejudiced, because no less than ten beautiful maidens took me for a row in a big canoe by moonlight on the still waters of Wellington Harbour,[61] and every one generally put aside everything for my behoof, instruction, amusement, and comfort. So, indeed, it has always been. For which reason I deserve no credit when my work happens to be accurate in detail. A friend long ago taxed me with having enjoyed the 'income of a Prince and the treatment of an Ambassador,' and with not appreciating it. He even called me, among other things, 'an ungrateful hound.' But what, I ask you, could I have done except go on with my work and try to add to the pleasure of those that had found it pleasant? One cannot repay the unrepayable by grins and handshakes.

From Wellington I went north towards Auckland[62] in a buggy with a small grey mare, and a most taciturn driver. It was bush country after rain. We crossed a rising river[63] twenty-three times in one day, and came out on great plains where wild horses stared at us, and caught their feet in long blown manes as they stamped and snorted. At one of our halts I was given for dinner a roast bird with a skin like pork crackling, but it had no wings nor trace of any. It was a kiwi—an apteryx. I ought to have saved its skeleton, for few men have eaten apteryx.[64] Hereabouts my driver—I had seen the like happen in lonely places before—exploded, as sometimes solitaries will. We passed a horse's skull beside the track, at which he began to swear horribly but without passion. He had, he said, driven and ridden past that skull for a very long time. To him it meant the lock on the chain of his bondage to circumstance, and why the hell did I come along talking about all those foreign, far places I had seen? Yet he made me go on telling him.

I had had some notion of sailing from Auckland to visit Robert Louis Stevenson[65] at Samoa, for he had done me the honour to write me about some of my tales; and moreover I was Eminent Past Master R.L.S. Even to-day I would back myself to take seventy-five per cent marks in written or *viva voce* examination on *The Wrong Box*[66] which, as the Initiated know, is the Test Volume of that Degree. I read it first in a small hotel in Boston in '89, when the negro waiter nearly turned me out of the dining-room for spluttering over my meal.[67]

But Auckland, soft and lovely in the sunshine, seemed the end of organised travel; for the captain of a fruit-boat, which might or might not go to Samoa at some time or other, was so devotedly drunk that I decided to turn south, and work back to India.[68] All I carried away from the magic town of Auckland was the face and voice of a woman who sold me beer at a little hotel there. They stayed at the back of my head till ten years later when, in a local train of the Cape Town suburbs, I heard a petty officer from Simons Town telling a companion about a woman in New Zealand who 'never scrupled to help a lame duck or put her foot on a scorpion.' Then—precisely as the removal of the key-log in a timber-jam starts the whole pile—those words gave me the key to the face and voice at

Auckland, and a tale called 'Mrs. Bathurst'[69] slid into my mind, smoothly and orderly as floating timber on a bank-high river.

The South Island, mainly populated by Scots, their sheep, and the Devil's own high winds, I tackled in another small steamer, among colder and increasing seas.[70] We cleared it at the Last Lamp-post in the World—Invercargill[71]—on a boisterous dark evening, when General Booth[72] of the Salvation Army came on board. I saw him walking backward in the dusk over the uneven wharf, his cloak blown upwards, tulip-fashion, over his grey head, while he beat a tambourine in the face of the singing, weeping, praying crowd who had come to see him off.

We stood out, and at once took the South Atlantic.[73] For the better part of a week we were swept from end to end, our poop was split, and a foot or two of water smashed through the tiny saloon. I remember no set meals. The General's cabin was near mine, and in the intervals between crashes overhead and cataracts down below he sounded like a wounded elephant; for he was in every way a big man.

I saw no more of him till I had picked up my P. & O., which also happened to be his, for Colombo at Adelaide.[74] Here all the world came out in paddle-boats and small craft to speed him on his road to India. He spoke to them from our upper deck, and one of his gestures—an imperative, repeated, downward sweep of the arm—puzzled me, till I saw that a woman crouching on the paddle-box of a crowded boat had rucked her petticoats well up to her knees. In those days righteous woman ended at the neck and instep. Presently, she saw what was troubling the General. Her skirts were adjusted and all was peace and piety. I talked much with General Booth during that voyage. Like the young ass I was, I expressed my distaste at his appearance on Invercargill wharf. 'Young feller,' he replied, bending great brows at me, 'if I thought I could win *one* more soul to the Lord by walking on my head and playing a tambourine with my toes, I'd—I'd learn how.'

He had the right of it ('if by any means I can save some'[75]) and I had decency enough to apologise. He told me about the beginnings of his mission, and how surely he would be in gaol were his accounts submitted to any sort of official inspection; and how his work *must* be a one-man despotism with only the Lord for supervisor. (Even so spoke Paul and, I am well sure, Muhammed.)

'Then why,' I asked, 'can't you stop your Salvation lassies from going out to India and living alone native-fashion among natives?'[76] I told him something of village conditions in India. The despot's defence was very human. 'But what *am* I to do?' he demanded. 'The girls *will* go, and one *can't* stop 'em.'

I think this first flare of enthusiasm was rationalised later, but not before some good lives had been expended. I conceived great respect and admiration for this man with the head of Isaiah and the fire of the Prophet, but, like the latter, rather at sea among women. The next time I met him was at Oxford when Degrees were being conferred.[77] He strode across to me in his Doctor's robes, which magnificently became him, and, 'Young feller,' said he, 'how's your soul?'

I have always liked the Salvation Army, of whose work outside England I have seen a little. They are, of course, open to all the objections urged against them by science and the regular creeds: but it seems to me that when a soul conceives itself as being reborn it may go through agonies both unscientific and unregulated. Haggard, who had worked with him and for the Army on several occasions, told me that for sheer luxury of attendance, kindliness, and good-will, nothing compared with travel under their care.

From Colombo I crossed over to the India of the extreme south which I did not know, and for four days and four nights in the belly of the train could not understand one word of the speech around me. Then came the open north and Lahore, where I was snatching a few days' visit with my people. They were coming 'Home' for good soon: so this was my last look round the only real home I had yet known.[78]

CHAPTER V

The Committee of
Ways and Means

Then down to Bombay where my *ayah*, so old but so unaltered, met me with blessings and tears; and then to London to be married in January '92[1] in the thick of an influenza epidemic, when the undertakers had run out of black horses and the dead had to be content with brown ones. The living were mostly abed. (We did not know then that this epidemic was the first warning that the plague—forgotten for generations—was on the move out of Manchuria.[2])

All of which touched me as much as it would any other young man under like circumstances. My concern was to get out of the pesthouse as soon as might be. For was I not a person of substance? Had I not several—more than two at least—thousand pounds in Fixed Deposits? Had not my own Bank's Manager himself suggested that I might invest some of my 'capital' in, say, indigo? But I preferred to invest once more in Cook's tickets—for two—on a voyage round the world. It was all arranged beyond any chance of failure.

So we were married in the church with the pencil-pointed steeple at Langham Place[3]—Gosse, Henry James,[4] and my cousin Ambrose Poynter[5] being all the congregation present—and we parted at the church door to the scandal of the Beadle, my wife to administer medicine to her mother, and I to a wedding breakfast with

Ambrose Poynter; after which, on returning to collect my wife, I saw, pinned down by weights on the rainy pavement as was the custom of those untroubled days, a newspaper poster announcing my marriage, which made me feel uncomfortable and defenceless.

And a few days afterwards we were on our magic carpet which was to take us round the earth, beginning with Canada deep in snow.[6] Among our wedding gifts was a generous silver flask filled with whisky, but of incontinent habit. It leaked in the valise where it lay with flannel shirts. And it scented the entire Pullman from end to end ere we arrived at the cause. But by that time all our fellow-passengers were pitying that poor girl who had linked her life to the shameless inebriate. Thus in a false atmosphere all of our innocent own, we came to Vancouver, where with an eye to the future and for proof of wealth we bought, or thought we had, twenty acres of a wilderness called North Vancouver, now part of the City. But there was a catch in the thing, as we found many years later when, after paying taxes on it for ever so long, we discovered it belonged to some one else. All the consolation we got then from the smiling people of Vancouver was: 'You bought that from Steve, did you? Ah-ah, *Steve*! You hadn't ought to ha' bought from Steve. No! Not from *Steve*.' And thus did the good Steve cure us of speculating in real estate.[7]

Then to Yokohama, where we were treated with all the kindliness in the world by a man and his wife on whom we had no shadow of any claim.[8] They made us more than welcome in their house, and saw to it that we should see Japan in wistaria and peony time. Here an earthquake[9] (prophetic as it turned out) overtook us one hot break of dawn, and we fled out into the garden, where a tall cryptomeria waggled its insane head back and forth with an 'I told you so' expression: though not a breath was stirring. A little later I went to the Yokohama branch of my Bank on a wet forenoon to draw some of my solid wealth. Said the Manager to me: 'Why not take more? It will be just as easy.' I answered that I did not care to have too much cash at one time in my careless keeping, but that when I had looked over my accounts I might come again in the afternoon. I did so; but in that little space my Bank, the notice on its shut door explained, had suspended payment.[10] (Yes, I should have done better to have invested my 'capital' as its London Manager had hinted.)

I returned with my news to my bride of three months and a child to be born. Except for what I had drawn that morning—the Manager had sailed as near to the wind as loyalty permitted—and the unexpended Cook vouchers, and our personal possessions in our trunks, we had nothing whatever. There was an instant Committee of Ways and Means, which advanced our understanding of each other more than a cycle of solvent matrimony. Retreat—flight, if you like— was indicated. What would Cook return for the tickets, not including the price of lost dreams? 'Every pound you've paid, of course,' said Cook of Yokohama. 'These things are all luck and— here's your refund.'

Back again, then,[11] across the cold North Pacific, through Canada on the heels of the melting snows, and to the outskirts of a little New England town where my wife's paternal grandfather (a Frenchman) had made his home and estate many years before.[12] The country was large-boned, mountainous, wooded, and divided into farms of from fifty to two hundred barren acres. Roads, sketched in dirt, connected white, clap-boarded farm-houses, where the older members of the families made shift to hold down the eating mortgages. The younger folk had gone elsewhere. There were many abandoned houses too; some decaying where they stood; others already reduced to a stone chimney-stack or mere green dimples still held by an undefeated lilac-bush. On one small farm was a building known as the Bliss Cottage,[13] generally inhabited by a hired man. It was of one storey and a half; seventeen feet high to the roof-tree; seventeen feet deep and, including the kitchen and wood-shed, twenty-seven feet wide over all. Its water-supply was a single half-inch lead pipe connecting with a spring in the neighbourhood. But it was habitable, and it stood over a deep if dampish cellar. Its rent was ten dollars or two pounds a month.

We took it. We furnished it with a simplicity that fore-ran the hire-purchase system. We bought, second or third hand, a huge, hot-air stove which we installed in the cellar. We cut generous holes in our thin floors for its eight-inch tin pipes (why we were not burned in our beds each week of the winter I never can understand) and we were extraordinarily and self-centredly content.

As the New England summer flamed into autumn I piled cut spruce boughs all round the draughty cottage sill, and helped to put up a tiny roofless verandah along one side of it for future needs. When winter shut down and sleigh-bells rang all over the white world that tucked us in, we counted ourselves secure. Sometimes we had a servant. Sometimes she would find the solitude too much for her and flee without warning, one even leaving her trunk. This troubled us not at all. There are always two sides to a plate, and the cleaning of frying- and saucepans is as little a mystery as the making of comfortable beds. When our lead pipe froze, we would slip on our coon-skin coats and thaw it out with a lighted candle. There was no space in the attic bedroom for a cradle, so we decided that a trunk-tray would be just as good. We envied no one—not even when skunks wandered into our cellar and, knowing the nature of the beasts, we immobilised ourselves till it should please them to depart.

But our neighbours saw no humour in our proceedings. Here was a stranger of an unloved race, currently reported to 'make as much as a hundred dollars out of a ten-cent bottle of ink,' and who had 'pieces in the papers' about him, who had married a 'Balestier girl.' Did not her grandmother[14] still live on the Balestier place, where 'old Balestier' instead of farming had built a large house, and there had dined late in special raiment, and drunk red wines after the custom of the French instead of decent whisky? And behold this Britisher, under pretext of having lost money, had settled his wife down 'right among her own folk' in the Bliss Cottage. It was not seemly on the face of it; so they watched as secretively as the New England or English peasant can, and what toleration they extended to the 'Britisher' was solely for the sake of 'the Balestier girl.'

But we had received the first shock of our young lives at the first crisis in them. The Committee of Ways and Means passed a resolution, never rescinded, that henceforth, at any price, it must own its collective self.

As money came in from the sale of books and tales, the first use we made of it was to buy back *Departmental Ditties*, *Plain Tales*, and the six paperbacked books that I had sold to get me funds for leaving

India in '89.[15] They cost something, but, owning them, the Bliss Cottage breathed more comfortably.

Not till much later did we realise the terrible things that 'folks thought of your doin's.' From their point of view they were right. Also, they were practical as the following will show.

One day a stranger[16] drove up to the Bliss Cottage. The palaver opened thus:—

'Kiplin', ain't ye?'

That was admitted.

'Write, don't ye?'

That seemed accurate. (Long pause.)

'Thet bein' so, you've got to live to please folk, hain't ye?'

That indeed was the raw truth. He sat rigid in the buggy and went on.

'Thet bein' so, you've got to please to live, I reckon?'

It was true. (I thought of my Adjutant of Volunteers at Lahore.)[17]

'Puttin' it thet way,' he pursued, 'we'll 'low thet, by and by, ye *can't* please. Sickness—accident—any darn thing. *Then*—what's liable to happen ye—both of ye?'

I began to see, and he to fumble in his breast pocket.

'Thet's where Life Insurance comes in. Naow, *I* represent,' etc. etc. It was beautiful salesmanship. The Company was reputable, and I effected my first American Insurance, Leuconoë agreeing with Horace to trust the future as little as possible.[18]

Other visitors were not so tactful. Reporters came from papers in Boston, which I presume believed itself to be civilised, and demanded interviews. I told them I had nothing to say. 'If ye hevn't, guess we'll *make* ye say something.' So they went away and lied copiously, their orders being to 'get the story.'[19] This was new to me at the time; but the Press had not got into its full free stride of later years.

My workroom in the Bliss Cottage was seven feet by eight, and from December to April the snow lay level with its window-sill. It chanced that I had written a tale about Indian Forestry work which included a boy who had been brought up by wolves.[20] In the stillness, and suspense, of the winter of '92 some memory of the Masonic Lions of my childhood's magazine, and a phrase in

Haggard's *Nada the Lily*,[21] combined with the echo of this tale. After blocking out the main idea in my head, the pen took charge, and I watched it begin to write stories about Mowgli and animals, which later grew into the *Jungle Books*.

Once launched there seemed no particular reason to stop, but I had learned to distinguish between the peremptory motions of my Daemon, and the 'carry-over' or induced electricity, which comes of what you might call mere 'frictional' writing. Two tales, I remember, I threw away and was better pleased with the remainder. More to the point, my Father thought well of the workmanship.

My first child and daughter[22] was born in three foot of snow on the night of December 29th, 1892. Her Mother's birthday being the 31st and mine the 30th of the same month, we congratulated her on her sense of the fitness of things, and she throve in her trunk-tray in the sunshine on the little plank verandah. Her birth brought me into contact with the best friend I made in New England—Dr. Conland.[23]

It seemed that the Bliss Cottage might be getting a little congested, so, in the following spring, the Committee of Ways and Means 'considered a field and bought it'[24]—as much as ten whole acres—on a rocky hillside looking across a huge valley to Wantastiquet, the wooded mountain across the Connecticut river.

That summer there came out of Quebec Jean Pigeon[25] with nine other *habitants* who put up a wooden shed for their own accommodation in what seemed twenty minutes, and then set to work to build us a house which we called 'Naulakha.'[26] Ninety feet was the length of it and thirty the width, on a high foundation of solid mortared rocks which gave us an airy and a skunk-proof basement. The rest was wood, shingled, roof and sides, with dull green hand-split shingles, and the windows were lavish and wide. Lavish too was the long open attic, as I realised when too late. Pigeon asked me whether I would have it finished in ash or cherry. Ignorant that I was, I chose ash, and so missed a stretch of perhaps the most satisfying interior wood that is grown. Those were opulent days, when timber was nothing regarded, and the best of cabinet work could be had for little money.

Next, we laid out a long drive to the road. This needed dynamite to soften its grades and a most mellow plumber brought up many sticks of it all rattling about under his buggy-seat among the tamping-rods. We dived, like woodchucks, into the nearest deepest hole. Next, needing water, we sunk a five-inch shaft three hundred foot into the New England granite, which nowhere was less than three, though some say thirty, thousand foot thick. Over that we set a windmill, which gave us not enough water and moaned and squeaked o' nights. So we knocked out its lowest bolts, hitched on two yoke of bullocks, and overthrew it, as it might have been the Vendôme Column: thus spiritually recouping ourselves for at least half the cost of erection. A low-power atmospheric pump, which it was my disgustful duty to oil, was its successor. These experiences gave us both a life-long taste for playing with timber, stone, concrete and such delightful things.

Horses were an integral part of our lives, for the Bliss Cottage was three miles from the little town, and half a mile from the house in building. Our permanent servitor was a big, philosophical black called Marcus Aurelius, who waited in the buggy as cars wait to-day, and when weary of standing up would carefully lie down and go to sleep between his shafts. After we had finished with him, we tied his reins short and sent him in charge of the buggy alone down the road to his stable-door, where he resumed his slumbers till some one came to undress him and put him to bed. There was a small mob of other horses about the landscape, including a meek old stallion with a permanently lame leg, who passed the evening of his days in a horse-power machine which cut wood for us.

I tried to give something of the fun and flavour of those days in a story called 'A Walking Delegate'[27] where all the characters are from horse-life.

The wife's passion, I discovered, was driving trotters. It chanced that our first winter in 'Naulakha' she went to look at the new patent safety heating-stove, which blew flame in her face and burnt it severely.[28] She recovered slowly, and Dr. Conland suggested that she needed a tonic. I had been in treaty for a couple of young, seal-brown, full brother and sister Morgans, good for a three-mile clip, and, on Conland's hint, concluded the deal. When I told the wife, she thought it would console her to try them and, that same afternoon, leaving one eye free of the bandages, she did so in three foot of snow and a failing light, while I suffered beside her. But Nip and Tuck were perfect roadsters and the 'tonic' succeeded. After that they took us all over the large countryside.

It would be hard to exaggerate the loneliness and sterility of life on the farms. The land was denuding itself of its accustomed inhabitants, and their places had not yet been taken by the wreckage of Eastern Europe or the wealthy city folk who later bought 'pleasure farms.' What might have become characters, powers and attributes perverted themselves in that desolation as cankered trees throw out branches akimbo, and strange faiths and cruelties, born of solitude to the edge of insanity, flourished like lichen on sick bark.

One day-long excursion up the flanks of Wantastiquet, our guardian mountain across the river, brought us to a farm-house where we were welcomed by the usual wild-eyed, flat-fronted woman of the place. Looking over sweeps of emptiness, we saw our 'Naulakha' riding on its hillside like a little boat on the flank of a far wave. Said the woman, fiercely: 'Be you the new lights 'crost the valley yonder? Ye don't know what a comfort they've been to me this winter. Ye aren't ever goin' to shroud 'em up—or *be* ye?' So, as long as we lived there, that broad side of 'Naulakha' which looked her-ward was always nakedly lit.

In the little town where we shopped there was another atmosphere. Vermont was by tradition a 'Dry' State.[29] For that reason, one found in almost every office the water-bottle and thick tooth-glass displayed openly, and in discreet cupboards or drawers the whisky bottle. Business was conducted and concluded with gulps of raw spirit, followed by a pledget[30] of ice-cold water. Then, both parties chewed cloves, but whether to defeat the Law, which no one ever regarded, or to deceive their women-folk, of whom they went in great fear (they were mostly educated up to College age by spinsters), I do not know.

But a promising scheme for a Country Club had to be abandoned because many men who would by right belong to it could not be trusted with a full whisky bottle. On the farms, of course, men drank cider, of various strengths, and sometimes achieved almost maniacal forms of drunkenness. The whole business seemed to me as unwholesomely furtive and false as many aspects of American life at that time.

Administratively, there was unlimited and meticulous legality, with a multiplication of semi-judicial offices and titles; but of law-abidingness, or of any conception of what that implied, not a trace. Very little in business, transportation, or distribution, that I had to deal with, was sure, punctual, accurate, or organised. But this they neither knew nor would have believed though angels affirmed it. Ethnologically, immigrants were coming into the States at about a million head a year. They supplied the cheap—almost slave—labour, lacking which all wheels would have stopped, and they were handled with a callousness that horrified me. The Irish had passed out of the market into 'politics' which suited their instincts of secrecy, plunder, and anonymous denunciation. The Italians were still at work, laying down trams, but were moving up, *via* small shops and curious activities, to the dominant position which they now occupy in well-organised society. The German, who had preceded even the Irish, counted himself a full-blooded American, and looked down gutturally on what he called 'foreign trash.' Somewhere in the background, though he did not know it, was the 'representative' American, who traced his blood through three or four generations and who, controlling nothing and affecting less, protested that the accepted lawlessness of life was not 'representative' of his country, whose moral, aesthetic, and literary champion he had appointed himself. He said too, almost automatically, that all foreign elements could and would soon be 'assimilated' into 'good Americans.' And not a soul cared what he said or how he said it! They were making or losing money.

The political background of the land was monotonous. When the people looked, which was seldom, outside their own borders, England was still the dark and dreadful enemy to be feared and guarded against. The Irish, whose other creed is Hate; the history books in the Schools; the Orators; the eminent Senators; and above all the Press; saw to that. Now John Hay,[31] one of the very few American Ambassadors to England with two sides to their heads, had his summer house a few hours north by rail from us. On a visit to him, we discussed the matter. His explanation was convincing. I quote the words which stayed textually in my memory. 'America's hatred of England is the hoop round the forty-four (as they were then) staves of the Union.' He said it was the only standard possible to apply to an enormously variegated population. 'So—when a man comes up out of the sea, we say to him: "See that big bully over there in the East? He's England! Hate him, and you're a good American."'

On the principle, 'if you can't keep a love affair going, start a row,' this is reasonable. At any rate the belief lifted on occasion the overwhelming vacuity of the national life into some contact with imponderable externals.

But how thoroughly the doctrine was exploited I did not realise till we visited Washington in '96,[32] where I met Theodore Roosevelt,[33] then Under-Secretary (I never caught the name of the Upper[34]) to the U.S. Navy. I liked him from the first and largely believed in him. He would come to our hotel, and thank God in a loud voice that he had not one drop of British blood in him; his ancestry being Dutch, and his creed conforming-Dopper,[35] I think it is called. Naturally I told him nice tales about his Uncles and Aunts in South Africa—only I called them Ooms and Tanties—who esteemed themselves the sole lawful Dutch under the canopy and dismissed Roosevelt's stock for 'Verdomder Hollanders.' Then he became really eloquent, and we would go off to the Zoo together, where he talked about grizzlies that he had met.[36] It was laid on him, at that time, to furnish his land with an adequate Navy; the existing collection of unrelated types and casual purchases being worn out. I asked him how he proposed to get it, for the American people did not love taxation. 'Out of *you*,' was the disarming reply. And so—to some extent—it was. The obedient and instructed Press explained how England—treacherous and jealous as ever—only waited round the corner to descend on the unprotected coasts of Liberty, and to that end was preparing, etc. etc. etc. (This in '96 when England had more than enough hay on her own trident to keep her busy![37]) But the trick worked, and all the Orators and Senators gave tongue, like the Hannibal Chollops[38] that they were. I remember the wife of a Senator who, apart from his politics, was very largely civilized, invited me to drop into the Senate and listen to her spouse 'twisting the Lion's tail.'[39] It seemed an odd sort of refreshment to offer a visitor. I could not go, but I read his speech. (At the present time (autumn '35) I have also read with interest the apology offered by an American Secretary of State to Nazi Germany for unfavourable comments on that land by a New York Police Court Judge.[40]) But those were great and spacious and friendly days in Washington which—politics apart—Allah had not altogether deprived of a sense of humour; and the food was a thing to dream of.

Through Roosevelt I met Professor Langley[41] of the Smithsonian, an old man who had designed a model aeroplane driven—for petrol had not yet arrived—by a miniature flash-boiler engine, a marvel of delicate craftsmanship. It flew on trial over two hundred yards, and drowned itself in the waters of the Potomac, which was cause of great mirth and humour to the Press of his country. Langley took it coolly enough and said to me that, though he would never live till then, I should see the aeroplane established.

The Smithsonian, specially on the ethnological side, was a pleasant place to browse in. Every nation, like every individual, walks in a vain show—else it could not live with itself—but I never got over the wonder of a people who, having extirpated the aboriginals of their continent more completely than any modern race had ever done, honestly believed that they were a godly little New England community, setting examples to brutal mankind. This wonder I used to explain to Theodore Roosevelt, who made the glass cases of Indian relics shake with his rebuttals.

The next time I met him[42] was in England, not long after his country had acquired the Philippines, and he—like an elderly lady with one babe—yearned to advise England on colonial administration. His views were sound enough, for his subject was Egypt as it was beginning to be then, and his text 'Govern or get out.' He consulted several people as to how far he could go. I assured him that the English would take anything from him, but were racially immune to advice.

I never met him again, but we corresponded through the years when he 'jumped' Panama from a brother-President there whom he described as 'Pithecanthropoid,'[43] and also during the War, in the course of which I met two of his delightful sons.[44] My own idea of him was that he was a much bigger man than his people understood or, at that time, knew how to use, and that he and they might have been better off had he been born twenty years later.

Meantime, our lives went on at the Bliss Cottage and, so soon as it was built, at 'Naulakha.' To the former one day came Sam Maclure,[45] credited with being the original of Stevenson's Pinkerton in *The Wrecker*,[46] but himself, far more original. He had been everything from a pedlar to a tin-type photographer along the highways, and had held intact his genius and simplicity. He entered, alight with the notion for a new Magazine to be called 'Maclure's.' I think the talk lasted some twelve—or it may have been seventeen— hours, before the notion was fully hatched out. He, like Roosevelt, was in advance of his age, for he looked rather straightly at practices and impostures which were in the course of being sanctified because they paid. People called it 'muck-raking' at the time, and it seemed to do no sort of good. I liked and admired Maclure more than a little, for he was one of the few with whom three and a half words serve for a sentence, and as clean and straight as spring water. Nor did I like him less when he made a sporting offer to take all my output for the next few years at what looked like fancy rates. But the Committee of Ways and Means decided that futures were not to be dealt in. (I here earnestly commend to the attention of the ambitious young a text in the thirty-third chapter of Ecclesiasticus which runs: '*So long as thou livest and hast breath in thee, give not thyself over to any.*')

To 'Naulakha,' on a wet day, came from Scribner's of New York a large young man called Frank Doubleday,[47] with a proposal, among other things, for a complete edition of my then works. One accepts or refuses things that really matter on personal and illogical grounds. We took to that young man at sight, and he and his wife[48] became of our closest friends. In due time, when he was building up what turned into the great firm of Doubleday, Page & Co., and later Doubleday, Doran & Co., I handed over the American side of my business to him. Whereby I escaped many distractions for the rest of my life. Thanks to the large and intended gaps in the American Copyright law, much could be done by the enterprising not only to steal, which was natural, but to add to and interpolate and embel- lish the thefts with stuff I had never written.[49] At first this annoyed me, but later I laughed; and Frank Doubleday chased the pirates up with cheaper and cheaper editions,[50] so that their thefts became less profitable. There was no more pretence to morality in these gentlemen than in their brethren, the bootleggers of later years. As a pillar of the Copyright League[51] (even *he* could not see the humour of it) once said, when I tried to bring him to book for a more than usually flagrant trespass: 'We thought there was money in it, so we did it.' It was, you see, his religion. By and large I should say that American pirates have made say half as many dollars out of my stuff as I am occasionally charged with having 'made' out of the legitimate market in that country.

Into this queer life the Father came to see how we fared, and we two went wandering into Quebec where, the temperature being 95 and all the world dressed all over after the convention of those days, the Father was much amazed.[52] Then we visited at Boston his old friend, Charles Eliot Norton[53] of Harvard, whose daughters I had known at The Grange in my boyhood and since. They were Brahmins of the Boston Brahmins,[54] living delightfully, but Norton himself, full of forebodings as to the future of his land's soul, felt the established earth sliding under him, as horses feel coming earth-tremors.

He told us a tale of old days in New England. He and another Professor, wandering round the country in a buggy and discussing high and moral matters, halted at the farm of an elderly farmer well known to them, who, in the usual silence of New England, set about getting the horse a bucket of water. The two men in the buggy went on with their discussion, in the course of which one of them said: 'Well, according to Montaigne,' and gave a quotation. Voice from the horse's head, where the farmer was holding the bucket: ''Tweren't Montaigne said that. 'Twere Montes-ki-ew.' And 'twas.

That, said Norton, was in the middle or late 'seventies. We two wandered about the back of Shady Hill[55] in a buggy, but nothing of that amazing kind befell us. And Norton spoke of Emerson[56] and Wendell Holmes[57] and Longfellow[58] and the Alcotts[59] and other influences of the past as we returned to his library, and he browsed aloud among his books; for he was a scholar among scholars.

But what struck me, and he owned to something of the same

75

feeling, was the apparent waste and ineffectiveness, in the face of the foreign inrush, of all the indigenous effort of the past generation. It was then that I first began to wonder whether Abraham Lincoln had not killed rather too many autochthonous 'Americans' in the Civil War, for the benefit of their hastily imported Continental supplant- ers.[60] This is black heresy, but I have since met men and women who have breathed it. The weakest of the old-type immigrants had been sifted and salted by the long sailing-voyage of those days. But steam began in the later 'sixties and early 'seventies, when human cargoes could be delivered with all their imperfections and infections in a fortnight or so. And one million more-or-less acclimatised Ameri- cans had been killed.

Somehow or other, between '92 and '96 we managed to pay two flying visits to England, where my people were retired and lived in Wiltshire;[61] and we learned to loathe the cold North Atlantic more and more. On one trip our steamer came almost atop of a whale, who submerged just in time to clear us, and looked up into my face with an unforgettable little eye the size of a bullock's. Eminent Masters R.L.S. will remember what William Dent Pitman saw of 'haughty and indefinable' in the hairdresser's waxen model.[62] When I was illustrating the *Just So Stories*, I remembered and strove after that eye.[63]

We went once or twice to Gloucester, Mass.,[64] on a summer visit, when I attended the annual Memorial Service to the men drowned or lost in the cod-fishing schooners fleet. Gloucester was then the metropolis of that industry.

Now our Dr. Conland had served in that fleet when he was young. One thing leading to another, as happens in this world, I embarked on a little book which was called *Captains Courageous*. My part was the writing; his the details. This book took us (he rejoicing to escape from the dread respectability of our little town) to the shore-front, and the old T-wharf of Boston Harbour,[65] and to queer meals in sailors' eating-houses, where he renewed his youth among ex-ship- mates or their kin. We assisted hospitable tug-masters to help haul three- and four-stick schooners of Pocahontas coal[66] all round the harbour; we boarded every craft that looked as if she might be useful, and we delighted ourselves to the limit of delight. Charts we got—old and new—and the crude implements of navigation such as they used off the Banks, and a battered boat-compass, still a treasure with me. (Also, by pure luck, I had sight of the first sickening uprush and vomit of iridescent coal-dusted water into the hold of a ship, a crippled iron hulk, sinking at her moorings.) And Conland took large cod and the appropriate knives with which they are prepared for the hold, and demonstrated anatomically and surgically so that I could make no mistake about treating them in print. Old tales, too, he dug up, and the lists of dead and gone schooners whom he had loved, and I revelled in profligate abundance of detail—not necessarily for publication but for the joy of it. And he sent me—may he be forgiven!—out on a pollock-fisher, which is ten times fouler than any cod-schooner, and I was immortally sick, even though they tried to revive me with a fragment of unfresh pollock.

As though this were not enough, when, at the end of my tale, I desired that some of my characters should pass from San Francisco[67] to New York in record time, and wrote to a railway magnate of my acquaintance asking what he himself would do, that most excellent man sent a fully worked-out time-table, with watering halts, changes of engine, mileage, track conditions and climates, so that a corpse could not have gone wrong in the schedule.[68] My characters arrived triumphantly; and, then, a real live railway magnate[69] was so moved after reading the book that he called out his engines and called out his men, hitched up his own private car, and set himself to beat *my* time on paper over the identical route, and succeeded. Yet the book was not all reporterage. I wanted to see if I could catch and hold something of a rather beautiful localised American atmosphere that was already beginning to fade. Thanks to Conland I came near this.

A million—or it may have been only forty—years later, a Super-film Magnate[70] was in treaty with me for the film rights of this book. At the end of the sitting, my Daemon led me to ask if it were proposed to introduce much 'sex appeal' into the great work. 'Why, certainly,' said he. Now a happily married lady cod-fish lays about three million eggs at one confinement. I told him as much. He said: 'Is that so?' And went on about 'ideals.' . . . Conland had been long since dead, but I prayed that wherever he was, he might have heard.

And so, in this unreal life, indoors and out, four years passed, and a good deal of verse and prose saw the light. Better than all, I had known a corner of the United States as a householder, which is the only way of getting at a country. Tourists may carry away impressions, but it is the seasonal detail of small things and doings (such as putting up fly-screens and stove-pipes, buying yeast-cakes and being lectured by your neighbours) that bite in the lines of mental pictures. They were an interesting folk, but behind their desperate activities lay always, it seemed to me, immense and unacknowledged boredom—the dead-weight of material things passionately worked up into Gods, that only bored their worshippers more and worse and longer. The intellectual influences of their Continental immigrants were to come later. At this time they were still more or less connected with the English tradition and schools, and the Semitic strain had not yet been uplifted in a too-much-at-ease Zion. So far as I was concerned, I felt the atmosphere was to some extent hostile. The idea seemed to be that I was 'making money' out of America—witness the new house and the horses—and was not sufficiently grateful for my privileges. My visits to England and the talk there persuaded me that the English scene might be shifting to some new developments, which would be worth watching. A meeting of the Committee of Ways and Means came to the conclusion that 'Naulakha,' desirable as it was, meant only 'a house' and not '*The* House' of our dreams. So we loosed hold[71] and, with another small daughter,[72] born in the early spring snows and beautifully tanned in a sumptuous upper verandah, we took ship for England, after clearing up all our accounts. As Emerson wrote:—

> Would'st thou seal up the Avenues of ill?
> Pay every debt as though God wrote the bill.[73]

The spring of '96[74] saw us in Torquay, where we found a house for our heads that seemed almost too good to be true. It was large and bright, with big rooms each and all open to the sun, the grounds embellished with great trees and the warm land dipping southerly to the clean sea under the Marychurch cliffs. It had been inhabited for thirty years by three old maids. We took it hopefully. Then we made two notable discoveries. Everybody was learning to ride things called 'bicycles.' In Torquay there was a circular cinder-track where, at stated hours, men and women rode solemnly round and round on them. Tailors supplied special costumes for this sport. Some one—I think it was Sam Maclure from America—had given us a tandem-bicycle, whose double steering-bars made good dependence for continuous domestic quarrel. On this devil's toast-rack we took exercise, each believing that the other liked it. We even rode it through the idle, empty lanes, and would pass or overtake without upset several carts in several hours. But, one fortunate day, it skidded, and decanted us on to the road-metal. Almost before we had risen from our knees, we made mutual confession of our common loathing of wheels, pushed the Hell-Spider home by hand, and rode it no more.

The other revelation came in the shape of a growing depression which enveloped us both—a gathering blackness of mind and sorrow of the heart, that each put down to the new, soft climate and, without telling the other, fought against for long weeks. It was the Feng-shui—the Spirit of the house itself—that darkened the sunshine and fell upon us every time we entered, checking the very words on our lips.

A talk about a doubtful cistern brought another mutual confession. 'But I thought *you* liked the place?' 'But I made sure *you* did,' was the burden of our litanies. Using the cistern for a stalking-horse, we paid forfeit and fled. More than thirty years later on a motor-trip we ventured down the steep little road to that house, and met, almost unchanged, the gardener and his wife in the large, open, sunny stable-yard, and, quite unchanged, the same brooding Spirit of deep, deep Despondency within the open, lit rooms.[75]

But while we were at Torquay there came to me the idea of beginning some tracts or parables on the education of the young. These, for reasons honestly beyond my control, turned themselves into a series of tales called *Stalky & Co*. My very dear Headmaster, Cormell Price, who had now turned into 'Uncle Crom' or just 'Crommy,' paid a visit at the time and we discussed school things generally. He said, with the chuckle that I had reason to know, that my tracts would be some time before they came to their own. On their appearance they were regarded as irreverent, not true to life,

79

and rather 'brutal.' This led me to wonder, not for the first time, at which end of their carcasses grown men keep their school memories.

Talking things over with 'Crommy,' I reviled him for the badness and scantiness of our food at Westward Ho! To which he replied: 'We-el! For one thing, we were all as poor as church mice. Can you remember any one who had as much as a bob a week pocket money? *I* can't. For another, a boy who is always hungry is more interested in his belly than in anything else.' (In the Boer War I learned that the virtue in a battalion living on what is known as 'Two and a half'—Army biscuits[76]—a day is severe.) Speaking of sickness and epidemics, which were unknown to us, he said: 'I expect you were healthy because you lived in the open almost as much as Dartmoor ponies.' *Stalky & Co.* became the illegitimate ancestor of several stories of school-life whose heroes lived through experiences mercifully denied to me. It is still read ('35) and I maintain it is a truly valuable collection of tracts.

Our flight from Torquay ended almost by instinct at Rottingdean where the beloved Aunt and Uncle had their holiday house, and where I had spent my very last days before sailing for India fourteen years back.[77] In 1882 there had been but one daily bus from Brighton, which took forty minutes; and when a stranger appeared on the village green the native young would stick out their tongues at him. The Downs poured almost direct into the one village street and lay out eastward unbroken to Russia Hill above Newhaven. It was little altered in '96.[78] My cousin, Stanley Baldwin, had married the eldest daughter of the Ridsdales[79] out of the Dene—the big house that flanked one side of the green. My Uncle's 'North End House' commanded the other, and a third house opposite the church was waiting to be taken according to the decrees of Fate. The Baldwin marriage, then, made us free of the joyous young brotherhood and sisterhood of the Dene, and its friends.

The Aunt and the Uncle had said to us: 'Let the child that is coming to you be born in our house,' and had effaced themselves till my son John[80] arrived on a warm August night of '97, under what seemed every good omen. Meantime, we had rented by direct interposition of Fate that third house opposite the church on the green.[81] It stood in a sort of little island behind flint walls which we then thought were high enough, and almost beneath some big ilex trees. It was small, none too well built, but cheap, and so suited us who still remembered a little affair at Yokohama.[82] Then there grew up great happiness between 'The Dene,' 'North End House,' and 'The Elms.' One could throw a cricket-ball from any one house to the other, but, beyond turning out at 2 A.M. to help a silly foxhound puppy who had stuck in a drain, I do not remember any violent alarms and excursions other than packing farm-carts filled with mixed babies—Stanley Baldwin's and ours—and despatching them into the safe clean heart of the motherly Downs for jam-smeared picnics. Those Downs moved me to write some verses called 'Sussex.'[83] To-day, from Rottingdean to Newhaven is almost fully developed suburb, of great horror.

When the Burne-Jones' returned to their own 'North End House,' all was more than well. My Uncle's world was naturally not mine, but his heart and brain were large enough to take in any universe, and in the matter of doing one's own work in one's own way he had no doubts. His golden laugh, his delight in small things, and the perpetual war of practical jokes that waged between us, was refreshment after working hours. And when we cousins, Phil, his son, Stanley Baldwin and I, went to the beach and came back with descriptions of fat bathers, he would draw them, indescribably swag-bellied, wallowing in the surf.[84] Those were exceedingly good days, and one's work came easily and fully.

Now even in the Bliss Cottage I had a vague notion of an Irish boy, born in India and mixed up with native life.[85] I went as far as to make him the son of a private in an Irish Battalion, and christened him 'Kim of the 'Rishti'—short, that is, for Irish. This done, I felt like Mr. Micawber[86] that I had as good as paid that I.O.U. on the future, and went after other things for some years.

In the meantime my people had left India for good,[87] and were established in a small stone house near Tisbury, Wilts. It possessed a neat little stone-walled stable with a shed or two, all perfectly designed for clay and plaster of Paris works, which are not desired indoors. Later, the Father put up a tin tabernacle which he had thatched, and there disposed his drawing portfolios, big photo and architectural books, gravers, modelling-tools, paints, siccatives, varnishes, and the hundred other don't-you-touch-'ems that every right-minded man who works with his hands naturally collects. (These matters are detailed because they all come into the story.)

Within short walk of him lay Fonthill, the great house of Arthur Morrison,[88] millionaire and collector of all manner of beautiful things, his wife contenting herself with mere precious and sub-precious stones. And my Father was free of all these treasures, and many others in such houses as Clouds, where the Wyndhams[89] lived, a few miles away. I think that both he and my Mother were happy in their English years, for they knew exactly what they did not want; and I knew that when I came over to see them I had no need to sing: 'Backward, turn backward, O Time in thy flight.'[90]

In a gloomy, windy autumn *Kim* came back to me[91] with insistence, and I took it to be smoked over with my Father. Under our united tobaccos it grew like the Djin released from the brass bottle, and the more we explored its possibilities the more opulence of detail did we discover. I do not know what proportion of an iceberg is below water-line, but *Kim* as it finally appeared was about one-tenth of what the first lavish specification called for.

As to its form there was but one possible to the author, who said that what was good enough for Cervantes was good enough for him.[92] To whom the Mother: 'Don't you stand in your wool-boots hiding behind Cervantes with *me*! You *know* you couldn't make a plot to save your soul.'

So I went home much fortified and *Kim* took care of himself. The only trouble was to keep him within bounds. Between us, we knew every step, sight, and smell on his casual road, as well as all the persons he met. Once only, as I remember, did I have to bother the India Office, where there are four acres of books and documents in the basements, for a certain work on Indian magic which I always sincerely regret that I could not steal. They fuss about receipts there.

At 'The Elms,' Rottingdean, the sou'-wester raged day and night, till the silly windows jiggled their wedges loose. (Which was why the Committee vowed never to have a house of their own with up-and-down windows. Cf. Charles Reade on that subject.) But I was quite unconcerned. I had my Eastern sunlight and if I wanted more I could get it at 'The Gables,' Tisbury. At last I reported *Kim* finished. 'Did *it* stop, or you?' the Father asked. And when I told him that it was *It*, he said: 'Then it oughtn't to be too bad.'

He would take no sort of credit for any of his suggestions, memories or confirmations—not even for that single touch of the low-driving sunlight which makes luminous every detail in the picture of the Grand Trunk Road at eventide.[93] The Himalayas I painted *all* by myself, as the children say. So also the picture of the Lahore Museum of which I had once been Deputy Curator for six weeks[94]—unpaid but immensely important. And there was a half-chapter of the Lama sitting down in the blue-green shadows at the foot of a glacier, telling Kim stories out of the Jatakas,[95] which was truly beautiful but, as my old Classics master would have said, 'otiose,' and it was removed almost with tears.

But the crown of the fun came when (in 1902) was issued an illustrated edition of my works, and the Father attended to *Kim*.[96] He had the notion of making low-relief plaques and photographing them afterwards. Here it was needful to catch the local photographer, who, till then, had specialised in privates of the Line with plastered hair and skin-tight uniforms, and to lead him up the strenuous path of photographing dead things so that they might show a little life. The man was a bit bewildered at first, but he had a teacher of teachers, and so grew to understand. The incidental muck-heaps in the stable-yard were quite noticeable, though a loyal housemaid fought them broom-and-bucket, and Mother allowed messy half-born 'sketches' to be dumped by our careless hands on sofas and chairs. Naturally when he got his final proofs he was sure that 'it all ought to be done again from the beginning,' which was rather how I felt about the letterpress, but, if it be possible, he and I will do that in a better world, and on a scale to amaze Archangels.

There is one picture that I remember of him in the tin tabernacle, hunting big photos of Indian architecture for some utterly trivial detail in a corner of some plaque. He looked up as I came in and, rubbing his beard and carrying on his own thought, quoted: 'If you get simple beauty and naught else, You get about the best thing God invents.'[97] It is the greatest of my many blessings that I was given grace to know them at the time, instead of having them brought to my remorseful notice too late.

I expect that is why I am perhaps a little impatient over the High Cannibalism[98] as practised to-day.

And so much for *Kim* which has stood up for thirty-five years. There was a good deal of beauty in it, and not a little wisdom; the best in both sorts being owed to my Father.

A great, but frightening, honour came to me when I was thirty-three (1897) and was elected to the Athenaeum[99] under Rule Two, which provides for admitting distinguished persons without ballot. I took council with Burne-Jones as to what to do. 'I don't dine there often,' said he. 'It frightens *me* rather, but we'll tackle it together.' And on a night appointed we went to that meal. So far as I recall we were the only people in that big dining-room, for in those days the Athenaeum, till one got to know it, was rather like a cathedral between services. But at any rate I had dined there, and hung my hat on Peg 33. (I have shifted it since.) Before long I realised that if one wanted to know anything from forging an anchor to forging antiquities one would find the world's ultimate expert in the matter at lunch. I managed to be taken into a delightful window-table, pre-empted by an old General,[100] who had begun life as a Middy in the Crimea before he entered the Guards. In his later years he was a fearless yachtsman, as well as several other things, and he dealt faithfully with me when I made technical errors in any tale of mine that interested him. I grew very fond of him, and of four or five others who used that table.

One afternoon, I remember, Parsons[101] of the *Turbinia* asked if I would care to see a diamond burned. The demonstration took place in a room crammed with wires and electric cells (I forget what their aggregate voltage was) and all went well for a while. The diamond's tip bubbled like cauliflower *au gratin*. Then there was a flash and a crash, and we were on the floor in darkness. But, as Parsons said, that was not the diamond's fault.

Among other pillars of the dear, dingy, old downstairs billiard-room was Hercules Ross,[102] of the British Museum on the Eastern Antiquities side. Externally, he was very handsome, but his professional soul was black, even for that of a Curator—and my Father had been a Curator. (*Note.* It is entirely right that the English should mistrust and disregard all the Arts and most of the Sciences, for on that indifference rests their moral grandeur, but their starvation in their estimates is sometimes too marked.)

At this present age I do not lunch very often at the Athenaeum, where it has struck me that the bulk of the members are scandalously young, whether elected under Rule Two or by ballot of their fellow-infants. Nor do I relish persons of forty calling me 'Sir.'

My life made me grossly dependent on Clubs for my spiritual comfort.[103] Three English ones, The Athenaeum, Carlton,[104] and Beefsteak,[105] met my wants, but the Beefsteak gave me most. Our company there was unpredictable, and one could say what one pleased at the moment without being taken at the foot of the letter. Sometimes one would draw a full house of five different professions, from the Bench to the Dramatic Buccaneer. Otherwhiles, three of a kind, chance-stranded in town, would drift into long, leisurely talk that ranged half earth over, and separate well pleased with themselves and their table-companions. And once, when I feared that I might have to dine alone, there entered a member whom I had never seen before, and have never met since, full of bird-preservation. By the time we parted what I did not know about bird sanctuaries was scarcely worth knowing. But it was best when of a sudden some one or something plunged us all in what you might call a general 'rag,' each man's tongue guarding his own head.

There is no race so dowered as the English with the gift of talking real, rich, allusive, cut-in-and-out 'skittles.' Americans are too much anecdotards; the French too much orators for this light-handed game, and neither race delivers itself so unreservedly to mirth as we do.

When I lived in Villiers Street,[106] I picked up with the shore-end of a select fishing-club, which met in a tobacconist's back-parlour. They were mostly small tradesmen, keen on roach, dace and such, but they too had that gift, as I expect their forebears had in Addison's time.

The late Doctor Johnson once observed that 'we shall receive no letters in the grave.'[107] I am perfectly sure, though Boswell never set it down, that he lamented the lack of Clubs in that same place.

85

CHAPTER VI

South Africa

But at the back of my head there was an uneasiness, based on things that men were telling me about affairs outside England. (The inhabitants of that country never looked further than their annual seaside resorts.) There was trouble too in South Africa after the Jameson Raid[1] which promised, men wrote me, further trouble. Altogether, one had a sense of 'a sound of a going in the tops of the mulberry trees'[2]—of things moving into position as troops move. And into the middle of it all came the Great Queen's Diamond Jubilee,[3] and a certain optimism that scared me. The outcome, as far as I was concerned, took the shape of a set of verses called 'Recessional,' which were published in *The Times* in '97[4] at the end of the Jubilee celebrations. It was more in the nature of a *nuzzur-wattu* (an averter of the Evil Eye), and—with the conservatism of the English—was used in choirs and places where they sing long after our Navy and Army alike had in the name of 'peace' been rendered innocuous. It was written just before I went off on Navy manoeuvres with my friend Captain Bagley.[5] When I returned it seemed to me that the time was ripe for its publication, so, after making one or two changes in it, I gave it to *The Times*. I say 'gave' because for this kind of work I did not take payment. It does not much matter what people think of a man after his death, but I should not like the people whose good opinion I valued to believe that I took money for verses on Joseph Chamberlain,[6] Rhodes, Lord Milner, or any of my South African verse in *The Times*.[7]

It was this uneasiness of mine which led us down to the Cape in the winter of '97,[8] taking the Father with us. There we lived in a boarding-house at Wynberg,[9] kept by an Irishwoman, who faithfully followed the instincts of her race and spread miseries and discomforts round her in return for good monies. But the children throve, and the colour, light, and half-oriental manners of the land bound chains round our hearts for years to come.

It was here that I first met Rhodes[10] to have any talk with. He was as inarticulate as a school-boy of fifteen. Jameson[11] and he, as I perceived later, communicated by telepathy. But Jameson was not with him at that time. Rhodes had a habit of jerking out sudden questions as disconcerting as those of a child—or the Roman Emperor he so much resembled. He said to me apropos of nothing in particular: 'What's your dream?' I answered that he was part of it, and I think I told him that I had come down to look at things. He showed me some of his newly established fruit-farms in the peninsula, wonderful old Dutch houses, stalled in deep peace, and lamented the difficulty of getting sound wood for packing-cases and the shortcomings of native labour. But it was his wish and his will that there should be a fruit-growing industry in the Colony, and his chosen lieutenants made it presently come to pass. The Colony then owed no thanks to any Dutch Ministry in that regard. The racial twist of the Dutch (they had taken that title to themselves and called the inhabitants of the Low Countries 'Hollanders') was to exploit everything they could which was being done for them, to put every obstacle in the way of any sort of development, and to take all the cash they could squeeze out of it. In which respect they were no better and no worse than many of their brethren. It was against their creed to try and stamp out cattle-plagues, to dip their sheep, or to combat locusts, which in a country overwhelmingly pastoral had its drawbacks. Cape Town, as a big distributing centre, was dominated in many ways by rather nervous shop-keepers, who wished to stand well with their customers up-country, and who served as Mayors and occasional public officials. And the aftermath of the Jameson Raid had scared many people.

During the South African War my position among the rank and file came to be unofficially above that of most Generals. Money was wanted to procure small comforts for the troops at the Front and, to this end, the *Daily Mail* started what must have been a very early 'stunt.' It was agreed that I should ask the public for subscriptions. That paper charged itself with the rest.[12] My verses ('The Absent-minded Beggar') had some elements of direct appeal but, as was pointed out, lacked 'poetry.' Sir Arthur Sullivan[13] wedded the words to a tune guaranteed to pull teeth out of barrel-organs. Anybody could do what they chose with the result, recite, sing, intone or reprint, etc., on condition that they turned in all fees and profits to the main account—'The Absent-minded Beggar Fund'— which closed at about a quarter of a million. Some of this was spent in tobacco. Men smoked pipes more than cigarettes at that epoch, and the popular brand was a cake—chewable also—called 'Hignett's True Affection.' My note-of-hand at the Cape Town depot was good for as much as I cared to take about with me. The rest followed. My telegrams were given priority by sweating R.E.[14] sergeants from all sorts of congested depots. My seat in the train was kept for me by British Bayonets in their shirt-sleeves. My small baggage was fought for and servilely carried by Colonial details, who are not normally meek, and I was *persona gratissima* at certain Wynberg Hospitals where the nurses found I was good for pyjamas. Once I took a bale of them to the wrong nurse (the red capes confused me) and, knowing the matter to be urgent, loudly announced: 'Sister, I've got your pyjamas.' That one was neither grateful nor very polite.

My attractions led to every sort of delightful or sometimes sorrowful wayside intimacies with all manner of men: and only once did I receive a snub. I was going up to Bloemfontein just after its capture[15] in a carriage taken from the Boers, who had covered its floors with sheep's guts and onions, and its side with caricatures of 'Chamberlain' on a gallows. Otherwise, there was nothing much except woodwork. Behind us was an open truck of British troops whom the Company wag was entertaining by mimicking their officers telling them how to pile horseshoes. As evening fell, I got from him a couple of three-wicked, signal-lamp candles, which gave us at least light to eat by. I naturally wanted to know how he had come by these desirable things. He replied: 'Look 'ere, Guv'nor, *I* didn't ask *you* 'ow you come by the baccy you dished out just now. *Can't* you bloody well leave me alone?'

In this same ghost-train an Indian officer's servant (Muhammedan) was worried on a point of conscience. 'Would this Government-issued tin of bully-beef be lawful food for a Muslim?' I told him that, when Islam wars with unbelievers, the Koran permits reasonable latitude of ceremonial obligations; and he need not hesitate. Next dawn, he was at my bunk-side with Anglo-India's morning cup of tea. (He must have stolen the hot water from the engine, for there was not a drop in the landscape.) When I asked how the miracle had come about, he replied, with the smile of my own Kadir Buksh:[16] 'Millar, Sahib,' signifying that he had found (or 'made') it.

My Bloemfontein trip was on Lord Roberts' order to report and do what I was told. This was explained at the station by two strangers, who grew into my friends for life, H. A. Gwynne,[17] then Head Correspondent of Reuter's, and Perceval Landon[18] of *The Times*. 'You've got to help us edit a paper for the troops,'[19] they said, and forthwith inducted me into the newly captured 'office,' for Bloemfontein had fallen—Boer fashion—rather like an outraged Sunday School a few days before.

The compositors and the plant were also captives of our bow and spear and rather cross about it—especially the ex-editor's wife, a German with a tongue. When one saw a compositor, one told him to compose Lord Roberts' Official Proclamation to the deeply injured enemy. I had the satisfaction of picking up from the floor a detailed account of how Her Majesty's Brigade of Guards had been driven into action by the fire of our artillery; and a proof of a really rude leader about myself.

There was in that lull a large trade in proclamations—and butter at half a crown the pound. We used all the old stereos, advertising long-since-exhausted comestibles, coal and groceries (face-powder, I think, was the only surviving commodity in the Bloemfontein

shops), and we enlivened their interstices with our own contributions, supplemented by the works of dusty men, who looked in and
gave us very fine copy—mostly libellous.

Julian Ralph,[20] the very best of Americans, was a co-editor also.
And he had a grown son[21] who went down with a fever unpleasantly
like typhoid. We searched for a competent doctor, and halted a
German who, so great was the terror of our arms after the 'capture,'
demanded haughtily: 'But who shall pay me for my trouble if I
come?' No one seemed to know, but several men explained who
would pay him if he dallied on the way. He took one look at the boy's
stomach, and said happily: 'Of *course* it is typhoid.' Then came the
question how to get the case over to hospital, which was rank with
typhoid, the Boers having cut the water supply. The first thing was
to fetch down the temperature with an alcohol swabbing. Here we
were at a standstill till some genius—I think it was Landon—said:
'I've noticed there's an officer's wife in the place who's wearing a
fringe.'[22] On this hint a man went forth into the wide dusty streets,
and presently found her, fringe and all. Heaven knows how she had
managed to wangle her way up, but she was a sportswoman of
purest water. 'Come to my room,' said she, and in passing over the
priceless bottle, only sighed: 'Don't use it *all*—unless you have to.'
We ran the boy down from 103 to a generous 99 and pushed him into
hospital, where it turned out that it was not typhoid after all but only
bad veldt-fever.

First and last there were, I think, eight thousand cases of typhoid
in Bloemfontein.[23] Often to my knowledge both 'ceremonial' Union
Jacks in a battalion would be 'in use' at the same time. Extra corpses
went to the grave under the service blanket.

Our own utter carelessness, officialdom and ignorance were responsible for much of the death-rate. I have seen a Horse Battery
'dead to the wide'[24] come in at midnight in raging rain and be
assigned, by some idiot saving himself trouble, the site of an evacu-
ated typhoid-hospital. Result—thirty cases after a month. I have
seen men drinking raw Modder-river[25] a few yards below where the
mules were staling; and the organisation and siting of latrines
seemed to be considered 'nigger-work.' The most important medical office in any Battalion ought to be Provost-Marshal of Latrines.

To typhoid was added dysentery, the smell of which is even more depressing than the stench of human carrion. One could wind the dysentery tents a mile off. And remember that, till we planted disease, the vast sun-baked land was antiseptic and sterilised—so much so that a clean abdominal Mauser-wound[26] often entailed no more than a week of abstention from solid food. I found this out on a hospital-train, where I had to head off a mob of angry 'abdominals' from regular rations. That was when we were picking up casualties after a small affair called Paardeberg,[27] and the lists—really about two thousand—were carefully minimised to save the English public from 'shock.' During this work I happened to fall unreservedly, in darkness, over a man near the train, and filled my palms with gravel. He explained in an even voice that he was 'fractured 'ip, sir. 'Ope you ain't 'urt yourself, sir.' I never got at this unknown Philip Sidney's name.[28] They were wonderful even in the hour of death— these men and boys—lodge-keepers and ex-butlers of the Reserve and raw town-lads of twenty.

But to return to Bloemfontein. In an interval of our editorial labours, I went out of the town and presently met the 'solitary horseman' of the novels. He was a Conductor—Commissariat Sergeant—who reported that the 'flower of the British Army' had been ambushed and cut up at a place called 'Sanna's Post,'[29] and passed on obviously discomposed. I had imagined the flower of that Army to be busied behind me reading our paper; but, a short while after, I met an officer who, in the old Indian days, was nicknamed 'the Sardine.' He was calm, but rather fuzzy as to the outlines of his uniform, which was frayed and ripped by bullets. Yes, there had been trouble where he came from, but he was fuller for the moment of professional admiration.

'What was it like? They got us in a donga.[30] Just like going into a theatre. "Stalls left, dress-circle right," don't you know? We just dropped into the trap, and it was "Infantry this way, please. Guns to the right, *if* you please." Beautiful bit of work! How many did they get of us? About twelve hundred, I think, and four—maybe six— guns. Expert job they made of it. *That's* the result of bill-stickin' expeditions.'[31] And with more compliments to the foe, he too passed on.

By the time that I returned to Bloemfontein the populace had it that eighty thousand Boers were closing in on the town at once, and the Press Censor (Lord Stanley, now Derby[32]) was besieged with persons anxious to telegraph to Cape Town. To him a non-Aryan pushed a domestic wire 'weather here changeable.' Stanley, himself a little worried for the fate of some of his friends in that ambuscaded column, rebuked the gentleman.

The Sardine was right about the 'bill-sticking' expeditions. Wandering columns had been sent round the country to show how kind the British desired to be to the misguided Boer. But the Transvaal Boer, not being a town-bird, was unimpressed by the 'fall' of the Free State capital, and ran loose on the veldt with his pony and Mauser.

So there had to be a battle, which was called the Battle of Kari Siding.[33] All the staff of the *Bloemfontein Friend* attended. I was put in a Cape cart, with native driver, containing most of the drinks, and with me was a well-known war-correspondent.[34] The enormous pale landscape swallowed up seven thousand troops without a sign, along a front of seven miles. On our way we passed a collection of neat, deep and empty trenches well undercut for shelter on the shrapnel-side. A young Guards officer, recently promoted to *Brevet*-Major—and rather sore with the paper that we had printed it *Branch*—studied them interestedly. They were the first dim lines of the dug-out, but his and our eyes were held. The Hun had designed them *secundum artem*, but the Boer had preferred the open within reach of his pony. At last we came to a lone farm-house in a vale adorned with no less than five white flags. Beyond the ridge was a sputter of musketry and now and then the whoop of a field-piece. 'Here,' said my guide and guardian, 'we get out and walk. Our driver will wait for us at the farm-house.' But the driver loudly objected. 'No, sar. They shoot. They shoot me.' 'But they are white-flagged all over,' we said. 'Yess, sar. That *why*,' was his answer, and he preferred to take his mules down into a decently remote donga and wait our return.

The farm-house (you will see in a little why I am so detailed) held two men and, I think, two women, who received us disinterestedly. We went on into a vacant world full of sunshine and distances, where now and again a single bullet sang to himself. What I most objected to was the sensation of being under aimed fire—being, as it were, required as a head. 'What are they doing this for?' I asked my friend. 'Because they think we are the Something Light Horse. They ought to be just under this slope.' I prayed that the particularly Something Light Horse would go elsewhere, which they presently did, for the aimed fire slackened and a wandering Colonial, bored to extinction, turned up with news from a far flank. 'No; nothing doing and no one to see.' Then more cracklings and a most cautious move forward to the lip of a large hollow where sheep were grazing. Some of them began to drop and kick. 'That's both sides trying sighting-shots,' said my companion. 'What range do you make it?' I asked. 'Eight hundred, at the nearest. That's close quarters nowadays. You'll never see anything closer than this. Modern rifles make it imposs-ible. We're hung up till something cracks somewhere.' There was a decent lull for meals on both sides, interrupted now and again by sputters. Then one indubitable shell—ridiculously like a pip-squeak in that vastness but throwing up much dirt. 'Krupp!'[35] Four or six pounder at extreme range,' said the expert. 'They still think we're the—Light Horse. They'll come to be fairly regular from now on.' Sure enough, every twenty minutes or so, one judgmatic shell pitched on our slope. We waited, seeing nothing in the emptiness, and hearing only a faint murmur as of wind along gas-jets, running in and out of the unconcerned hills.

Then pom-poms[36] opened. These were nasty little one-pounders, ten in a belt (which usually jammed about the sixth round). On soft ground they merely thudded. On rock-face the shell breaks up and yowls like a cat. My friend for the first time seemed interested. 'If these are *their* pom-poms, it's Pretoria[37] for us,' was his diagnosis. I looked behind me—the whole length of South Africa down to Cape Town—and it seemed very far. I felt that I could have covered it in five minutes under fair conditions, but—*not* with those aimed shots up my back. The pom-poms opened again at a bare rock-reef that gave the shells full value. For about two minutes a file of racing ponies, their tails and their riders' heads well down, showed and vanished northward. 'Our pom-poms,' said the correspondent. 'Le Gallais,[38] I expect. *Now* we shan't be long.' All this time the absurd Krupp was faithfully feeling for us, *vice*—Light Horse, and, given a few more hours, might perhaps hit one of us. Then to the left, almost under us, a small piece of hanging woodland filled and fumed with our shrapnel much as a man's moustache fills with cigarette-smoke. It was most impressive and lasted for quite twenty minutes. Then silence; then a movement of men and horses from our side up the slope, and the hangar[39] our guns had been hammering spat steady fire at them. More Boer ponies on more skylines; a last flurry of pom-poms on the right and a little frieze of far-off meek-tailed ponies, already out of rifle range.

'*Maffeesh*,'[40] said the correspondent, and fell to writing on his knee. 'We've shifted 'em.'

Leaving our infantry to follow men on pony-back towards the Equator, we returned to the farm-house. In the donga where he was waiting someone squibbed off a rifle just after we took our seats, and our driver flogged out over the rocks to the danger of our sacred bottles.

Then Bloemfontein, and Gwynne storming in late with his ac-counts complete—one hundred and twenty-five casualties, and the general opinion that 'French[41] was a bit of a butcher' and a tale of the General commanding the cavalry[42] who absolutely refused to break up his horses by galloping them across raw rock—'not for any dam' Boer.'

Months later, I got a cutting from an American paper, on information from Geneva—even then a pest-house of propa-ganda—describing how I and some officers—names, date, and place correct—had entered a farm-house where we found two men and three women. We had dragged the women from under the bed where they had taken refuge (I assure you that no Tantie Sannie[43] of that day could bestow herself beneath any known bed) and, giving them a hundred yards' start, had shot them down as they ran.[44]

Even then, the beastliness struck me as more comic than signifi-cant. But by that time I ought to have known that it was the Hun's reflection of his own face as he spied at our back-windows. He had thrown in the 'hundred yards' start' touch as a tribute to our national sense of fair play.

From the business point of view the war was ridiculous. We charged ourselves step by step with the care and maintenance of all

Boerdom—women and children included. Whence horrible tales of our atrocities in the concentration-camps.[45]

One of the most widely exploited charges was our deliberate cruelty in making prisoners' tents and quarters open to the north. A Miss Hobhouse[46] among others was loud in this matter, but she was to be excused.

We were showing off our newly-built little 'Woolsack'[47] to a great lady on her way up-country, where a residence was being built for her. At the larder the wife pointed out that it faced south—that quarter being the coldest when one is south of the Equator. The great lady considered the heresy for a moment. Then, with the British sniff which abolishes the absurd, 'Hmm. I shan't allow *that* to make any difference to *me*.'

Some Army and Navy Stores Lists were introduced into the prisoners' camps, and the women returned to civil life with a knowledge of corsets, stockings, toilet-cases, and other accessories frowned upon by their clergymen and their husbands. *Qua* women they were not very lovely, but they made their men fight, and they knew well how to fight on their own lines.

In the give-and-take of our work our troops got to gauge the merits of the commando-leaders they were facing. As I remember the scale, De Wet,[48] with two hundred and fifty men, was to be taken seriously. With twice that number he was likely to fall over his own feet. Smuts[49] (of Cambridge), warring, men assured me, in a black suit, trousers rucked to the knees, and a top-hat, could handle five hundred but, beyond that, got muddled. And so with the others. I had the felicity of meeting Smuts as a British General, at the Ritz during the Great War.[50] Meditating on things seen and suffered, he said that being hunted about the veldt on a pony made a man think quickly, and that perhaps Mr. Balfour[51] (as he was then) would have been better for the same experience.

Each commando had its own reputation in the field, and the grizzlier their beards the greater our respect. There was an elderly contingent from Wakkerstroom which demanded most cautious handling. They shot, as you might say, for the pot. The young men were not so good. And there were foreign contingents who insisted on fighting after the manner of Europe. These the Boers wisely put in the forefront of the battle and kept away from. In one affair the Zarps—the Transvaal Police—fought brilliantly and were nearly all killed. But they were Swedes for the most part, and we were sorry.

Occasionally foreign prisoners were gathered in. Among them I remember a Frenchman who had joined for pure logical hatred of England, but, being a professional, could not resist telling us how we ought to wage the war. He was quite sound but rather cantankerous.

The 'war' became an unpleasing composte of 'political considerations,' social reform, and housing; maternity-work and variegated absurdities. It is possible, though I doubt it, that first and last we may have killed four thousand Boers. Our own casualties, mainly from preventible disease, must have been six times as many.[52]

The junior officers agreed that the experience ought to be a 'first-class dress-parade for Armageddon,' but their practical conclusions were misleading. Long-range, aimed rifle-fire would do the work of the future: troops would never get nearer each other than half a mile, and Mounted Infantry would be vital. This was because, having found men on foot cannot overtake men on ponies, we created eighty thousand of as good Mounted Infantry as the world had seen. For these Western Europe had no use. Artillery preparation of wire-works, such as were not at Magersfontein,[53] was rather overlooked in the reformers' schemes, on account of the difficulty of bringing up ammunition by horse-power. The pom-poms, and Lord Dundonald's[54] galloping light gun-carriages, ate up their own weight in shell in three or four minutes.

In the ramshackle hotel at Bloemfontein, where the Correspondents lived and the Officers dropped in, one heard free and fierce debate as points came up, but—since no one dreamt of the internal-combustion engine that was to stand the world on its thick head, and since our wireless apparatus did not work in those landscapes—we were all beating the air.[55]

Eventually the 'war' petered out on political lines. Brother Boer—and all ranks called him that—would do everything except die. Our men did not see why they should perish chasing stray commandos, or festering in block-houses, and there followed a sort of demoralising 'handy-pandy' of alternate surrenders complicated by Exchange of Army tobacco for Boer brandy which was bad for both sides.

At long last, we were left apologising to a deeply-indignant people, whom we had been nursing and doctoring for a year or two; and who now expected, and received, all manner of free gifts and appliances for the farming they had never practised. We put them in a position to uphold and expand their primitive lust for racial domination, and thanked God we were 'rid of a knave.'

.   .   .   .   .

Into these shifts and changes we would descend yearly for five or six months from the peace of England to the deeper peace of the 'Woolsack,' and life under the oak-trees overhanging the patio, where mother-squirrels taught their babies to climb, and in the stillness of hot afternoons the fall of an acorn was almost like a shot. To one side of us was a pine and eucalyptus grove, heavy with mixed scent; in front our garden, where anything one planted out in May became a blossoming bush by December. Behind all, tiered the flank of Table Mountain and its copses of silver-trees, flanking scarred ravines. To get to Rhodes' house, 'Groote Schuur,' one used a path through a ravine set with hydrangeas, which in autumn (England's spring) were one solid packed blue river. To this Paradise we moved each year-end from 1900 to 1907[56]—a complete equipage of governess, maids and children, so that the latter came to know and therefore, as children will, to own the Union Castle Line—stewards and all: and on any change of governess to instruct the new hand how cabins were set away for a long voyage and 'what went where.' Incidentally we lost two governesses and one loved cook by marriage, the tepid seas being propitious to such things.

Ship-board life, going and coming, was a mere prolongation of South Africa and its interests. There were Jews a plenty from the Rand; Pioneers; Native Commissioners dealing with Basutos or Zulus; men of the Matabele Wars[57] and the opening of Rhodesia; prospectors; politicians of all stripes, all full of their business; Army officers also, and from one of these, when I expected no such jewel, I got a tale called 'Little Foxes'[58]—so true in detail that an awed

Superintendent of Police wrote me out of Port Sudan, demanding how I had come to know the very names of the hounds in the very pack to which he had been Whip in his youth. But, as I wrote him back, I had been talking with the Master.

Jameson, too, once came home with us,[59] and disgraced himself at the table which we kept for ourselves. A most English lady with two fair daughters had been put there our first day out, and when she rightly enough objected to the quality of the food, and called it prison fare, Jameson said: 'Speaking as one of the criminal classes, I assure you it is worse.' At the next meal the table was all our own.

But the outward journey was the great joy because it always included Christmas near the Line, where there was no room for memories; seasonable inscriptions written in soap on the mirrors by skilly[60] stewards; and a glorious fancy-dress ball. Then, after the Southern Cross had well risen above the bows, the packing away of heavy kit, secure it would not be needed till May, the friendly, well-known Mountain and the rush to the garden to see what had happened in our absence; the flying barefoot visit to our neighbours the Strubens at Strubenheim,[61] where the children were regularly and lovingly spoiled; the large smile of the Malay laundress, and the easy pick-up-again of existence.

Life went well then, and specially for the children, who had all the beasts on the Rhodes estate to play with. Uphill lived the lions, Alice and Jumbo, whose morning voices were the signal for getting up. The zebra paddock, which the emus also used, was immediately behind the 'Woolsack'—a slope of scores of acres. The zebras were always play-fighting like Lions and Unicorns on the Royal Arms; the game being to grab the other's fore-leg below the knee if it could not snatch it away. No fence could hold them when they cared to shift. Jameson and I once saw a family of three returning from an excursion. A heavy sneeze-wood-post fence and wires lay in the path, blind-tight except where the lowest wire spanned a small ditch. Here Papa kneeled, snouted under the wire till it slid along his withers, hove it up, and so crawled through. Mamma and Baby followed in the same fashion. At this, an aged lawn-mower pony who was watching conceived he might also escape, but got no further than backing his fat hind-quarters against one of the posts, and turning round from time to time in wonder that it had not given way. It was, as Jameson said, the complete allegory of the Boer and the Briton.

In another paddock close to the house lived a spitting llama, whose peculiarity the children learned early. But their little visitors did not, and, if they were told to stand close to the fence and make noises, they did—once. You can see the rest.

But our most interesting visitor was a bull-kudu of some eighteen hands. He would jump the seven-foot fence round our little peach orchard, hook a loaded branch in the great rings of his horns, rend it off with a jerk, eat the peaches, leaving the stones, and lift himself over the wires, like a cloud, up the flank of Table Mountain. Once, coming home after dinner, we met him at the foot of the garden,[62] gigantic in the moonlight, and fetched a compass round him, walking delicately, the warm red dust in our shoes: because we knew that a few days before the keepers had given him a dose of small shot in his stern for chasing somebody's cook.

The children's chaperon on their walks was a bulldog—Jumbo— of terrific aspect, to whom all Kaffirs gave full right of way. There was a legend that he had once taken hold of a native and, when at last removed, came away with his mouth full of the native. Normally, he lay about the house and apologised abjectly when anyone stepped on him. The children fed him with currant buns and then, remembering that currants were indigestible, would pick them out of his back teeth while he held his dribbling jaws carefully open.

A baby lion was another of our family for one winter. His mother, Alice, desiring to eat him when born, he was raked out with broomsticks from her side and taken to 'Groote Schuur' where, in spite of the unwilling attentions of a she-dog foster-mother (he had of course the claws of a cat) he pined. The wife hinted that, with care, he might recover. 'Very good,' said Rhodes. 'I'll send him over to the "Woolsack" and you can try.' He came, with corrugated-iron den and foster-mother complete. The latter the wife dismissed; went out and bought stout motor-gloves, and the largest of babies' bottles, and fed him forthwith. He highly approved of this, and ceased not to pull at the bottle till it was all empty. His tummy was then slapped, as it might have been a water-melon, to be sure that it rang full, and he went to sleep. Thus he lived and throve in his den, which the children were forbidden to enter, lest their caresses should injure him.

When he was about the size of a large rabbit, he cut little pins of teeth, and made coughing noises which he was persuaded were genuine roars. Later, he developed rickets, and I was despatched to an expert at Cape Town to ask for a cure. 'Too much milk,' said the expert. 'Give him real, not cold-storage, boiled mutton-broth.' This at first he refused to touch in the saucer, but was induced to lick the wife's dipped finger, whence he removed the skin. His ears were boxed, and he was left alone with the saucer to learn table-manners. He wailed all night, but in the morning lapped like a lion among Christians, and soon got rid of his infirmity. For three months he was at large among us, incessantly talking to himself as he wandered about the house or in the garden where he stalked butterflies. He dozed on the stoep, I noticed, due north and south, looking with slow eyes up the length of Africa—always a little aloof, but obedient to the children, who at that time wore little more than one garment apiece. We returned him in perfect condition on our departure for England, and he was then the size of a bull-terrier but not so high. Rhodes and Jameson were both away. He was put in a cage, fed, like his family, on imperfectly thawed cold-storage meats fouled in the grit of his floor, and soon died of colic. But M'Slibaan, which we made Matabele for 'Sullivan,' as fitted his Matabele ancestry, was always honoured among the many kind ghosts that inhabited the 'Woolsack.'[63]

Lions, as pets, are hardly safe after six months old; but here is an exception. A man kept a lioness up-country till she was a full year old, and then, with deep regret on both sides, sent her to Rhodes' Zoo. Six months later he came down, and with a girl who did not know what fear was entered her cage, where she received him fawning, rolling, crooning—almost weeping with love and delight. Theoretically, of course, he and the girl ought to have been killed, but they took no hurt at all.

During the war, by some luck our water-supply had not been restricted, and our bath was of the type you step down into and soak in at full length. Hence also Gwynne, filthy after months of the veldt, standing afar off like a leper. ('I say, I want a bath and—there's my kit in the garden. No, I haven't left it on the stoep. It's crawling.') Many came. As the children put it: 'There's always lots of dirty ones.'

When Rhodes was hatching his scheme of the Scholarships,[64] he would come over and, as it were, think aloud or discuss, mainly with the wife, the expense side of the idea. It was she who suggested that £250 a year was not enough for scholars who would have to carry themselves through the long intervals of an Oxford 'year.' So he made it three hundred. My use to him was mainly as a purveyor of words; for he was largely inarticulate. After the idea had been presented—and one had to know his code for it—he would say: 'What am I trying to express? Say it, *say* it.' So I would say it, and if the phrase suited not, he would work it over, chin a little down, till it satisfied him.

The order of his life at 'Groote Schuur' was something like this. The senior guest [*sic*] allotted their rooms to men who wished to 'see' him. They did not come except for good reason connected with their work, and they stayed till Rhodes 'saw' them, which might be two or three days. His heart compelled him to lie down a good deal on a huge couch on the marble-flagged verandah facing up Table Mountain towards the four-acre patch of hydrangeas, which lay out like lapiz-lazuli on the lawns. He would say: 'Well, So-and-so. I see you. What is it?' And the case would be put.

There was a man laying the Cape-to-Cairo telegraph, who had come to a stretch of seventy miles beside a lake, where the ladies of those parts esteemed copper above gold, and took it from the poles for their adornment. What to do? When he had finished his exposition Rhodes, turning heavily on his couch, said: 'You've got some sort of lake there, haven't you? Lay it like a cable. Don't bother me with a little thing like that.' Palaver done set,[65] and at his leisure the man returned.

One met interesting folk at 'Groote Schuur' meals, which often ended in long talks of the days of building up Rhodesia.

During the Matabele War Rhodes, with some others, under a guide, had wandered on horseback beyond the limits of safety, and had to take refuge in some caves. The situation was eminently unhealthy, and in view of some angry Matabeles hunting them they had to spur out of it. But the guide, just when the party were in the open, was foolish enough to say something to the effect that Rhodes's 'valuable life' was to be considered. Upon which Rhodes pulled up and said: 'Let's get this straight before we go on. *You* led us into this mess, didn't you?' 'Yes, sir, yes. But *please* come on.' 'No. Wait a minute. Consequently you're running to save your own hide, aren't you?' 'Yes, sir. We all are.' 'That's all right. I only wanted to have it settled. *Now* we'll come on.' And they did, but it was a close shave. I heard this at his table, even as I heard his delayed reply to a query by a young officer who wished to know what Rhodes thought of him and his career. Rhodes postponed his answer till dinner and then, in his characteristic voice, laid down that the young man would eminently succeed, but only to a certain point, because he was always thinking of his career and not of the job he was doing. Thirty later years proved the truth of his verdict.

Chapter VII

The Very-Own House

How can I turn from any fire
On any man's hearth-stone?
I know the wonder and desire
That went to build my own.
The Fires.[1]

All this busy while the Committee of Ways and Means kept before them the hope of a house of their very own—a real House in which to settle down for keeps—and took trains on rails and horsed carriages of the age to seek it. Our adventures were many and sometimes grim—as when a 'comfortable nursery' proved to be a dark padded cell at the end of a discreet passage! Thus we quested for two or three years, till one summer day a friend cried at our door: 'Mr. Harmsworth[2] has just brought round one of those motor-car things. Come and try it!'

It was a twenty-minute trip. We returned white with dust and dizzy with noise. But the poison worked from that hour. Somehow, an enterprising Brighton agency hired us a Victoria-hooded, carriage-sprung, carriage-braked, single-cylinder, belt-driven, fixed-ignition Embryo which, at times, could cover eight miles an hour. Its hire, including 'driver,' was three and a half guineas a week. The beloved Aunt, who feared nothing created, said 'Me too!' So we three house-hunted together taking risks of ignorance that made me shudder through after-years. But we went to Arundel and back, which was sixty miles, and returned in the same ten-hour day! We, and a few other desperate pioneers, took the first shock of outraged public opinion. Earls stood up in their belted barouches and cursed us. Gipsies, governess-carts, brewery waggons—all the world except the poor patient horses who would have been quite quiet if left alone joined in the commination service, and *The Times* leaders on 'motor-cars' were eolithic in outlook.

Then I bought me a steam-car called a 'Locomobile,' whose nature and attributes I faithfully drew in a tale called 'Steam Tactics.'[3] She reduced us to the limits of fatigue and hysteria, all up and down Sussex. Next came the earliest Lanchester,[4] whose springing, even at that time, was perfect. But no designer, manufacturer, owner, nor chauffeur knew anything about anything. The heads of the Lanchester firm[5] would, after furious telegrams, visit us as friends (we were all friends in those days) and sit round our hearth speculating Why What did That. Once, the proud designer—she was his newest baby—took me as far as Worthing, where she fainted opposite a vacant building-plot. This we paved completely with every other fitting that she possessed ere we got at her trouble. We then re-assembled her, a two hours' job. After which, she spat boiling water over our laps, but we stuffed a rug into the geyser and so spouted home.[6]

But it was the heart-breaking Locomobile that brought us to the house called 'Bateman's.'[7] We had seen an advertisement of her, and we reached her down an enlarged rabbit-hole of a lane. At very first sight the Committee of Ways and Means said: 'That's her! The Only She! Make an honest woman of her—quick!' We entered and felt her Spirit—her Feng Shui—to be good. We went through every room and found no shadow of ancient regrets, stifled miseries, nor any menace, though the 'new' end of her was three hundred years old. To our woe the Owner said: 'I've just let it for twelve months.' We withdrew, each repeatedly telling the other that no sensible person would be found dead in the stuffy little valley where she stood. We lied thus while we pretended to look at other houses till, a year later, we saw her advertised again, and got her.

When all was signed and sealed, the seller said: 'Now I can ask you something. How are you going to manage about getting to and from the station? It's nearly four miles, and I've used up two pair of horses on the hill here.' 'I'm thinking of using this sort of contraption,' I replied from my seat in—Jane Cakebread Lanchester,[8] I think, was her dishonourable name. 'Oh! *Those* things haven't come to stay!' he returned. Years afterwards I met him, and he confided that had he known what I had guessed, he would have asked twice the money. In three years from our purchase the railway station had passed out of our lives. In seven, I heard my chauffeur[9] say to an under-powered visiting sardine-tin: 'Hills? There ain't any hills on the London road.'

The House was not of a type to present to servants by lamp or candle-light. Hence electricity, which in 1902 was a serious affair. We chanced, at a week-end visit, to meet Sir William Willcocks,[10] who had designed the Assouan Dam—a trifling affair on the Nile. Not to be over-crowed, we told him of our project for de-clutching the water-wheel from an ancient mill at the end of our garden, and using its microscopical mill-pond to run a turbine. That was enough! 'Dam?' said he. '*You* don't know anything about dams or turbines. *I'll* come and look.' That Monday morn he came with us, explored the brook and the mill-sluit,[11] and foretold truly the exact amount of horse-power that we should get out of our turbine— 'Four and a half and no more.' But he called me Egyptian names for the state of my brook, which, till then, I had deemed picturesque. 'It's all messed up with trees and bushes. Cut 'em down and slope the banks to one in three.' 'Lend me a couple of Fellahîn Battalions[12] and I'll begin,' I said.

He said also: 'Don't run your light cable on poles. Bury it.' So we got a deep-sea cable which had failed under test at twelve hundred volts—our voltage being one hundred and ten—and laid him in a trench from the Mill to the house, a full furlong, where he worked for a quarter of a century. At the end of that time he was a little fatigued, and the turbine had worn as much as one-sixteenth of an inch on her bearings. So we gave them both honourable demission—and never again got anything so faithful.

Of the little one-street village up the hill we only knew that, according to the guide-books, they came of a smuggling, sheep-stealing stock, brought more or less into civilisation within the past three generations. Those of them who worked for us, and who I presume would to-day be called 'Labour,' struck for higher pay than they had agreed on as soon as we were committed to our first serious works. My foreman and general contractor, himself of their race, and soon to become our good friend, said: 'They think they've got ye. They think there's no harm in tryin' it.' There was not. I had sense enough to feel that most of them were artists and craftsmen, either in stone or timber, or wood-cutting, or drain-laying or—which is a gift—the aesthetic disposition of dirt; persons of contrivance who could conjure with any sort of material. As our electric-light campaign developed, a London contractor came down to put a fifteen-inch eduction-pipe through the innocent-seeming mill-dam. His imported gang came across a solid core of ancient brick-work about as workable as obsidian. They left, after using very strong words. But every other man of 'our folk' had known exactly where and what that core was, and when 'Lunnon' had sufficiently weakened it, they 'conjured' the pipe quietly through what remained.

The only thing that ever shook them was when we cut a little under the Mill foundations to fix the turbine; and found that she sat on a crib or raft of two-foot-square elm logs. What we took came out, to all appearance, as untouched as when it had been put under water. Yet, in an hour, the great baulk, exposed to air, became silver dust, and the men stood round marvelling. There was one among them, close upon seventy when we first met, a poacher by heredity and instinct, a gentleman who, when his need to drink was on him, which was not too often, absented himself and had it out alone; and he was more 'one with Nature' than whole parlours full of poets. He became our special stay and counsellor. Once we wanted to shift a lime and a witch-elm into the garden proper. He said not a word till we talked of getting a tree-specialist from London. 'Have it *as* you're minded. *I* dunno as I should if I was you,' was his comment. By this we understood that he would take charge when the planets were favourable. Presently, he called up four of his own kin (also artists) and brushed us aside. The trees came away kindly. He placed them, with due regard for their growth for the next two or three generations; supported them, throat and bole, with stays and stiffenings, and bade us hold them thus for four years. All fell out as he had foretold. The trees are now close on forty foot high and have never flinched. Equally, a well-grown witch-elm that needed discipline, he climbed into and topped, and she carries to this day the graceful dome he gave her. In his later years—he lived to be close on eighty-five—he would, as I am doing now, review his past, which held incident enough for many unpublishable volumes. He spoke of old loves, fights, intrigues, anonymous denunciations 'by such folk as knew writing,' and vindictive conspiracies carried out with oriental thoroughness. Of poaching he talked in all its branches, from buying *Cocculus Indicus*[13] for poisoning fish in ponds, to the art of making silk-nets for trout-brooks—mine among them, and he left a specimen to me; and of pitched battles (guns barred) with heavy-handed keepers in the old days in Lord Ashburnham's[14] woods where a man might pick up a fallow-deer. His sagas were lighted with pictures of nature as he, indeed, knew her; night-pieces and dawn-breakings; stealthy returns and the thinking out of alibis, all naked by the fire, while his clothes dried; and of the face and temper of the next twilight under which he stole forth to follow his passion. His wife, after she had known us for ten years, would range through a past that accepted magic, witchcraft and love-philtres, for which last there was a demand as late as the middle 'sixties.

She described one midnight ritual at the local 'wise woman's' cottage, when a black cock was killed with curious rites and words, and '*all* de time dere was, like, *someone* trying to come *through* at ye from outside in de dark. Dunno as I believe so much in such things *now*, but when I was a maid I—I justabout *did*!' She died well over ninety, and to the last carried the tact, manner and presence, for all she was so small, of an old-world Duchess.

There were interesting and helpful outsiders, too. One was a journeyman bricklayer who, I remember, kept a store of gold sovereigns loose in his pocket, and kindly built us a wall; but so leisurely that he came to be almost part of the establishment. When we wished to sink a well opposite some cottages, he said he had the gift of water-finding, and I testify that, when he held one fork of the hazel Y and I the other, the thing bowed itself against all the grip of my hand over an unfailing supply.

Then, out of the woods that know everything and tell nothing, came two dark and mysterious Primitives. They had heard. They would sink that well, for they had the 'gift.' Their tools were an enormous wooden trug,[15] a portable windlass whose handles were curved, and smooth as ox-horns, and a short-handled hoe. They made a ring of brickwork on the bare ground and, with their hands at first, grubbed out the dirt beneath it. As the ring sank they heightened it, course by course, grubbing out with the hoe, till the shaft, true as a rifle-barrel, was deep enough to call for their Father of Trugs, which one brother down below would fill, and the other haul up on the magic windlass. When we stopped, at twenty-five feet, we had found a Jacobean tobacco-pipe, a worn Cromwellian latten[16] spoon and, at the bottom of all, the bronze cheek of a Roman horse-bit.

In cleaning out an old pond which might have been an ancient marl-pit or mine-head, we dredged two intact Elizabethan 'sealed quarts' that Christopher Sly affected,[17] all pearly with the patina of centuries. Its deepest mud yielded us a perfectly polished Neolithic axe-head with but one chip on its still venomous edge.

These things are detailed that you may understand how, when my cousin, Ambrose Poynter, said to me: 'Write a yarn about Roman times here,' I was interested. 'Write,' said he, 'about an old Centurion of the Occupation telling his experiences to his children.' 'What is his name?' I demanded, for I move easiest from a given point. 'Parnesius,' said my cousin; and the name stuck in my head. I was then on Committee of Ways and Means (which had grown to include Public Works and Communications) but, in due season, the name came back—with seven other inchoate devils. I went off Committee, and began to 'hatch,' in which state I was 'a brother to dragons and a companion to owls.'[18] Just beyond the west fringe of our land, in a little valley running from Nowhere to Nothing-at-all, stood the long, overgrown slag-heap of a most ancient forge, supposed to have been worked by the Phoenicians and Romans and, since then, uninterruptedly till the middle of the eighteenth century. The bracken and rush-patches still hid stray pigs of iron, and if one scratched a few inches through the rabbit-shaven turf, one came on the narrow mule-tracks of peacock-hued furnace-slag laid down in Elizabeth's day. The ghost of a road climbed up out of this dead arena, and crossed our fields, where it was known as 'The Gunway,' and popularly connected with Armada times. Every foot of that little corner was alive with ghosts and shadows. Then, it pleased our children to act for us, in the open, what they remembered of *A Midsummer-Night's Dream*. Then a friend gave them a real birch-bark canoe, drawing at least three inches, in which they went adventuring on the brook.[19] And in a near pasture of the water-meadows lay out an old and unshifting Fairy Ring.

You see how patiently the cards were stacked and dealt into my hands? The Old Things of our Valley glided into every aspect of our outdoor works. Earth, Air, Water and People had been—I saw it at last—in full conspiracy to give me ten times as much as I could compass, even if I wrote a complete history of England, as that might have touched or reached our Valley.

I went off at score[20]—not on Parnesius, but a story told in a fog by a petty Baltic pirate, who had brought his galley to Pevensey and, off Beachy Head—where in the War we heard merchant-ships being torpedoed—had passed the Roman fleet abandoning Britain to her doom. That tale may have served as a pipe-opener, but one could not see its wood for its trees, so I threw it away.

I carried the situation to the little house in Wiltshire, where my Father and Mother were installed; and smoked it over with the Father, who said—not for the first time: 'Most things in this world are accomplished by judicious leaving alone.' So we played cribbage (he had carved a perfect Lama and a little Kim for my two pegs), while the Mother worked beside us, or, each taking a book, lapsed into the silence of entire mutual comprehension. One night, apropos of nothing at all, the Father said: 'And you'll have to look up your references rather more carefully, won't you?' That had *not* been my distinction on the little *Civil and Military*.

This led me on another false scent. I wrote a tale told by Daniel Defoe in a brickyard (we had a real one of our own at that time where we burned bricks for barns and cottages to the exact tints we desired) of how he had been sent to stampede King James II, then havering about Thames mouth, out of an England where no party had any use for him. It turned out a painstaken and meritorious piece of work, overloaded with verified references, with about as much feeling to it as a walking-stick. So it also was discarded, with a tale of Doctor Johnson telling the children how he had once thrown his spurs out of a boat in Scotland, to the amazement of one Boswell.[21] Evidently my Daemon would not function in brickyards or schoolrooms. Therefore, like Alice in Wonderland, I turned my back on the whole thing and walked the other way.[22] Therefore, the whole thing set and linked itself. I fell first upon Normans and Saxons. Parnesius came later, directly out of a little wood above the Phoenician forge; and the rest of the tales in *Puck of Pook's Hill* followed in order. The Father came over to see us and, hearing 'Hal o' the Draft,' closed in with fore-reaching pen, presently ousted me from my table, and inlaid the description of Hal's own drawing-knife. He liked that tale, and its companion piece 'The Wrong Thing' (*Rewards and Fairies*), which latter he embellished, notably in respect to an Italian fresco-worker, whose work never went 'deeper than the plaster.'[23] He said that 'judicious leaving alone' did not apply between artists.

Of 'Dymchurch Flit,' with which I was always unashamedly content, he asked: 'Where did you get that lighting from?' It had come of itself. *Qua* workmanship, that tale and two night-pieces in 'Cold Iron' (*Rewards and Fairies*) are the best in that kind I have ever made, but somehow 'The Treasure and the Law' (*Puck of Pook's Hill*) always struck me as too heavy for its frame.

Yet that tale brought me a prized petty triumph. I had put a well into the wall of Pevensey Castle *circa* A.D. 1100, because I needed it there. Archaeologically, it did not exist till this year (1935) when excavators brought such a well to light.[24] But that I maintain was a reasonable gamble. Self-contained castles must have self-contained water supplies. A longer chance that I took in my Roman tales was when I quartered the Seventh Cohort of the Thirtieth (Ulpia Victrix) Legion on the Wall, and asserted that there Roman troops used arrows against the Picts. The first shot was based on honest 'research'; the second was legitimate inference. Years after the tale was told, a digging-party on the Wall sent me some heavy four-sided, Roman made, 'killing' arrows found *in situ* and—most marvellously—a rubbing of a memorial-tablet to the Seventh Cohort of the Thirtieth Legion! Having been brought up in a suspicious school, I suspected a 'leg-pull' here, but was assured that the rubbing was perfectly genuine.[25]

I embarked on *Rewards and Fairies*—the second book—in two minds. Stories a plenty I had to tell, but how many would be authentic and how many due to 'induction'? There was moreover the old Law: 'As soon as you find you can do anything, do something you can't.'

My doubt cleared itself with the first tale 'Cold Iron,' which gave me my underwood: 'What else could I have done?'—the plinth of all structures. Yet, since the tales had to be read by children, before people realised that they were meant for grown-ups; and since they had to be a sort of balance to, as well as a seal upon, some aspects of my 'Imperialistic' output in the past, I worked the material in three or four overlaid tints and textures, which might or might not reveal themselves according to the shifting light of sex, youth, and experience. It was like working lacquer and mother o' pearl, a natural combination, into the same scheme as niello and grisaille,[26] and trying not to let the joins show.

So I loaded the book up with allegories and allusions, and verified references until my old Chief would have been almost pleased with me; put in three or four really good sets of verses; the bones of one entire historical novel for any to clothe who cared; and even slipped in a cryptogram, whose key I regret I must have utterly forgotten.[27] It was glorious fun; and I knew it must be very good or very bad because the series turned itself off just as *Kim* had done.

Among the verses in *Rewards* was one set called 'If,' which escaped from the book, and for a while ran about the world. They were drawn from Jameson's character, and contained counsels of perfection most easy to give. Once started, the mechanism of the age made them snowball themselves in a way that startled me. Schools, and places where they teach, took them for the suffering Young—which did me no good with the Young when I met them later. ('Why did you write that stuff? I've had to write it out twice as an impot.') They were printed as cards to hang up in offices and bedrooms; illuminated text-wise and anthologised to weariness. Twenty-seven of the Nations of the Earth translated them into their seven-and-twenty tongues, and printed them on every sort of fabric.

Some years after the War a kind friend hinted that my two innocent little books might have helped towards begetting the

'Higher Cannibalism' in biography. By which I understood him to mean the exhumation of scarcely cold notorieties, defenceless females for choice, and tricking them out with sprightly inferences and 'sex'-deductions to suit the mood of the market. It was an awful charge, and anyway I felt that others had qualified as Chief Morticians to that trade.[28]

For rest and refreshment and dearly-loved experiments and anxieties, during the six months or so of each year that we stayed in England, there was always the House and the land, and on occasion the Brook at the foot of our garden, which would flood devastatingly. As she supplied the water for our turbine, and as the little weir which turned her current into the little mill-race was of a frail antiquity, one had to attend to her often and at once, and always at the most inconvenient moment.

Undiscerning folks would ask: 'What do you find to *do* in the country?' Our answer was: 'Everything except time to do it.'

We began with tenants—two or three small farmers on our very few acres—from whom we learned that farming was a mixture of farce, fraud, and philanthropy that stole the heart out of the land. After many, and some comic experiences, we fell back on our own county's cattle—the big, red Sussex breed who make beef and not milk. One got something at least for one's money from the mere sight of them, and they did not tell lies. Rider Haggard would visit us from time to time and give of his ample land-wisdom. I remember I planted some apple-trees in an old orchard then rented by an Irishman, who at once put in an agile and hungry goat. Haggard met the combination suddenly one morning. He had gifts of speech, and said very clearly indeed that one might as well put Satan in an orchard as a goat. I forget what—though I acted on it—he said about tenants. His comings were always a joy to us and the children, who followed him like hounds in the hope of 'more South African stories.' Never was a better tale-teller or, to my mind, a man with a more convincing imagination. We found by accident that each could work at ease in the other's company. So he would visit me, and I him, with work in hand; and between us we could even hatch out tales together—a most exacting test of sympathy.

I was honoured till he died by the friendship of a Colonel Wemyss

Feilden,[29] who moved into the village to inherit a beautiful little William and Mary house on the same day as we came to take over 'Bateman's.' He was in soul and spirit Colonel Newcome;[30] in manner as diffident and retiring as an old maid out of *Cranford*;[31] and up to his eighty-second year could fairly walk me off my feet, and pull down pheasants from high heaven. He had begun life in the Black Watch, with whom, outside Delhi during the Mutiny, he heard one morning as they were all shaving that a 'little fellow called Roberts'[32] had captured single-handed a rebel Standard and was coming through the Camp. 'We all turned out. The boy was on horseback looking rather pleased with himself, and his mounted Orderly carried the Colour behind him. We cheered him with the lather on our faces.'

After the Mutiny he sold out, and having interests in Natal went awhile to South Africa. Next, he ran the blockade of the U.S. Civil War, and wedded his Southern wife in Richmond with a ring hammered out of an English sovereign 'because there wasn't any gold in Richmond just then.' Mrs. Feilden at seventy-five was in herself fair explanation of all the steps he had taken—and forfeited.

He came to be one of Lee's aides-de-camp,[33] and told me how once on a stormy night, when he rode in with despatches, Lee had ordered him to take off his dripping cloak and lie by the fire; and how when he waked from badly needed sleep, he saw the General on his knees before the flame drying the cloak. 'That was just before the surrender,' said he. 'We had finished robbing the grave, and we'd begun on the cradle. For those last three months I was with fifteen thousand boys under seventeen, and I don't remember any one of them even smiling.'

Bit by bit I came to understand that he was a traveller and an Arctic explorer, in possession of the snow-white Polar ribbon; a botanist and naturalist of reputation; and himself above all.

When Rider Haggard heard these things, he rested not till he had made the Colonel's acquaintance. They cottoned to each other on sight and sound; South Africa in the early days being their bond. One evening, Haggard told us how his son had been born on the edge of Zulu, I think, territory, the first white child in those parts. 'Yes,' said the Colonel, quietly out of his corner. 'I and'—he named two men—'rode twenty-seven miles to look at him. We hadn't seen a white baby for some time.' Then Haggard remembered that visit of strangers.[34]

And once there came to us with her married daughter the widow of a Confederate Cavalry leader; both of them were what you might call 'unreconstructed' rebels. Somehow, the widow mentioned a road and a church beside a river in Georgia. 'It's still there, then?' said the Colonel, giving it its name. 'Why do you ask?' was the quick reply. 'Because, if you look in such-and-such a pew, you might find my initials. I cut them there the night ——'s Cavalry stabled their horses there.' There was a pause. ''Fore God, then, *who* are you?' she gasped. He told her. 'You knew my husband?' 'I served under him. He was the only man in our corps who wore a white collar.' She pelted him with questions, and the names of the old dead. 'Come away,' whispered her daughter to me. 'They don't want *us*.' Nor did they for a long hour.

Sooner or later, all sorts of men cast up at our house. From India naturally; from the Cape increasingly after the Boer War and our half-yearly visits there; from Rhodesia when that province was in the making; from Australia, with schemes for emigration which one knew Organised Labour would never allow to pass its legislatures; from Canada, when 'Imperial Preference'[35] came to the fore, and Jameson, after one bitter experience, cursed 'that dam' dancing-master (Laurier)[36] who had bitched the whole show'; and from off main-line Islands and Colonies—men of all makes, each with his life-tale, grievance, idea, ideal, or warning.

There was an ex-Governor of the Philippines,[37] who had slaved his soul out for years to pull his charge into some sort of shape and—on a turn of the political wheel at Washington—had been dismissed at literally less notice than he would have dared to give a native orderly. I remembered not a few men whose work and hope had been snatched from under their noses, and my sympathy was very real. His account of Filipino political 'leaders,' writing and shouting all day for 'independence' and running round to him after dark to be assured that there was no chance of the dread boon being granted—'because then we shall most probably all be killed'—was cheeringly familiar.

The difficulty was to keep these interests separate in the head; but the grind of adjusting the mental eye to new perspectives was good for the faculties. Besides this *viva voce*, there was always heavy written work, three-fourths of which was valueless, but for the sake of the possibly worth-while residue all had to be gone through. This was specially the case during the three years before the War, when warnings came thick and fast, and the wise people to whom I conveyed them said: 'Oh, but you're *so-o*—extreme.'

Blasts of extravagant publicity alternated with my office-work. In the late summer of '06,[38] for example, we took ship to Canada, which I had not seen in any particularity for many years, and of which I had been told that it was coming out of its spiritual and material subjection to the United States. Our steamer was an Allen Liner[39] with the earliest turbines and wireless. In the wireless-room, as we were feeling our way blind through the straits of Belle Isle, a sister ship, sixty miles ahead, morsed that the fog with her was even thicker. Said a young engineer in the doorway: 'Who's yon talking, Jock? Ask him if he's done drying his socks.' And the old professional jest crackled out through the smother. It was my first experience of practical wireless.

At Quebec we met Sir William Van Horne,[40] head of the whole C.P.R. system, but, on our wedding trip fifteen years before, a mere Divisional Superintendent who had lost a trunk of my wife's and had stood his Division on its head to find it. His deferred, but ample revenge was to give us one whole Pullman car with coloured porter complete, to take and use and hitch on to and declutch from any train we chose, to anywhere we fancied, for as long as we liked. We took it, and did all those things to Vancouver and back again. When we wished to sleep in peace, it slid off into still, secret freight-yards till morning. When we would eat, *chefs* of the great mail trains, which it had honoured by its attachment, asked us what we would like. (It was the season of blueberries and wild duck.) If we even looked as though we wanted anything, that thing would be waiting for us a few score miles up the line. In this manner and in such state we progressed, and the procession and the progress was meat and drink to the soul of William the coloured porter, our Nurse, Valet, Seneschal, and Master of Ceremonies. (More by token, the wife understood coloured folk, and that put William at ease.) Many people would come aboard to visit us at halting-places, and there were speeches of sorts to be prepared and delivered at the towns. In the first case: ' 'Nother depytation, Boss,' from William behind enormous flower-pieces; 'and more bo-kays for de Lady.' In the second: 'Dere's a speech doo at ——. You go right ahaid with what you're composin', Boss. Jest put your feets out an' I'll shine 'em meanwhile.' So, brushed up and properly shod, I was ushered into the public eye by the immortal William.

In some ways it was punishing 'all out' work, but in all ways worth it. I had been given an honorary degree, my first, by the McGill University at Montreal.[41] That University received me with interest, and after I had delivered a highly moral discourse,[42] the students dumped me into a fragile horse-vehicle, which they hurtled through the streets. Said one nice child sitting in the hood of it: 'You gave us a dam' dull speech. Can't you say anything amusin' now?' I could but express my fears for the safety of the conveyance, which was disintegrating by instalments.

In '15 I met some of those boys digging trenches in France.

No words of mine can give any notion of the kindness and goodwill lavished on us through every step of our road. I tried, and failed to do so in a written account of it. (*Letters to the Family*.)[43] And always the marvel—to which the Canadians seemed insensible—was that on one side of an imaginary line should be Safety, Law, Honour, and Obedience, and on the other frank, brutal decivilisation; and that, despite this, Canada should be impressed by any aspect whatever of the United States. Some hint of this too I strove to give in my *Letters*.

Before we parted, William told us a tale of a friend of his who was consumed with desire to be a Pullman porter 'bekase he had watched me doin' it, an' thought he could do it—jest by watchin' me.' (This was the burden of his parable, like a deep-toned locomotive bell.) Overborne at last, William wangled for his friend the coveted post—'next car ahaid to mine . . . I got *my* folks to baid early 'kase I guessed he'd be needin' me soon. . . . But *he* thought he could do it. And den all *his* folk in *his* car, dey all wanted to go to baid at de same time—like they allus do. An' he tried—Gawd knows he tried—to 'commodate 'em all de same time an' he couldn't. He jes' couldn't. . . . He didn't know haow. He thought he did bekase he had,' etc. etc. 'An' den he quit . . . he jes' quit.' A long pause.

'Jumped out of window?' we demanded.

'No. Oh no. Dey wasn't no jump to him dat night. He went into de broom-closet—'kase I found him dar—an' he cried, an' all his folk slammin' on de broom-house door an' cussin' him 'kase dey wanted to go to baid. An' he couldn't put 'em dar. He couldn't put 'em. He thought,' etc. etc. 'An' den? Why, o' course I jes' whirled in an' put 'em to baid for him an' when I told 'em how t'wuz with dat sorerful cryin' nigger, dey laughed. Dey laughed heaps an' heaps. . . . But he thought he could do it by havin' watched me do it.'

A few weeks after we returned from the wonderful trip, I was notified that I had been awarded the Nobel Prize of that year for Literature.[44] It was a very great honour, in all ways unexpected.

It was necessary to go to Stockholm. Even while we were on the sea, the old King of Sweden died. We reached the city, snow-white under sun, to find all the world in evening dress, the official mourning, which is curiously impressive. Next afternoon, the prize-winners were taken to be presented to the new King.[45] Winter darkness in those latitudes falls at three o'clock, and it was snowing. One half of the vast acreage of the Palace sat in darkness, for there lay the dead King's body. We were conveyed along interminable corridors looking out into black quadrangles, where snow whitened the cloaks of the sentries, the breeches of old-time cannon, and the shot-piles alongside of them. Presently, we reached a living world of more corridors and suites all lighted up, but wrapped in that Court hush which is like no other silence on earth. Then, in a great lit room, the weary-eyed, over-worked, new King, saying to each the words appropriate to the occasion. Next, the Queen,[46] in marvellous Mary Queen of Scots mourning, a few words, and the return piloted by soft-footed Court officials through a stillness so deep that one heard the click of the decorations on their uniforms. They said that the last words of the old King had been: 'Don't let them shut the theatres for me.' So Stockholm that night went soberly about her pleasures, all dumbed down under the snow.

Morning did not come till ten o'clock; and one lay abed in thick dark, listening to the blunted grind of the trams speeding the people to their work-day's work. But the ordering of their lives was reasonable, thought out, and most comfortable for all classes in the matters of food, housing, the lesser but more desirable decencies, and the consideration given to the Arts. I had only known the Swede as a first-class immigrant in various parts of the earth. Looking at his native land I could guess whence he drew his strength and directness. Snow and frost are no bad nurses.

At that epoch staid women attached to the public wash-houses washed in a glorious lather of soap, worked up with big bunches of finest pine-shavings (when you think of it, a sponge is almost as dirty a tool as the permanent tooth-brush of the European), men desirous of the most luxurious bath known to civilisation. But foreigners did not always catch the idea. Hence this tale told to me at a winter resort in the deep, creamy contralto of the North by a Swedish lady who took, and pronounced, her English rather biblically. The introit you can imagine for yourself. Here is the finale: 'And then she—the old woman com-ed—came—in to wash that man. But he was angered—angry. He wented—he went dee-ep into the water and he say-ed—said—"Go a-way!" And she sayed, "But I comm to wash you, sare." And she made to do that. But he tur-ned over up-on his fa-ace, and wa-ved his legs in the airs and he sayed: "Go a-damway away!" So she went to the Direktor and she say-ed: "Comm he-ere. There are a mads in my bath, which will not let me wash of him." But the Direktor say-ed to her: "Oh, that are not a mads. That are an Englishman. He will himself—he will wash himself."'

CHAPTER VIII

Working-Tools[1]

Every man must be his own law in his own work, but it is a poor-spirited artist in any craft who does not know how the other man's work should be done or could be improved. I have heard as much criticism among hedgers and ditchers and woodmen of a companion's handling of spade, bill-hook, or axe, as would fill a Sunday paper. Carters and cattle-men are even more meticulous, since they must deal with temperaments and seasonal instabilities. We had once on the farms a pair of brothers between ten and twelve. The younger could deal so cunningly with the intractable cart-mare who rushed her gates, and for choice diagonally, that he was called in to take charge of her as a matter of course. The elder, at eleven, could do all that his strength allowed, and the much more that ancestral craft had added, with any edged tool or wood. Modern progress has turned them into meritorious menials.

One of my cattle-men had a son who at eight could appraise the merits and character of any beast in his father's care, and was on terms of terrifying familiarity with the herd-bull, whom he would slap on the nose to make him walk disposedly before us when visitors came. At eighteen, he would have been worth two hundred a year to begin with on any ranch in the Dominions. But he was 'good at his books,' and is now in a small grocery, but wears a black coat on the Sabbath. Which things are a portent.

I have told what my early surroundings were, and how richly they furnished me with material. Also, how rigorously newspaper spaces limited my canvases and, for the reader's sake, prescribed that within these limits must be some sort of beginning, middle, and end. My ordinary reporting, leader- and note-writing carried the same lesson, which took me an impatient while to learn. Added to this, I was almost nightly responsible for my output to visible and often brutally voluble critics at the Club. They were not concerned with my dreams. They wanted accuracy and interest, but first of all accuracy.

My young head was in a ferment of new things seen and realised at every turn and—that I might in any way keep abreast of the flood— it was necessary that every word should tell, carry, weigh, taste and, if need were, smell. Here the Father helped me incomparably by his 'judicious leaving alone.' 'Make your own experiments,' said he. 'It's the only road. If I helped, I'd hinder.' So I made my own experiments and, of course, the viler they were the more I admired them.

Mercifully, the mere act of writing was, and always has been, a physical pleasure to me. This made it easier to throw away anything that did not turn out well: and to practice, as it were, scales.

Verse, naturally, came first, and here the Mother was at hand, with now and then some shrivelling comment that infuriated me. But, as she said: 'There's no Mother in Poetry, my dear.' It was she, indeed, who had collected and privately printed verses written at school up to my sixteenth year, which I faithfully sent out from the little House of the Dear Ladies.[2] Later, when the notoriety came, 'in they broke, those people of importance,'[3] and the innocent thing 'came on to the market,' and Philadelphia lawyers,[4] a breed by itself, wanted to know, because they had paid much money for an old copy, what I remembered about its genesis. They had been first written in a stiff, marble-backed MS. book, the front page of which the Father had inset with a scandalous sepia-sketch of Tennyson and Browning in procession, and a spectacled school-boy bringing up the rear.[5] I gave it, when I left school, to a woman[6] who returned it to me many years later—for which she will take an even higher place in Heaven than her natural goodness ensures—and I burnt it, lest it should fall into the hands of 'lesser breeds without the (Copyright) law.'[7]

I forget who started the notion of my writing a series of Anglo-Indian tales,[8] but I remember our council over the naming of the series.[9] They were originally much longer than when they appeared, but the shortening of them, first to my own fancy after rapturous re-readings, and next to the space available, taught me that a tale from which pieces have been raked out is like a fire that has been poked. One does not know that the operation has been performed, but every one feels the effect. Note, though, that the excised stuff must have been honestly written for inclusion. I found that when, to save trouble, I 'wrote short' *ab initio* much salt went out of the work. This supports the theory of the chimaera which, having bombinated and been removed, *is* capable of producing secondary causes *in vacuo*.[10]

This leads me to the Higher Editing. Take of well-ground Indian Ink as much as suffices and a camel-hair brush proportionate to the inter-spaces of your lines. In an auspicious hour, read your final draft and consider faithfully every paragraph, sentence and word, blacking out where requisite. Let it lie by to drain as long as possible. At the end of that time, re-read and you should find that it will bear a second shortening. Finally, read it aloud alone and at leisure. Maybe a shade more brushwork will then indicate or impose itself. If not, praise Allah and let it go, and 'when thou hast done, repent not.' The shorter the tale, the longer the brushwork and, normally, the shorter the lie-by, and *vice versa*. The longer the tale, the less brush but the longer lie-by. I have had tales by me for three or five years which shortened themselves almost yearly. The magic lies in the Brush and the Ink. For the Pen, when it is writing, can only scratch; and bottled ink is not to compare with the ground Chinese stick. *Experto crede*.

Let us now consider the Personal Daemon of Aristotle and others, of whom it has been truthfully written, though not published:—

This is the doom of the Makers—their Daemon lives in their pen.
If he be absent or sleeping, they are even as other men.

But if he be utterly present, and they swerve not from his behest,
The word that he gives shall continue, whether in earnest or jest.[11]

Most men, and some most unlikely, keep him under an alias which varies with their literary or scientific attainments. Mine came to me early when I sat bewildered among other notions, and said: 'Take this and no other.' I obeyed, and was rewarded. It was a tale in the little Christmas Magazine *Quartette* which we four wrote together, and it was called 'The Phantom Rickshaw.'[12] Some of it was weak, much was bad and out of key; but it was my first serious attempt to think in another man's skin.

After that I learned to lean upon him and recognise the sign of his approach. If ever I held back, Ananias fashion, anything of myself (even though I had to throw it out afterwards) I paid for it by missing what I *then* knew the tale lacked. As an instance, many years later I wrote about a mediaeval artist, a monastery, and the premature discovery of the microscope. ('The Eye of Allah.'[13]) Again and again it went dead under my hand, and for the life of me I could not see why. I put it away and waited. Then said my Daemon—and I was meditating something else at the time—'Treat it as an illuminated manuscript.' I had ridden off on hard black-and-white decoration, instead of pumicing the whole thing ivory-smooth, and loading it with thick colour and gilt. Again, in a South African, post-Boer War tale called 'The Captive,'[14] which was built up round the phrase 'a first-class dress parade for Armageddon,' I could not get my lighting into key with the tone of the monologue. The background insisted too much. My Daemon said at last: 'Paint the background first once for all, as hard as a public-house sign, and leave it alone.' This done, the rest fell into place with the American accent and outlook of the teller.

My Daemon was with me in the *Jungle Books*, *Kim*, and both Puck books, and good care I took to walk delicately, lest he should withdraw. I know that he did not, because when those books were finished they said so themselves with, almost, the water-hammer click of a tap turned off. One of the clauses in our contract was that I should never follow up 'a success,' for by this sin fell Napoleon and a few others. *Note here*. When your Daemon is in charge, do not try to think consciously. Drift, wait, and obey.

I am afraid that I was not much impressed by reviews. But my early days in London were unfortunate. As I got to know literary circles and their critical output, I was struck by the slenderness of some of the writers' equipment. I could not see how they got along with so casual a knowledge of French work and, apparently, of much English grounding that I had supposed indispensable. Their stuff seemed to be a day-to-day traffic in generalities, hedged by trade considerations. Here I expect I was wrong, but, making my own tests (the man who had asked me out to dinner to discover what I had read gave me the notion), I would ask simple questions, misquote or misattribute my quotations; or (once or twice) invent an author. The result did not increase my reverence. Had they been newspaper men in a hurry, I should have understood; but the gentlemen were presented to me as Priests and Pontiffs. And the generality of them seemed to have followed other trades—in banks or offices—before coming to the Ink; whereas I was free born. It was pure snobism on my part, but it served to keep me inside myself, which is what snobbery is for.

I would not to-day recommend any writer to concern himself overly with reviews. London is a parish, and the Provincial Press has been syndicated, standardised, and smarmed down[15] out of individuality. But there remains still a little fun in that fair. In Manchester was a paper called *The Manchester Guardian*. Outside the mule-lines I had never met anything that could kick or squeal so continuously, or so completely round the entire compass of things. It suspected me from the first, and when my 'Imperialistic' iniquities were established after the Boer War, it used each new book of mine for a shrill recount of my previous sins (exactly as C———[16] used to do) and, I think, enjoyed itself. In return I collected and filed its more acid but uncommonly well-written leaders for my own purposes. After many years, I wrote a tale ('The Wish House'[17]) about a woman of what was called 'temperament' who loved a man and who also suffered from a cancer on her leg—the exact situation carefully specified. The review came to me with a gibe on the margin from a faithful friend: 'You threw up a catch *that* time!' The review said that I had revived Chaucer's Wife of Bath even to the 'mormal on her shinne.' And it looked just like that too! There was no possible answer, so, breaking my rule not to have commerce with any paper, I wrote to *The Manchester Guardian* and gave myself 'out—caught to leg.' The reply came from an evident human being (I had thought red-hot linotypes composed their staff) who was pleased with the tribute to his knowledge of Chaucer.[18]

Per contra, I have had miraculous escapes in technical matters, which make me blush still. Luckily the men of the seas and the engine-room do not write to the Press, and my worst slip is still underided.[19]

The nearest shave that ever missed me was averted by my Daemon. I was at the moment in Canada, where a young Englishman gave me, as a personal experience, a story of a body-snatching episode in deep snow, perpetrated in some lonely prairie-town and culminating in purest horror. To get it out of the system I wrote it detailedly, and it came away just a shade too good; too well-balanced; too slick. I put it aside, not that I was actively uneasy about it, but I wanted to make sure. Months passed, and I started a tooth which I took to the dentist in the little American town near 'Naulakha.'[20] I had to wait a while in his parlour, where I found a file of bound *Harper's Magazines*—say six hundred pages to the volume—dating from the 'fifties. I picked up one, and read as undistractedly as the tooth permitted. There I found my tale, identical in every mark—frozen ground, frozen corpse stiff in its fur robes in the buggy—the inn-keeper offering it a drink—and so on to the ghastly end. Had I published that tale, what could have saved me from the charge of deliberate plagiarism? *Note here.* Always, in our trade, look a gift horse at both ends and in the middle. He may throw you.

But here is a curious case. In the late summer, I think, of '13,[21] I was invited to Manœuvres round Frensham Ponds at Aldershot. The troops were from the Eighth Division of the coming year—Guardsmen, Black Watch, and the rest, down to the horsed maxims—two per battalion. Many of the officers had been juniors in the Boer War, known to Gwynne, one of the guests, and some to me.

When the sham fight was developing, the day turned blue-hazy, the sky lowered, and the heat struck like the Karroo,[22] as one scuttled among the heaths, listening to the uncontrolled clang of the musketry fire. It came over me that anything might be afoot in such weather, pom-poms for instance, half heard on a flank, or the glint of a helio[23] through a cloud-drift. In short I conceived the whole pressure of our dead of the Boer War flickering and re-forming as the horizon flickered in the heat; the galloping feet of a single horse, and a voice once well-known that passed chanting ribaldry along the flank of a crack battalion. ('But Winnie is one of the lost—poor dear!'[24] was that song, if any remember it or its Singer in 1900–1901.) In an interval, while we lay on the grass, I told Gwynne what was in my head; and some officers also listened. The finale was to be manœuvres abandoned and a hurried calling-off of all arms by badly frightened Commandants—the men themselves sweating with terror though they knew not why.

Gwynne played with the notion, and added details of Boer fighting that I did not know; and I remember a young Duke of Northumberland,[25] since dead, who was interested. The notion so obsessed me that I wrote out the beginning at once. But in cold blood it seemed more and more fantastic and absurd, unnecessary and hysterical. Yet, three or four times I took it up and, as many, laid it down. After the War I threw the draft away. It would have done no good, and might have opened the door, and my mail, to unprofitable discussion. For there is a type of mind that dives after what it calls 'psychical experiences.' And I am in no way 'psychic.'[26] Dealing as I have done with large, superficial areas of incident and occasion, one is bound to make a few lucky hits or happy deductions. But there is no need to drag in the 'clairvoyance,' or the rest of the modern jargon. I have seen too much evil and sorrow and wreck of good minds on the road to Endor to take one step along that perilous track. Once only was I sure that I had 'passed beyond the bounds of ordinance.'[27] I dreamt that I stood, in my best clothes, which I do not wear as a rule, one in a line of similarly habited men, in some vast hall, floored with rough-jointed stone slabs. Opposite me, the width of the hall, was another line of persons and the impression of a crowd behind them. On my left some ceremony was taking place that I wanted to see, but could not unless I stepped out of my line because the fat stomach of my neighbour on my left barred my vision. At the ceremony's close, both lines of spectators broke up and moved forward and met, and the great space filled with people. Then a man came up behind me, slipped his hand beneath my arm, and said: 'I want a word with you.' I forget the rest: but it had been a perfectly clear dream, and it stuck in my memory. Six weeks or more later, I attended in my capacity of a Member of the War Graves Commission a ceremony at Westminster Abbey,[28] where the Prince of Wales dedicated a plaque to 'The Million Dead' of the Great War. We Commissioners lined up facing, across the width of the Abbey Nave, more members of the Ministry and a big body of the public behind them, all in black clothes. I could see nothing of the ceremony because the stomach of the man on my left barred my vision. Then, my eye was caught by the cracks of the stone flooring, and I said to myself: 'But here is where I have been!' We broke up, both lines flowed forward and met, and the Nave filled with a crowd, through which a man came up and slipped his hand upon my arm saying: 'I want a word with you, please.' It was about some utterly trivial matter that I have forgotten.

But how, and why, had I been shown an unreleased roll of my life-film? For the sake of the 'weaker brethren'—and sisters—I made no use of the experience.

In respect to verifying one's references, which is a matter in which one can help one's Daemon, it is curious how loath a man is to take his own medicine. Once, on a Boxing Day, with hard frost coming greasily out of the ground, my friend, Sir John Bland-Sutton,[29] the head of the College of Surgeons, came down to 'Bateman's' very full of a lecture which he was to deliver on 'gizzards.' We were settled before the fire after lunch, when he volunteered that So-and-so had said that if you hold a hen to your ear, you can hear the click in its gizzard of the little pebbles that help its digestion. 'Interesting,' said I. 'He's an authority.' 'Oh yes, but'—a long pause—'have you any hens about here, Kipling?' I owned that I had, two hundred yards down a lane, but why not accept So-and-so? 'I can't,' said John simply, 'till I've tried it.' Remorselessly, he worried me into taking him to the hens, who lived in an open shed in front of the gardener's cottage. As we skated over the glairy[30] ground, I saw an eye at the corner of the drawn-down Boxing-Day blind, and knew that my character for sobriety would be blasted all over the farms before night-fall. We caught an outraged pullet. John soothed her for a while (he said her pulse was a hundred and twenty-six), and held her to his ear. 'She clicks all right,' he announced. 'Listen.' I did, and there was click enough for a lecture. '*Now* we can go back to the house,' I pleaded. 'Wait a bit. Let's catch that cock. He'll click better.' We caught him after a loud and long chase, and he clicked like a solitaire-board. I went home, my ears alive with parasites, so wrapped up in my own indignation that the fun of it escaped me. It had not been *my* verification, you see.

But John was right. Take nothing for granted if you can check it. Even though that seem waste-work, and has nothing to do with the essentials of things, it encourages the Daemon. There are always men who by trade or calling know the fact or the inference that you put forth. If you are wrong by a hair in this, they argue: 'False in one thing, false in all.' Having sinned, I know. Likewise, never play down to your public—not because some of them do not deserve it, but because it is bad for your hand. All your material is drawn from the lives of men. Remember, then, what David did with the water brought to him in the heat of battle.[31]

And, if it be in your power, bear serenely with imitators. My *Jungle Books* begat Zoos of them. But the genius of all the genii was one who wrote a series called *Tarzan of the Apes*.[32] I read it, but regret I never saw it on the films, where it rages most successfully. He had 'jazzed' the motif of the *Jungle Books* and, I imagine, had thoroughly enjoyed himself. He was reported to have said that he wanted to find out how bad a book he could write and 'get away with,' which is a legitimate ambition.

Another case was verses of the sort that are recited. An Edinburgh taxi-driver in the War told me that they were much in vogue among the shelters and was honoured to meet me, their author. Afterwards, I found that they were running neck-and-neck with 'Gunga Din' in the military go-as-you-pleases[32] and on the Lower Deck, and were always ascribed to my graceful hand. They were called 'The Green Eye of the Little Yellow God.'[34] They described an English Colonel and his daughter at Khatmandhu in Nepal where there was a military Mess; and her lover of the name of 'mad Carew' which rhymed comfortably. The refrain was more or less 'And the green-eyed yellow Idol looking down.' It was luscious and rampant, with a touch, I thought, of the suburban Toilet-Club school favoured by the late Mr. Oscar Wilde.[35] Yet, and this to me was the Devil of it, it carried for one reader an awesome suggestion of 'but for the Grace of God there goes Richard Baxter.'[36] (Refer again to the hairdresser's model which so moved Mr. Dent Pitman.[37]) Whether the author had done it out of his own head, or as an inspired parody of the possibilities latent in a fellow-craftsman, I do not know. But I admired him.

Occasionally one could test a plagiarist. I had to invent a tree, with name to match, for a man who at that time was rather riding in my pocket. In about eighteen months—the time it takes for a 'test' diamond thrown over the wires into a field of 'blue' rock to turn up on the Kimberley sorting-tables—my tree appeared in his 'nature-studies'—name as spelt by me and virtues attributed. Since in our trade we be all felons, more or less, I repented when I had caught him, but not too much.[38]

And I would charge you for the sake of your daily correspondence, never to launch a glittering generality, which an older generation used to call 'Tupperism.'[39] Long ago I stated that 'East was East and West was West and never the twain should meet.'[40] It seemed right, for I had checked it by the card, but I was careful to point out circumstances under which cardinal points ceased to exist. Forty years rolled on, and for a fair half of them the excellent and uplifted of all lands would write me, apropos of each new piece of broad-minded folly in India, Egypt, or Ceylon, that East and West *had* met—as, in their muddled minds, I suppose they had. Being a political Calvinist,[41] I could not argue with these condemned ones. But their letters had to be opened and filed.

Again. I wrote a song called 'Mandalay'[42] which, tacked to a tune with a swing, made one of the waltzes of that distant age. A private soldier reviews his loves and, in the chorus, his experiences in the Burma campaign. One of his ladies lives at Moulmein, which is not on the road to anywhere, and he describes the *amour* with some minuteness, but always in his chorus deals with 'the road to Manda-lay,' his golden path to romance. The inhabitants of the United States, to whom I owed most of the bother, 'Panamaed' that song (this was before copyright), set it to their own tunes, and sang it in their own national voices. Not content with this, they took to pleasure cruising, and discovered that Moulmein did not command any view of any sun rising across the Bay of Bengal. They must have interfered too with the navigation of the Irrawaddy Flotilla steam-ers,[43] for one of the Captains S.O.S.-ed me to give him 'something to tell these somethinged tourists about it.' I forget what word I sent, but I hoped it might help.

Had I opened the chorus of the song with 'Oh' instead of 'On the road,' etc., it might have shown that the song was a sort of general mix-up of the singer's Far-Eastern memories against a background of the Bay of Bengal as seen at dawn from a troop-ship taking him there. But 'On' in this case was more singable than 'Oh.' That simple explanation may stand as a warning.

Lastly—and this got under my skin because it touched something that mattered—when, after the Boer War, there seemed an off-chance of introducing conscription into England, I wrote verses called 'The Islanders'[44] which, after a few days' newspaper corre-spondence, were dismissed as violent, untimely, and untrue. In them I had suggested that it was unwise to 'grudge a year of service to the lordliest life on earth.' In the immediate next lines I described the life to which the year of service was grudged as:—

> Ancient, effortless, ordered—cycle on cycle set—
> Life so long untroubled that ye who inherit forget
> It was not made with the mountains; it is not one with the deep.
> Men, not Gods, devised it. Men, not Gods, must keep.

In a very little while it was put about that I had said that 'a year of compulsory service' would be 'effortless, ordered,' etc. etc.—with the rider that I didn't know much about it. This perversion was perversified by a man who ought to have known better; and I, I suppose, should have known that it was part of the 'effortless, ordered' drift towards Armageddon. You ask: 'Why inflict on us legends of your Middle Ages?' Because in life as in literature, its sole enduring record, is no age. Men and Things come round again, eternal as the seasons.

But, attacking or attacked, so long as you have breath, on no provocation explain. What you have said may be justified by things or some man, but never take a hand in a 'dog-fight' that opens: 'My attention has been drawn to,' etc.

I came near to breaking this Law with *Punch*, an institution I always respected for its continuity and its utter Englishdom, and from whose files I drew my modern working history. I had written during the Boer War a set of verses based on unofficial criticisms of many serious junior officers.[45] (Incidentally they contained one jewel of a line that opened 'And which it may subsequently transpire'[46]—a galaxy of words I had long panted to place in the literary firmament.) Nobody loved them, and indeed they were not conciliatory; but *Punch* took them rather hard. This was a pity because *Punch* would have been useful at that juncture. I knew none of its staff, but I asked questions and learned that *Punch* on this particular issue was—non-Aryan 'and German at that.'[47] It is true that the Children of Israel are 'people of the Book,' and in the second Surah of the Koran Allah is made to say: 'High above mankind have I raised you.' Yet, later, in the fifth Surah, it is written: 'Oft as they kindle a beacon-fire for war, shall God quench it. And their aim will be to abet disorder on the earth: but God loveth not the abettors of disorder.'[48] More important still, my bearer in Lahore never announced our good little Jew Tyler but he spat loudly and openly in the verandah. I swallowed my spittle at once. Israel is a race to leave alone. It abets disorder.

Many years later, during the War, *The Times*, with which I had had no dealings for a dozen years or so,[49] was 'landed' with what purported to be some verses by me, headed 'The Old Volunteer.'[50] They had been sent in by a Sunday mail with some sort of faked postmark and without any covering letter. They were stamped with a rubber-stamp from the village office, they were written on an absolutely straight margin, which is beyond my powers, and in an un-European fist. (I had never since typewriters began sent out press-work unless it was typed.) From my point of view the contribution should not have deceived a messenger-boy. Ninthly and lastly, they were wholly unintelligible.

Human nature being what it is, *The Times* was much more annoyed with me than anyone else, though goodness knows—this, remember, was in '17[51]—I did not worry them about it, beyond hinting that the usual week-end English slackness, when no one is in charge, had made the mess. They took the matter up with the pomp of the Public Institution which they were, and submitted the MS. to experts, who proved that it must be the work of a man who had all but 'spoofed' *The Times* about some fragments of Keats. He happened to be an old friend of mine, and when I told him of his magnified 'characteristic' letters, and the betraying slopes at which they lay—*his*, as I pointed out, 'very C's and U's and T's,' he was wrath and, being a poet, swore a good deal that if he could not have done a better parody of my 'stuff' with his left hand he would retire from business.[52] This I believed, for, on the heels of my modest disclaimer which appeared, none too conspicuously, in *The Times*, I had had a letter in a chaffing vein about 'The Old Volunteer' from a non-Aryan who never much appreciated me; and the handwriting of it, coupled with the subtlety of choosing a week-end (as the Hun had chosen August Bank Holiday of '14) for the work, *plus* the Oriental detachedness and insensitiveness of playing that sort of game in the heart of a life-and-death struggle, made me suspect him more than a little. He is now in Abraham's bosom, so I shall never know.[53] But *The Times* seemed very happy with its enlarged letters, and measurements of the alphabet, and—there really *was* a war on which filled my days and nights. Then *The Times* sent down a detective to my home.[54] I didn't see the drift of this, but naturally was interested. And It was a Detective out of a book, down to the very creaks of Its boots. (On the human side at lunch It knew a lot about second-hand furniture.) Officially, It behaved like all the detectives in the literature of that period. Finally, It settled Its self, back to the light, facing me at my work-table, and told me a long yarn about a man who worried the Police with complaints of anonymous letters addressed to him from unknown sources, all of which, through the perspicacity of the Police, turned out to have been written by himself to himself for the purpose of attracting notoriety. As in the case of the young man on the Canadian train, that tale felt as though it had come out of a magazine of the 'sixties; and I was so interested in its laborious evolution that I missed its implication till quite the end. Then I got to thinking of the psychology of the detective, and what a gay life of plots It must tramp through; and of the psychology of *The Times*-in-a-hole, which is where no one shows to advantage; and of how Moberly Bell,[55] whose bows I had crossed in the old days, would have tackled the matter; what Buckle,[56] whom I loved for his sincerity and gentlehood, would have thought of it all. Thus I forgot to defend my 'injured honour.' The thing had passed out of reason into the Higher Hysterics. What could I do but offer It some more sherry and thank It for a pleasant interview?

I have told this at length because Institutions of idealistic tendencies sometimes wait till a man is dead, and then furnish their own evidence. Should this happen, try to believe that in the deepest trough of the War I did not step aside to play with *The Times*, Printing House Square, London, E.C.

In the come-and-go of family talk there was often discussion as to whether I could write a 'real novel.' The Father thought that the setting of my work and life would be against it, and Time justified him.

Now here is a curious thing. At the Paris Exhibition of 1878 I saw, and never forgot, a picture of the death of Manon Lescaut,[57] and asked my Father many questions. I read that amazing 'one book' of the Abbé Prévost,[58] in alternate slabs with Scarron's *Roman Comique*,[59] when I was about eighteen, and it brought up the picture. My theory is that a germ lay dormant till my change of life to London (though that is not Paris) woke it up, and that *The Light that Failed*[60] was a sort of inverted, metagrobolised[61] phantasmagoria based on *Manon*. I was confirmed in my belief when the French took to that *conte* with relish, and I always fancied that it walked better in translation than in the original. But it was only a *conte*—not a built book.

Kim, of course, was nakedly picaresque and plotless—a thing imposed from without.[62]

Yet I dreamed for many years of building a veritable three-decker out of chosen and long-stored timber—teak, green-heart, and ten-year-old oak knees—each curve melting deliciously into the next that the sea might nowhere meet resistance or weakness; the whole suggesting motion even when, her great sails for the moment furled, she lay in some needed haven—a vessel ballasted on ingots of pure research and knowledge, roomy, fitted with delicate cabinet-work below-decks, painted, carved, gilt and wreathed the length of her, from her blazing stern-galleries outlined by bronzy palm-trunks, to her rampant figure-head—an East Indiaman worthy to lie along-side *The Cloister and the Hearth.*[63]

Not being able to do this, I dismissed the ambition as 'beneath the thinking mind.' So does a half-blind man dismiss shooting and golf.

Nor did I live to see the day when the new three-deckers should hoist themselves over the horizon, quivering to their own power, over-loaded with bars, ball-rooms, and insistent chromium plumbing; hellishly noisy from the sports' deck to the barber's shop; but serving their generation as the old craft served theirs. The young men were already laying down the lines of them, fondly believing that the old laws of design and construction were for them abrogated.

And with what tools did I work in my own mould-loft?[64] I had always been choice, not to say coquettish in this respect. In Lahore for my *Plain Tales* I used a slim, octagonal-sided, agate penholder with a Waverley nib.[65] It was a gift, and when in an evil hour it snapped I was much disturbed. Then followed a procession of impersonal hirelings each with a Waverley, and next a silver pen-holder with a quill-like curve, which promised well but did not perform. In Villiers Street I got me an outsize office pewter ink-pot, on which I would gouge the names of the tales and books I wrote out of it. But the housemaids of married life polished those titles away till it grew as faded as a palimpsest.[66]

I then abandoned hand-dipped Waverleys—a nib I never changed—and for years wallowed in the pin-pointed 'stylo' and its successor the 'fountain' which for me meant geyser-pens. In later years I clung to a slim, smooth, black treasure (Jael was her office name) which I picked up in Jerusalem. I tried pump-pens with glass insides, but they were of 'intolerable entrails.'[67]

For my ink I demanded the blackest, and had I been in my Father's house, as once I was, would have kept an ink-boy to grind me Indian-ink. All 'blue-blacks' were an abomination to my Daemon, and I never found a bottled vermilion fit to rubricate initials when one hung in the wind waiting.

My writing-blocks were built for me to an unchanged pattern of large, off-white, blue sheets, of which I was most wasteful. All this old-maiderie did not prevent me when abroad from buying and using blocks, and tackle, in any country.

With a lead pencil I ceased to express—probably because I had to use a pencil in reporting. I took very few notes except of names, dates, and addresses. If a thing didn't stay in my memory, I argued it was hardly worth writing out. But each man has his own method. I rudely drew what I wanted to remember.

Like most men who ply one trade in one place for any while, I always kept certain gadgets on my work-table, which was ten feet long from North to South and badly congested. One was a long, lacquer, canoe-shaped pen-tray full of brushes and dead 'fountains'; a wooden box held clips and bands; another, a tin one, pins; yet another, a bottle-slider, kept all manner of unneeded essentials from emery-paper to small screw-drivers; a paper-weight, said to have been Warren Hastings';[68] a tiny, weighted fur-seal and a leather crocodile sat on some of the papers; an inky foot-rule and a Father of Penwipers which a much-loved housemaid of ours presented yearly, made up the main-guard of these little fetishes.[69]

My treatment of books, which I looked upon as tools of my trade, was popularly regarded as barbarian. Yet I economised on my multitudinous pen-knives, and it did no harm to my fore-finger. There were books which I respected, because they were put in locked cases. The others, all the house over, took their chances.

Left and right of the table were two big globes, on one of which a great airman[70] had once outlined in white paint those air-routes to the East and Australia which were well in use before my death.

"BAA BAA, BLACK SHEEP"

(*The Week's News*, December 22, 1888;
collected in *Wee Willie Winkie*
[Allahabad, A.H. Wheeler, 1889])

EDITOR'S NOTE

This story was written in Allahabad, in the house of Mr. and Mrs. S.A. Hill, where Kipling was then living as a paying guest. Mrs. Hill, the details of whose recollections are not always to be trusted, gives the following account of the story's composition:

> *The Week's News* demanded a Christmas story which would fill a whole sheet of the paper. R.K. brooded over this awhile; the result was "Baa, Baa, Black Sheep," which is a true story of his early life when he was sent with his little sister to England to be educated . . . It was pitiful to see Kipling living over the experience, pouring out his soul in the story, as the drab life was worse than he could possibly describe it . . . When he was writing this he was a sorry guest, as he was in a towering rage at the recollection of those days.
>
> ("THE YOUNG KIPLING," *Atlantic Monthly, 157, 413–14*)

In his *Rudyard Kipling* (New York, 1978), Lord Birkenhead, presumably on the authority of Kipling's sister Trix, states that

> it was a grievous blow to the Lockwood Kiplings when they read these savage outpourings in cold print, and, unwilling to recognize their own contribution to this suffering, they tried to make Trix say it was all exaggerated and untrue, but even to comfort them she could not pretend that they had ever been happy. (*pp. 27–28*)

The conclusion to "Baa Baa, Black Sheep" is in striking contrast to Kipling's later summing up of his experience of desolation in childhood. In *Something of Myself* (see p. 12, above), he writes that his sufferings then "drained me of any capacity for real, personal hate for the rest of my days." But "Baa Baa, Black Sheep" affects no such view: "when young lips have drunk deep of the bitter waters of Hate, Suspicion, and Despair, all the Love in the world will not wholly take away that knowledge."

The illustrations accompanying this reprint of "Baa Baa, Black Sheep" are by Kipling himself in a holograph of the story now in the Berg Collection of the New York Public Library. They have not been previously published. The manuscript appears to be a fair copy of the completed story, no doubt made by Kipling for Mrs. Hill before the story had yet been published.

The text of this reprint is that of the first collected edition, in the *Wee Willie Winkie* volume of the Indian Railway Library, 1889. It varies in a number of details from the text in the English trade edition, and is much closer to that of the manuscript in the Berg Collection.

Baa Baa, Black Sheep

Baa Baa, Black Sheep,
Have you any wool?
Yes Sir, yes Sir, three bags full.
One for the Master, one for the Dame—
None for the Little Boy that cries down the lane.

Nursery Rhyme

THE FIRST BAG

'When I was in my father's house, I was in a better place.'[1]

They were putting Punch[2] to bed—the *ayah* and the *hamal* and Meeta the big *Surti*[3] boy with the red and gold turban. Judy, already tucked inside her mosquito-curtains, was nearly asleep. Punch had been allowed to stay up for dinner. Many privileges had been accorded to Punch within the last ten days, and a greater kindness from the people of his world had encompassed his ways and works, which were mostly obstreperous. He sat on the edge of his bed and swung his bare legs defiantly.

'Punch-*baba* going to bye-lo?' said the *ayah* suggestively.

'No,' said Punch. 'Punch-*baba* wants the story about the Ranee that was turned into a tiger. Meeta must tell it, and the *hamal* shall hide behind the door and make tiger-noises at the proper time.'

'But Judy-*baba* will wake up,' said the *ayah*.

'Judy-*baba* is waking,' piped a small voice from the mosquito-curtains. 'There was a Ranee that lived at Delhi. Go on Meeta,' and she fell fast asleep again while Meeta began the story.

Never had Punch secured the telling of that tale with so little opposition. He reflected for a long time. The *hamal* made the tiger-noises in twenty different keys.

''Top!' said Punch, authoritatively. 'Why doesn't Papa come in and say he is going to give me *put-put*?'

'Punch-*baba* is going away,' said the *ayah*. 'In another week there will be no Punch-*baba* to pull my hair any more.' She sighed softly, for the boy of the household was very dear to her heart.

'Up the Ghauts in a train?' said Punch, standing on his bed. 'All the way to Nassick[4] where the Ranee-Tiger lives?'

'Not to Nassick this year, little *Sahib*,' said Meeta, lifting him on his shoulder. 'Down to the sea where the cocoa-nuts are thrown, and across the sea in a big ship. Will you take Meeta with you to *Belait*?'

'You shall all come,' said Punch, from the height of Meeta's strong arms. 'Meeta and the *ayah* and the *hamal*, and Bhini-in-the-Garden, and the *salaam-Captain-Sahib*-snake-man.'

There was no mockery in Meeta's voice when he replied—'Great is the *Sahib's* favour,' and laid the little man down in the bed, while the *ayah*, sitting in the moonlight at the doorway, lulled him to sleep with an interminable canticle such as they sing in the Roman Catholic Church at Parel.[5] Punch curled himself into a ball and slept.

Next morning Judy shouted that there was a rat in the nursery, and thus he forgot to tell her the wonderful news. It did not much matter, for Judy was only three and she would not have understood. But Punch was five; and he knew that going to England would be much nicer than a trip to Nassick.

．　　　．　　　．　　　．　　　．

And Papa and Mamma sold the brougham and the piano, and stripped the house, and curtailed the allowance of crockery for the daily meals, and took long council together over a bundle of letters bearing the Rocklington post-mark.

'The worst of it is that one can't be certain of anything,' said Papa pulling his moustache. 'The letters in themselves are excellent, and the terms are moderate enough.'

'The worst of it is that the children will grow up away from me,' thought Mamma; but she did not say it aloud.

'We are only one case among hundreds,' said Papa, bitterly. 'You shall go Home again in five years, dear.'

'Punch will be ten then—and Judy eight. Oh how long and long and long the time will be! And we have to leave them among strangers.'

'Punch is a cheery little chap. He's sure to make friends wherever he goes.'

'And who could help loving my Ju?'

They were standing over the cots in the nursery late at night, and I think that Mamma was crying softly. After Papa had gone away, she knelt down by the side of Judy's cot. The *ayah* saw her and put up a prayer that the *memsahib* might never find the love of her children taken away from her and given to a stranger.

Mamma's own prayer was a slightly illogical one. Summarized it ran:— 'Let strangers love my children and be as good to them as I should be, but let *me* preserve their love and their confidence for ever and ever. Amen.' Punch scratched himself in his sleep, and Judy moaned a little. That seems to be the only answer to the prayer: and, next day, they all went down to the sea, and there was a scene at the Apollo Bunder[6] when Punch discovered that Meeta could not come too, and Judy learned that the *ayah* must be left behind. But Punch found a thousand fascinating things in the rope, block and steam-pipe line on the big P. and O. Steamer, long before Meeta and the *ayah* had dried their tears.

'Come back, Punch-*baba*,' said the *ayah*.

'Come back,' said Meeta, 'and be a *Burra Sahib*.'

'Yes,' said Punch, lifted up in his father's arms to wave good-bye. 'Yes, I will come back, and I will be a *Burra Sahib Bahadur*!'

At the end of the first day Punch demanded to be set down in England, which he was certain must be close at hand. Next day there was a merry breeze, and Punch was very sick. 'When I come back to Bombay,' said Punch on his recovery, 'I will come by the road—in a broom-*gharri*. This is a very naughty ship.'

The Swedish boatswain consoled him, and he modified his opinions as the voyage went on. There was so much to see and to handle and ask questions about that Punch nearly forgot the *ayah* and Meeta and the *hamal*, and with difficulty remembered a few words of the Hindustani, once his second-speech.

But Judy was much worse. The day before the steamer reached Southampton, Mamma asked her if she would not like to see the *ayah* again. Judy's blue eyes turned to the stretch of sea that had swallowed all her tiny past, and she said:— '*Ayah*! What *Ayah*?'

Mamma cried over her and Punch marvelled. It was then that he heard for the first time Mamma's passionate appeal to him never to let Judy forget Mamma. Seeing that Judy was young, ridiculously young, and that Mamma every evening for four weeks past, had come into the cabin to sing her and Punch to sleep with a mysterious rune that he called 'Sonny, my soul,'[7] Punch could not understand what Mamma meant. But he strove to do his duty; for, the moment Mamma left the cabin, he said to Judy:— 'Ju, you bemember Mamma?'

''Torse I do,' said Judy.

'Then *always* bemember Mamma, 'r else I won't give you the paper ducks that the red-haired Captain-*Sahib* cut out for me.'

So Judy promised always to 'bemember Mamma.'

Many and many a time was Mamma's command laid upon Punch, and Papa would say the same thing with an insistence that awed the child.

'You must make haste and learn to write, Punch,' said Papa, 'and then you'll be able to write letters to us in Bombay.'

'I'll come into your room,' said Punch, and Papa choked.

Papa and Mamma were always choking in those days. If Punch took Judy to task for not 'bemembering,' they choked. If Punch sprawled on the sofa in the Southampton lodging-house and sketched his future in purple and gold, they choked; and so they did if Judy put up her mouth for a kiss.

Through many days all four were vagabonds on the face of the earth:— Punch with no one to give orders to, Judy too young for anything, and Papa and Mamma, grave, distracted and choking.

'Where,' demanded Punch, wearied of a loathsome contrivance on four wheels with a mound of luggage atop—'*Where* is our broom-

gharri? This thing talks so much that *I* can't talk. Where is our *own* broom-*gharri*? When I was at Bandstand before we comed away, I asked Inverarity *Sahib* why he was sitting in it, and he said it was his own. And I said, "I will *give* it you"—I like Inverarity *Sahib*—and I said, "Can you put your legs through the pully-wag loops by the window?" And Inverarity *Sahib* said No, and laughed. *I* can put my legs through the pully-wag loops. I can put my legs through *these* pully-wag loops. Look! Oh Mamma's crying again! I didn't know. I wasn't not to do *so*.'

Punch drew his legs out of the loops of the four-wheeler; the door opened and he slid to the earth, in a cascade of parcels, at the door of an austere little villa whose gates bore the legend 'Downe Lodge.'⁸ Punch gathered himself together and eyed the house with disfavour. It stood on a sandy road, and a cold wind tickled his knicker-bockered legs.

'Let us go away,' said Punch. 'This is not a pretty place.'

But Mamma and Papa and Judy had quitted the cab, and all the luggage was being taken into the house. At the doorstep stood a woman in black, and she smiled largely, with dry chapped lips. Behind her was a man, big, bony, grey and lame as to one leg— behind him a boy of twelve, black-haired and oily in appearance.⁹ Punch surveyed the trio, and advanced without fear, as he had been accustomed to do in Bombay when callers came and he happened to be playing in the verandah.

'How do you do?' said he. 'I am Punch.' But they were all looking at the luggage—all except the grey man, who shook hands with Punch and said he was 'a smart little fellow.' There was much running about and banging of boxes, and Punch curled himself up on the sofa in the dining-room and considered things.

'I don't like these people,' said Punch. 'But never mind. We'll go away soon. We have always went away soon from everywhere. I wish we was gone back to Bombay *soon*.'

The wish bore no fruit. For six days Mamma wept at intervals, and showed the woman in black all Punch's clothes—a liberty which Punch resented. 'But p'raps she's a new white *ayah*,' he thought. 'I'm to call her Antirosa, but she doesn't call *me Sahib*. She says just Punch,' he confided to Judy. 'What is Antirosa?'

Judy didn't know. Neither she nor Punch had heard anything of an animal called an aunt. Their world had been Papa and Mamma who knew everything, permitted everything, and loved everybody—even Punch when he used to go into the garden at Bombay and fill his nails with mould after the weekly nail-cutting, because, as he explained between two strokes of the slipper to his sorely-tried Father, his fingers 'felt so new at the ends.'

In an undefined way Punch judged it advisable to keep both parents between himself, and the woman in black and the boy in black hair. He did not approve of them. He liked the grey man who had expressed a wish to be called 'Uncleharri.' They nodded at each other when they met, and the grey man showed him a little ship with rigging that took up and down.

'She is a model of the *Brisk*—the little *Brisk* that was sore exposed that day at Navarino.' The grey man hummed the last words and fell into a reverie. 'I'll tell you about Navarino, Punch, when we go for walks together; and you mustn't touch the ship because she's the *Brisk*.'[10]

Long before that walk, the first of many, was taken, they roused Punch and Judy in the chill dawn of a February morning to say Good-bye;[11] and of all people in the wide earth to Papa and Mamma—both crying this time. Punch was very sleepy and Judy was cross.

'Don't forget us,' pleaded Mamma. 'Oh my little son, don't forget us, and see that Judy remembers too.'

'I've told Judy to bemember,' said Punch wriggling, for his father's beard tickled his neck. 'I've told Judy—ten—forty—'leven thousand times. But Ju's so young—quite a baby—isn't she?'

'Yes,' said Papa, 'quite a baby, and you must be good to Judy, and make haste to learn to write and—and—and' . . . .

Punch was back in his bed again. Judy was fast asleep, and there was the rattle of a cab below. Papa and Mamma had gone away. Not to Nassick; that was across the sea. To some place much nearer, of course, and equally of course they would return. They came back after dinner-parties, and Papa had come back after he had been to a place called 'The Snows,' and Mamma with him, to Punch and Judy at Mrs. Inverarity's house in Marine Lines. Assuredly they would come back again. So Punch fell asleep till the true morning, when the black-haired boy met him with the information that Papa and Mamma had gone to Bombay, and that he and Judy were to stay at Downe Lodge 'for ever.' Antirosa, tearfully appealed to for a contradiction, said that Harry had spoken the truth, and that it behoved Punch to fold up his clothes neatly on going to bed. Punch went out and wept bitterly with Judy, into whose fair head he had driven some ideas of the meaning of separation.

When a matured man discovers that he has been deserted by Providence, deprived of his God, and cast without help, comfort or sympathy upon a world which is new and strange to him, his despair, which may find expression in evil-living, the writing of his experiences, or the more satisfactory diversion of suicide, is generally supposed to be impressive. A child, under exactly similar circumstances as far as its knowledge goes, cannot very well curse God and die. It howls till its nose is red, its eyes are sore, and its head aches. Punch and Judy, through no fault of their own, had lost all their world. They sat in the hall and cried; the black-haired boy looking on from afar.

The model of the ship availed nothing, though the grey man assured Punch that he might pull the rigging up and down as much as he pleased; and Judy was promised free entry into the kitchen. They wanted Papa and Mamma gone to Bombay beyond the seas, and their grief while it lasted was without remedy.

When the tears ceased the house was very still. Antirosa had decided it was better to let the children 'have their cry out,' and the boy had gone to school. Punch raised his head from the floor and sniffed mournfully. Judy was nearly asleep. Three short years had not taught her how to bear sorrow with full knowledge. There was a distant, dull boom in the air—a repeated heavy thud. Punch knew that sound in Bombay in the Monsoon. It was the sea—the sea that must be traversed before any one could get to Bombay.

'Quick, Ju!' he cried, 'We're close to the sea. I can hear it! Listen! That's where they've went. P'raps we can catch them if we was in time. They didn't mean to go without us. They've only forgot.'

'Iss,' said Judy. 'They've only forgotted. Less go to the sea.'

The hall-door was open and so was the garden-gate.

'It's very, very big, this place,' he said, looking cautiously down the road, 'and we will get lost; but *I* will find a man and order him to take me back to my house—like I did in Bombay.'

He took Judy by the hand, and the two fled hatless in the direction of the sound of the sea. Downe Villa was almost the last range of newly-built houses running out, through a chaos of brick-mounds, to a heath where gipsies occasionally camped and where the Garri-son Artillery of Rocklington practised. There were few people to be seen, and the children might have been taken for those of the soldiery who ranged far. Half an hour the wearied little legs tramped across heath, potato-field, and sand-dune.

'I'se so tired,' said Judy, 'and Mamma will be angry.'

'Mamma's *never* angry. I suppose she is waiting at the sea now while Papa gets tickets. We'll find them and go along with. Ju, you mustn't sit down. Only a little more and we'll come to the sea. Ju, if you sit down I'll *thmack* you!' said Punch.

They climbed another dune, and came upon the great grey sea at low tide. Hundreds of crabs were scuttling about the beach, but there was no trace of Papa or Mamma, not even of a ship upon the waters—nothing but sand and mud for miles and miles.

And 'Uncleharri' found them by chance—very muddy and very forlorn—Punch dissolved in tears, but trying to divert Judy with an 'ickle trab,' and Judy wailing to the pitiless horizon for 'Mamma, Mamma!'—and again 'Mamma!'

The Second Bag

Ah, welladay, for we are souls bereaved!
Of all the creatures under Heaven's wide scope
We are most hopeless who had once most hope,
And most beliefless who had most believed.
The City of Dreadful Night.[12]

All this time not a word about Black Sheep. He came later and Harry the black-haired boy was mainly responsible for his coming.

Judy—who could help loving little Judy?—passed, by special permit, into the kitchen and thence straight to Aunty Rosa's heart. Harry was Aunty Rosa's one child, and Punch was the extra boy about the house. There was no special place for him or his little

THE LITTLE BRISK

NURSERY WINDOW

affairs, and he was forbidden to sprawl on sofas and explain his ideas about the manufacture of this world and his hopes for his future. Sprawling was lazy and wore out sofas, and little boys were not expected to talk. They were talked to, and the talking to was intended for the benefit of their morals. As the unquestioned despot of the house at Bombay, Punch could not quite understand how he came to be of no account in this his new life.

Harry might reach across the table and take what he wanted; Judy might point and get what she wanted. Punch was forbidden to do either. The grey man was his great hope and standby for many months after Mamma and Papa left and he had forgotten to tell Judy to 'bemember Mamma.'

This lapse was excusable, because in the interval he had been introduced by Aunty Rosa to two very impressive things—an

145

abstraction called God, the intimate friend and ally of Aunty Rosa, generally believed to live behind the kitchen-range because it was hot there—and a dirty brown book filled with unintelligible dots and marks. Punch was always anxious to oblige everybody. He, therefore, welded the story of the Creation on to what he could recollect of his Indian fairy tales, and scandalised Aunty Rosa by repeating the result to Judy. It was a sin, a grievous sin, and Punch was talked to for a quarter of an hour. He could not understand where the iniquity came in, but was careful not to repeat the offence, because Aunty Rosa told him that God had heard every word he had said and was very angry. If this were true why didn't God come and say so, thought Punch, and dismissed the matter from his mind. Afterwards he learned to know the Lord as the only thing in the world more awful than Aunty Rosa—as a Creature that stood in the background and counted the strokes of the cane.

But the reading was, just then, a much more serious matter than any creed. Aunty Rosa sat him upon a table and told him that A B meant ab.

'Why?' said Punch. 'A is a and B is bee. *Why* does A B mean ab?'

'Because I tell you it does,' said Aunty Rosa, 'and you've got to say it.'

Punch said it accordingly, and for a month, hugely against his will, stumbled through the brown book not in the least comprehending what it meant. But Uncle Harry who walked much and generally alone was wont to come into the nursery and suggest to Aunty Rosa that Punch should walk with him. He seldom spoke, but he showed Punch all Rocklington, from the mudbanks and the sand of the back-bay to the great harbours where ships lay at anchor, and the dockyards where the hammers were never still, and the marine storeshops, and the shiny brass counters in the offices where Uncle Harry went once every three months with a slip of blue paper and received sovereigns in exchange; for he held a wound-pension. Punch heard, too, from his lips the story of the battle of Navarino, where the sailors of the Fleet, for three days afterwards, were deaf as posts and could only sign to each other. 'That was because of the noise of the guns,' said Uncle Harry, 'and I have got the wadding of a bullet somewhere inside me now.'

Punch regarded him with curiosity. He had not the least idea what wadding was, and his notion of a bullet was a dockyard cannon-ball bigger than his own head. How could Uncle Harry keep a cannon-ball inside him? He was ashamed to ask, for fear Uncle Harry might be angry.

Punch had never known what anger—real anger—meant until one terrible day when Harry had taken his paint-box to paint a boat with, and Punch had protested with a loud and lamentable voice. Then Uncle Harry had appeared on the scene and, muttering something about 'strangers' children' had with a stick smitten the black-haired boy across the shoulders till he wept and yelled, and Aunty Rosa came in and abused Uncle Harry for cruelty to his own flesh and blood, and Punch shuddered to the tips of his shoes. 'It wasn't my fault,' he explained to the boy, but both Harry and Aunty Rosa said that it was, and that Punch had told tales, and for a week there were no more walks with Uncle Harry.

But that week brought a great joy to Punch.

He had repeated till he was thrice weary the statement that 'the Cat lay on the Mat and the Rat came in.'

'Now I can truly read,' said Punch, 'and now I will never read anything in the world.'

He put the brown book in the cupboard where his school books lived and accidentally tumbled out a venerable volume, without covers, labelled *Sharpe's Magazine*.[13] There was the most portentous picture of a griffin on the first page with verses below. The griffin carried off one sheep a day from a German village, till a man came with a 'falchion' and split the griffin open. Goodness only knew what a falchion was, but there was the Griffin, and his history was an improvement upon the eternal Cat.

'This,' said Punch, 'means things, and now I will know all about everything in all the world.' He read till the light failed, not understanding a tithe of the meaning, but tantalized by glimpses of new worlds hereafter to be revealed.

'What is a "falchion"? What is a "e-wee lamb"? What is a "base *uss*urper"? What is a "verdant me-ad"?' he demanded, with flushed cheeks at bed-time of the astonished Aunt Rosa.

'Say your prayers and go to sleep,' she replied, and that was all the

help Punch then or afterwards found at her hands in the new and delightful exercise of reading.

'Aunt Rosa only knows about God and things like that,' argued Punch. 'Uncle Harry will tell me.'

The next walk proved that Uncle Harry could not help either; but he allowed Punch to talk, and even sat down on a bench to hear about the Griffin. Other walks brought other stories as Punch ranged further afield, for the house held large store of old books that no one ever opened—from *Frank Fairlegh*[14] in serial numbers, and the earlier poems of Tennyson, contributed anonymously[15] to *Sharpe's Magazine*, to '62 Exhibition Catalogues,[16] gay with colours and delightfully incomprehensible, and odd leaves of *Gulliver's Travels*.

As soon as Punch could string a few pothooks together, he wrote to Bombay, demanding by return of post 'all the books in all the world.' Papa could not comply with this modest indent, but sent *Grimm's Fairy Tales* and a Hans Andersen. That was enough. If he were only left alone Punch could pass, at any hour he chose, into a land of his own, beyond reach of Aunty Rosa and her God, Harry and his teasements, and Judy's claims to be played with.

'Don't disturve me, I'm reading. Go and play in the kitchen,' grunted Punch. 'Aunty Rosa lets *you* go there.' Judy was cutting her second teeth and was fretful. She appealed to Aunty Rosa, who descended on Punch.

'I was reading,' he explained, 'reading a book. I *want* to read.'

'You're only doing that to show off,' said Aunty Rosa, 'But we'll see. Play with Judy now, and don't open a book for a week.'

Judy did not pass a very enjoyable play-time with Punch, who was consumed with indignation. There was a pettiness at the bottom of the prohibition which puzzled him.

'It's what I like to do,' he said, 'and she's found out that and stopped me. Don't cry Ju—it wasn't your fault—*please* don't cry, or she'll say I made you.'

Ju loyally mopped up her tears, and the two played in their nursery, a room in the basement and half under-ground, to which they were regularly sent after the midday dinner while Aunty Rosa slept. She drank wine—that is to say, something from a bottle in the cellaret—for her stomach's sake, but if she did not fall asleep she would sometimes come into the nursery to see that the children were really playing. Now bricks, wooden hoops, ninepins and china-ware cannot amuse for ever, especially when all Fairyland is to be won by the mere opening of a book and, as often as not, Punch would be discovered reading to Judy or telling her interminable tales. That was an offence in the eyes of the law, and Judy would be whisked off by Aunty Rosa, while Punch was left to play alone, 'and be sure that I hear you doing it.'

It was not a cheering employ for he had to make a playful noise. At last, with infinite craft, he devised an arrangement whereby the table could be supported as to three legs on toy bricks, leaving the fourth clear to bring down on the floor. He could work the table with one hand and hold a book with the other. This he did till an evil day when Aunty Rosa pounced upon him unawares and told him that he was 'acting a lie.'

'If you're old enough to do that,' she said—her temper was always worst after dinner—'you're old enough to be beaten.'

'But—I'm—I'm not a animal!' said Punch aghast.

He remembered Uncle Harry and the stick, and turned white. Aunty Rosa had hidden a light cane behind her, and Punch was beaten then and there over the shoulders. It was a revelation to him. The room-door was shut and he was left to weep himself into repentance and work out his own Gospel of Life.

Aunty Rosa, he argued, had the power to beat him with many stripes. It was unjust and cruel, and Mamma and Papa would never have allowed it. Unless perhaps, as Aunty Rosa seemed to imply, they had sent secret orders. In which case he was abandoned indeed. It would be discreet in the future to propitiate Aunty Rosa, but, then again, even in matters in which he was innocent, he had been accused of wishing to 'show off.' He had 'shown off' before visitors when he had attacked a strange gentleman—Harry's uncle, not his own—with requests for information about the Griffin and the falchion, and the precise nature of the Tilbury in which Frank Fairlegh rode—all points of paramount interest which he was bursting to understand. Clearly it would not do to pretend to care for Aunty Rosa.

At this point Harry entered and stood afar off, eyeing Punch, a dishevelled heap in the corner of the room, with disgust.

'You're a liar—a young liar,' said Harry, with great unction, 'and you're to have tea down here because you're not fit to speak to us. And you're not to speak to Judy again till Mother gives you leave. You'll corrupt her. You're only fit to associate with the servant. Mother says so.'

Having reduced Punch to a second agony of tears, Harry departed upstairs with the news that Punch was still rebellious.

Uncle Harry sat uneasily in the dining-room. 'Damn it all, Rosa,' said he at last, 'can't you leave the child alone? He's a good enough little chap when I meet him.'

'He puts on his best manners with you, Harry,' said Aunty Rosa, 'but I'm afraid, I'm very much afraid, that he is the Black Sheep of the family.'

Harry heard and stored up the name for future use. Judy cried till she was bidden to stop, her brother not being worth tears; and the evening concluded with the return of Punch to the upper regions and a private sitting at which all the blinding horrors of Hell were revealed to Punch with such store of imagery as Aunty Rosa's narrow mind possessed.

Most grievous of all was Judy's round-eyed reproach, and Punch went to bed in the depths of the Valley of Humiliation. He shared his room with Harry and knew the torture in store. For an hour and a half he had to answer that young gentleman's question as to his motives for telling a lie, and a grievous lie, the precise quantity of punishment inflicted by Aunty Rosa, and had also to profess his deep gratitude for such religious instruction as Harry thought fit to impart.

From that day began the downfall of Punch, now Black Sheep.

'Untrustworthy in one thing, untrustworthy in all,' said Aunty Rosa, and Harry felt that Black Sheep was delivered into his hands. He would wake him up in the night to ask him why he was such a liar.

'I don't know,' Punch would reply.

'Then don't you think you ought to get up and pray to God for a new heart?'

'Y-yess.'

'Get out and pray, then!' And Punch would get out of bed with raging hate in his heart against all the world, seen and unseen. He was always tumbling into trouble. Harry had a knack of cross-examining him as to his day's doings which seldom failed to lead him, sleepy and savage, into half-a-dozen contradictions—all duly reported to Aunty Rosa next morning.

'But it *wasn't* a lie,' Punch would begin, charging into a laboured explanation that landed him more hopelessly in the mire. 'I said that I didn't say my prayers *twice* over in the day, and *that* was on Tuesday. *Once* I did. I *know* I did, but Harry said I didn't,' and so forth, till the tension brought tears, and he was dismissed from the table in disgrace.

'You usen't to be as bad as this,' said Judy, awe-stricken at the catalogue of Black Sheep's crimes. 'Why are you so bad now?'

'I don't know,' Black Sheep would reply. 'I'm not, if I only wasn't bothered upside down. I knew what I *did* and I want to say so, but Harry always makes it out different somehow, and Aunty Rosa doesn't believe a word I say. Oh Ju, don't *you* say I'm bad too.'

'Aunty Rosa says you are,' said Judy. 'She told the Vicar so when he came yesterday.'

'Why does she tell all the people outside the house about me? It isn't fair,' said Black Sheep. 'When I was in Bombay, and was bad—*doing* bad, not made-up bad like this—Mamma told Papa, and

Papa told me he knew, and that was all. *Outside* people didn't know too—even Meeta didn't know.'

'I don't remember,' said Judy wistfully. 'I was all little then. Mamma was just as fond of you as she was of me, wasn't she?'

''Course she was. So was Papa. So was everybody.'

'Aunt Rosa likes me more than she does you. She says that you are a Trial and a Black Sheep, and I'm not to speak to you more than I can help.'

'Always? Not outside of the times when you mustn't speak to me at all?'

Judy nodded her head mournfully. Black Sheep turned away in despair, but Judy's arms were round his neck.

'Never mind, Punch,' she whispered. 'I *will* speak to you just the same as ever and ever. You're my own own brother though you are—though Aunty Rosa says you're Bad, and Harry says you're a little coward. He says that if I pulled your hair hard, you'd cry.'

'Pull, then,' said Punch.

Judy pulled gingerly.

'Pull harder—as hard as you can! There! I don't mind how much you pull it *now*. If you'll speak to me same as ever I'll let you pull it as much as you like—pull it out if you like. But I know if Harry came and stood by and made you do it, I'd cry.'

So the two children sealed the compact with a kiss, and Black Sheep's heart was cheered within him, and by extreme caution and careful avoidance of Harry he acquired virtue and was allowed to read undisturbed for a week. Uncle Harry took him for walks and consoled him with rough tenderness, never calling him Black Sheep. 'It's good for you, I suppose, Punch,' he used to say. 'Let us sit down. I'm getting tired.' His steps led him now not to the beach, but to the Cemetery of Rocklington amid the potato-fields. For hours the grey man would sit on a tombstone, while Black Sheep read epitaphs, and then with a sigh would stump home again.

'I shall lie there soon,' said he to Black Sheep, one winter evening, when his face showed white as a worn silver coin under the lights of the chapel-lodge. 'You needn't tell Aunty Rosa.'

A month later, he turned sharp round, ere half a morning walk was completed, and stumped back to the house. 'Put me to bed,

Rosa,' he muttered. 'I've walked my last. The wadding has found me out.'

They put him to bed, and for a fortnight the shadow of his sickness lay upon the house, and Black Sheep went to and fro unobserved. Papa had sent him some new books, and he was told to keep quiet. He retired into his own world and was perfectly happy. Even at night his felicity was unbroken. He could lie in bed and string himself tales of travel and adventure while Harry was downstairs.

'Uncle Harry's going to die,' said Judy, who now lived almost entirely with Aunty Rosa.

'I'm very sorry,' said Black Sheep soberly. 'He told me that a long time ago.'

Aunty Rosa heard the conversation. 'Will nothing check your wicked tongue?' she said angrily. There were blue circles round her eyes.

Black Sheep retreated to the nursery and read *'Cometh up as a Flower'*[17] with deep and uncomprehending interest. He had been forbidden to read it on account of its 'sinfulness,' but the bonds of the Universe were crumbling and Aunty Rosa was in great grief.

'I'm glad,' said Black Sheep. 'She's unhappy now. It wasn't a lie, though. *I* knew. He told me not to tell.'

That night Black Sheep woke with a start. Harry was not in the room, and there was a sound of sobbing on the next floor. Then the voice of Uncle Harry singing the song of the Battle of Navarino, cut through the darkness:—

> 'Our vanship was the *Asia*—
> 'The *Albion* and *Genoa*.'

'He's getting well,' thought Black Sheep, who knew the song through all its seventeen verses. But the blood froze at his little heart as he thought. The voice leapt an octave and rang shrill as a boatswain's pipe:—

> 'And next came on the lovely *Rose*,
> 'The *Philomel*, her fire-ship, closed,
> 'And the little *Brisk* was sore exposed
> 'That day at Navarino.'[18]

NYPL

'That day at Navarino, Uncle Harry!' shouted Black Sheep, half wild with excitement and fear of he knew not what.

A door opened and Aunty Rosa screamed up the staircase:— 'Hush! For God's sake hush, you little devil. Uncle Harry is *dead*!'[19]

THE THIRD BAG

> Journeys end in lovers' meeting,
> Every wise man's son doth know.[20]

'I wonder what will happen to me now,' thought Black Sheep, when the semi-pagan rites peculiar to the burial of the Dead in middle-class houses had been accomplished, and Aunty Rosa awful in black crape, had returned to this life. 'I don't think I've done anything bad that she knows of. I suppose I will soon. She will be very cross after Uncle Harry's dying, and Harry will be cross too. I'll keep in the nursery.'

Unfortunately for Punch's plans, it was decided that he should be sent to a day-school[21] which Harry attended. This meant a morning walk with Harry, and perhaps an evening one; but the prospect of freedom in the interval was refreshing. 'Harry'll tell everything I do, but I won't do anything,' said Black Sheep. Fortified with this virtuous resolution he went to school only to find that Harry's version of his character had preceded him, and that life was a burden in consequence. He took stock of his associates. Some of them were unclean, some of them talked in dialect, many dropped their h's, and there were two Jews and a negro, or some one quite as dark, in the

154

assembly. 'That's a *hubshi*,' said Black Sheep to himself. 'Even Meeta used to laugh at a *hubshi*. I don't think this is a proper place.' He was indignant for at least an hour, till he reflected that any expostulation on his part would be by Aunty Rosa construed into 'showing off,' and that Harry would tell the boys.

'How do you like school?' said Aunty Rosa at the end of the day.

'I think it is a very nice place,' said Punch quietly.

'I suppose you warned the boys of Black Sheep's character?' said Aunty Rosa to Harry.

'Oh yes,' said the censor of Black Sheep's morals. 'They know all about him.'

'If I was with my father,' said Black Sheep stung to the quick, 'I shouldn't *speak* to those boys. He wouldn't let me. They live in shops. I saw them go into shops—where their fathers live and sell things.'

'You're too good for that school, are you?' said Aunty Rosa, with a bitter smile. 'You ought to be grateful, Black Sheep, that those boys speak to you at all. It isn't every school that takes little liars.'

Harry did not fail to make much capital out of Black Sheep's ill-considered remark; with the result that several boys, including the *hubshi*, demonstrated to Black Sheep the eternal equality of the human race by smacking his head, and his consolation from Aunty Rosa was that it 'served him right for being vain.' He learned, however, to keep his opinions to himself, and by propitiating Harry in carrying books and the like to secure a little peace. His existence was not too joyful. From nine till twelve he was at school, and from two to four, except on Saturdays. In the evenings he was sent down into the nursery to prepare his lessons for the next day, and every night came the dreaded cross-questionings at Harry's hand. Of Judy he saw but little. She was deeply religious—at six years of age Religion is easy to come by—and sorely divided between her natural love for Black Sheep and her love for Aunty Rosa who could do no wrong.

The lean woman returned that love with interest and Judy, when she dared, took advantage of this for the remission of Black Sheep's penalties. Failures in lessons at school were punished at home by a week without reading other than school-books, and Harry brought the news of such a failure with glee. Further, Black Sheep was then bound to repeat his lessons at bedtime to Harry, who generally succeeded in making him break down, and consoled him by gloomiest forebodings for the morrow. Harry was at once spy, practical joker, inquisitor and Aunty Rosa's deputy executioner. He filled his many posts to admiration. From his actions, now that Uncle Harry was dead, there was no appeal. Black Sheep had not been permitted to keep any self-respect at school: at home he was of course utterly discredited and grateful for any pity that the servant girls—they changed frequently at Downe Lodge because they, too, were liars— might show. 'You're just fit to row in the same boat with Black Sheep,' was a sentiment that each new Jane or Eliza might expect to hear, before a month was over, from Aunty Rosa's lips; and Black Sheep was used to ask new girls whether they had yet been compared to him. Harry was 'Master Harry' in their mouths; Judy was officially 'Miss Judy'; but Black Sheep was never anything more than Black Sheep *tout court*.

As time went on and the memory of Papa and Mamma became wholly overlaid by the unpleasant task of writing them letters, under Aunty Rosa's eye, each Sunday, Black Sheep forgot what manner of life he had led in the beginning of things. Even Judy's appeals to 'try and remember about Bombay,' failed to quicken him.

'I can't remember,' he said. 'I know I used to give orders and Mamma kissed me.'

'Aunty Rosa will kiss you if you are good,' pleaded Judy.

'Ugh! I don't want to be kissed by Aunty Rosa. She'd say I was doing it to get something more to eat.'

The weeks lengthened into months, and the holidays came; but just before the holidays Black Sheep fell into deadly sin.

Among the many boys whom Harry had incited to 'punch Black Sheep's head because he daren't hit back,' was one more aggravating than the rest who in an unlucky moment, fell upon Black Sheep when Harry was not near. The blows stung and Black Sheep struck back at random with all the power at his command. The boy dropped and whimpered. Black Sheep was astounded at his own act, but feeling the unresisting body under him, shook it with both his hands in blind fury and then began to throttle his enemy; meaning honestly to slay him. There was a scuffle and Black Sheep was torn off the body by Harry and some colleagues, and cuffed home tingling but exultant. Aunty Rosa was out: pending her arrival Harry set himself to lecture Black Sheep on the sin of murder—which he described as the offence of Cain.

'Why didn't you fight him fair? What did you hit him when he was down for, you little cur?'

Black Sheep looked up at Harry's throat and then at a knife on the dinner-table.

'I don't understand,' he said wearily. 'You always set him on me and told me I was a coward when I blubbed. Will you leave me alone until Aunty Rosa comes in? She'll beat me if you tell her I ought to be beaten; so it's all right.'

'It's all wrong,' said Harry, magisterially. 'You nearly killed him, and I shouldn't wonder if he dies.'

'Will he die?' said Black Sheep.

'I dare say,' said Harry, 'and then you'll be hanged.'

'All right,' said Black Sheep, possessing himself of the table-knife. 'Then I'll kill you now. You say things and do things and . . . and *I* don't know how things happen, and you never leave me alone—and I don't care *what* happens!'

He ran at the boy with the knife, and Harry fled upstairs to his room, promising Black Sheep the finest thrashing in the world when Aunty Rosa returned. Black Sheep sat at the bottom of the stairs, the table-knife in his hand, and wept for that he had not killed Harry. The servant-girl came up from the kitchen, took the knife away and consoled him. But Black Sheep was beyond consolation. He would be badly beaten by Aunty Rosa; then there would be another beating at Harry's hands; then Judy would not be allowed to speak to him; then the tale would be told at school and then . . . .

There was no one to help and no one to care, and the best way out of the business was by death. A knife would hurt, but Aunty Rosa had told him, a year ago, that if he sucked paint he would die. He went into the nursery, unearthed the now disused Noah's Ark and sucked the paint off as many animals as remained. It tasted abominable, but he had licked Noah's Dove clean by the time Aunty Rosa and Judy returned. He went upstairs and greeted them with:— 'Please Aunty Rosa, I believe I've nearly killed a boy at school, and

I've tried to kill Harry, and when you've done all about God and Hell, will you beat me and get it over?'

The tale of the assault as told by Harry could only be explained on the ground of possession by the Devil. Wherefore Black Sheep was not one only most excellently beaten, once by Aunty Rosa and once, when thoroughly cowed down, by Harry, but he was further prayed for at family prayers, together with Jane who had stolen a cold rissole from the pantry and snuffled audibly as her enormity was brought before the Throne of Grace. Black Sheep was sore and stiff but triumphant. He would die that very night and be rid of them all. No, he would ask for no forgiveness from Harry, and at bedtime would stand no questioning at Harry's hands, even though addressed as 'Young Cain.'

'I've been beaten,' said he, 'and I've done other things. I don't care what I do. If you speak to me to-night, Harry, I'll get out and try to kill you. Now you can kill me if you like.'

Harry took his bed into the spare room, and Black Sheep lay down to die.

It may be, that the makers of Noah's Arks know that their animals are likely to find their way into young mouths, and paint them accordingly. Certain it is that the common, weary next-morning broke through the windows and found Black Sheep quite well and a good deal ashamed of himself, but richer by the knowledge that he could, in extremity, secure himself against Harry for the future.

When he descended to breakfast on the first day of the holidays, he was greeted with the news that Harry, Aunty Rosa and Judy were going away to Brighton, while Black Sheep was to stay in the house with the servant. His latest outbreak suited Aunty Rosa's plans admirably. It gave her good excuse for leaving the extra boy behind. Papa in Bombay, who really seemed to know a young sinner's wants to the hour, sent, that week, a package of new books. And with these and the society of Jane on board-wages, Black Sheep was left alone for a month.

The books lasted for ten days. They were eaten too quickly, in long gulps of four and twenty hours at a time. Then came days of doing absolutely nothing, of dreaming dreams and marching imaginary armies up and down stairs, of counting the number of banisters, and of measuring the length and breadth of every room in hand-spans —fifty down the side, thirty across and fifty back again. Jane made many friends, and, after receiving Black Sheep's assurance that he would not tell of her absences, went out daily for long hours. Black Sheep would follow the rays of the sinking sun from the kitchen to the dining-room and thence upward to his own bed-room until all was grey dark, and he ran down to the kitchen fire and read by its light. He was happy in that he was left alone and could read as much as he pleased. But, later, he grew afraid of the shadows of window-curtains and the flapping of doors and the creaking of shutters. He went out into the garden and the rustling of the laurel-bushes frightened him.

He was glad when they all returned—Aunty Rosa, Harry and Judy—full of news, and Judy laden with gifts. Who could help loving loyal little Judy? In return for all her merry babblement, Black Sheep confided to her that the distance from the hall-door to the top of the first landing was exactly one hundred and eighty-four handspans. He had found it out himself.

Then the old life recommenced; but with a difference, and a new sin. To his other iniquities Black Sheep had now added a phenom-enal clumsiness—was as unfit to trust in action as he was in word. He himself could not account for spilling everything he touched, upset-ting glasses as he put his hand out, and bumping his head against doors that were manifestly shut. There was a grey haze upon all his world, and it narrowed month by month, until at last it left Black Sheep almost alone with the flapping curtains that were so like ghosts, and the nameless terrors of broad daylight that were only coats on pegs after all.

Holidays came and holidays went and Black Sheep was taken to see many people whose faces were all exactly alike; was beaten when occasion demanded, and tortured by Harry on all possible occa-sions; but defended by Judy through good and evil report, though she hereby drew upon herself the wrath of Aunty Rosa.

The weeks were interminable and Papa and Mamma were clean forgotten. Harry had left school and was a clerk in a banking-office. Freed from his presence, Black Sheep resolved that he should no longer be deprived of his allowance of pleasure-reading. Consequently when he failed at school he reported that all was well, and conceived a large contempt for Aunty Rosa as he saw how easy it was to deceive her. 'She says I'm a little liar when I don't tell lies, and now I do, she doesn't know,' thought Black Sheep. Aunty Rosa had credited him in the past with petty cunning and stratagem that had never entered into his head. By the light of the sordid knowledge that she had revealed to him he paid her back full tale. In a household where the most innocent of his motives, his natural yearning for a little affection, had been interpreted into a desire for more bread and jam or to ingratiate himself with strangers and so put Harry into the background, his work was easy. Aunty Rosa could penetrate certain kinds of hypocrisy, but not all. He set his child's wits against hers and was no more beaten. It grew monthly more and more of a trouble to read the school-books, and even the pages of the open-print story-books danced and were dim. So Black Sheep brooded in the shadows that fell about him and cut him off from the world, inventing horrible punishments for 'dear Harry,' or plotting another line of the tangled web of deception that he wrapped round Aunty Rosa.

Then the crash came and the cobwebs were broken. It was impossible to foresee everything. Aunty Rosa made personal enquiries as to Black Sheep's progress and received information that startled her. Step by step, with a delight as keen as when she convicted an underfed housemaid of the theft of cold meats, she followed the trail of Black Sheep's delinquencies. For weeks and weeks, in order to escape banishment from the book-shelves, he had made a fool of Aunty Rosa, of Harry, of God, of all the world! Horrible, most horrible, and evidence of an utterly depraved mind.

Black Sheep counted the cost. 'It will only be one big beating and then she'll put a card with "Liar" on my back, same as she did before. Harry will whack me and pray for me, and she will pray for me at prayers and tell me I'm a Child of the Devil and give me hymns to learn. But I've done all my reading and she never knew. She'll say she knew all along. She's an old liar too,' said he.

For three days Black Sheep was shut in his own bedroom—to prepare his heart. 'That means two beatings. One at school and one here. *That* one will hurt most.' And it fell even as he thought. He was thrashed at school before the Jews and the *Hubshi*, for the heinous crime of bringing home false reports of progress. He was thrashed at home by Aunty Rosa on the same count, and then the placard was produced. Aunty Rosa stitched it between his shoulders and bade him go for a walk with it upon him.

'If you make me do that,' said Black Sheep very quietly, 'I shall burn this house down, and perhaps I'll kill you. I don't know whether I *can* kill you—you're so bony—but I'll try.'

No punishment followed this blasphemy, though Black Sheep held himself ready to work his way to Aunty Rosa's withered throat and grip there till he was beaten off. Perhaps Aunty Rosa was afraid, for Black Sheep having reached the Nadir of Sin, bore himself with a new recklessness.

In the midst of all the trouble there came a visitor from over the seas to Downe Lodge, who knew Papa and Mamma, and was commissioned to see Punch and Judy. Black Sheep was sent to the drawing-room and charged into a solid tea-table laden with china.

'Gently, gently, little man,' said the visitor, turning Black Sheep's face to the light slowly. 'What's that big bird on the palings?'

'What bird?' asked Black Sheep.

The visitor looked deep down into Black Sheep's eyes for half a minute and then said suddenly:— 'Good God, the little chap's nearly blind!'

It was a most business-like visitor. He gave orders, on his own responsibility, that Black Sheep was not to go to school or open a book until Mamma came home. 'She'll be here in three weeks, as you know, of course,' said he, 'and I'm Inverarity *Sahib*. I ushered you into this wicked world, young man, and a nice use you seem to have made of your time. You must do Nothing Whatever. Can you do that?'

'Yes,' said Punch, in a dazed way. He had known that Mamma was coming. There was a chance, then, of another beating. Thank Heaven Papa wasn't coming too. Aunty Rosa had said of late that he ought to be beaten by a man.

For the next three weeks Black Sheep was strictly allowed to do nothing. He spent his time in the old nursery looking at the broken toys, for all of which account must be rendered to Mamma. Aunty Rosa hit him over the hands if even a wooden boat were broken. But that sin was of small importance compared to the other revelations, so darkly hinted at by Aunty Rosa. 'When your Mother comes, and hears what I have to tell her, she may appreciate you properly,' she said grimly and mounted guard over Judy lest that small maiden should attempt to comfort her brother, to the peril of her own soul.

And Mamma came—in a four-wheeler and a flutter of tender excitement. Such a Mamma! She was young, frivolously young, and beautiful, with delicately flushed cheeks, eyes that shone like stars, and a voice that needed no additional appeal of outstretched arms to draw little ones to her heart. Judy ran straight to her, but Black Sheep hesitated. Could this wonder be 'showing off?' She would not put out her arms when she knew of his crimes. Meantime was it possible that by fondling she wanted to get anything out of Black Sheep? Only all his love and all his confidence; but that Black Sheep did not know. Aunty Rosa withdrew and left Mamma, kneeling between her children, half laughing, half crying, in the very hall where Punch and Judy had wept five years before.

'Well, chicks, do you remember me?'

'No,' said Judy frankly, 'but I said "God bless Papa and Mamma," ev'vy night.'

'A little,' said Black Sheep. 'Remember I wrote to you every week, anyhow. That isn't to show off, but 'cause of what comes afterwards.'

'What comes after! What should come after, my darling boy?' And she drew him to her again. He came awkwardly, with many angles. ' 'Not used to petting,' said the quick Mother-soul. 'The girl is.'

'She's too little to hurt anyone,' thought Black Sheep, 'and if I said I'd kill her, she'd be afraid. I wonder what Aunty Rosa will tell.'

There was a constrained late dinner, at the end of which Mamma picked up Judy and put her to bed with endearments manifold. Faithless little Judy had shown her defection from Aunty Rosa already. And that lady resented it bitterly. Black Sheep rose to leave the room.

'Come and say good night,' said Aunty Rosa, offering a withered cheek.

'Huh!' said Black Sheep. 'I never kiss you, and I'm not going to show off. Tell that woman what I've done and see what she says.'

Black Sheep climbed into bed feeling that he had lost Heaven after a glimpse through the gates. In half an hour 'that woman' was bending over him. Black Sheep flung up his right arm. It wasn't fair to come and hit him in the dark. Even Aunty Rosa never tried that. But no blow followed.

'Are you showing off? I won't tell you anything more than Aunty Rosa has, and *she* doesn't know everything,' said Black Sheep as clearly as he could for the arms round his neck.

'Oh my son—my little, little son! It was my fault—*my* fault, darling—and yet how could we help it? Forgive me, Punch.' The voice died out in a broken whisper and two hot tears fell on Black Sheep's forehead.

'Has she been making you cry too?' he asked. 'You should see Jane cry. But you're nice, and Jane is a Born Liar—Aunty Rosa says so.'

'Hush, Punch, hush! My boy, don't talk like that. Try to love me a little bit—a little bit. You don't know how I want it. Punch-*baba*, come back to me! I am your Mother—your own Mother—and never mind the rest. I know—yes, I know, dear. It doesn't matter now. Punch, won't you care for me a little?'

It is astonishing how much petting a big boy of ten can endure when he is quite sure that there is no one to laugh at him. Black Sheep had never been made much of before, and here was this beautiful woman treating him—Black Sheep, the Child of the Devil and the Inheritor of Undying Flame—as though he were a small God.

'I care for you a great deal, Mother dear,' he whispered at last, 'and I'm glad you've come back; but are you sure Aunty Rosa told you everything?'

'Everything. What *does* it matter? But—' the voice broke with a sob that was also laughter—'Punch, my poor, dear, half-blind darling, don't you think it was a little foolish of you?'

'*No.* It saved a lickin'.'

Mamma shuddered and slipped away in the darkness to write a long letter to Papa. Here is an extract:—

.... *Judy is a dear, plump little prig who adores the woman, and wears with as much gravity as her religious opinions—only eight Jack!—a venerable horse-hair atrocity which she calls her Bustle! I have just burnt it, and the child is asleep in my bed as I write. She will come to me at once. Punch I cannot quite understand. He is well nourished, but seems to have been worried into a system of small deceptions which the woman magnifies into deadly sins. Don't you recollect our own up-bringing, dear, when the Fear of the Lord was so often the beginning of falsehood? I shall win Punch to me before long. I am taking the children away into the country to get them to know me and, on the whole, I am content, or shall be when you come home, dear boy, and then, thank God, we shall be all under one roof again at last!*

Three months later, Punch, no longer Black Sheep, has discovered that he is the veritable owner of a real, live, lovely Mamma, who is also a sister, comforter and friend, and that he must protect her till the Father comes home. Deception does not suit the part of a protector, and, when one can do anything without question, where is the use of deception?

'Mother would be awfully cross if you walked through that ditch,' says Judy, continuing a conversation.

'Mother's never angry,' says Punch. 'She'd just say, "You're a little *pagal*"; and that's not nice, but I'll show.'

Punch walks through the ditch and mires himself to the knees. 'Mother, dear,' he shouts, 'I'm just as dirty as I can pos-*sib*-ly be!'

'Then change your clothes as quickly as you pos-*sib*-ly can!' rings out Mother's clear voice from the house. 'And don't be a little *pagal*!'

'There! Told you so,' says Punch. 'It's all different now and we are just as much Mother's as if she had never gone.'

Not altogether, O Punch, for when young lips have drunk deep of the bitter waters of Hate, Suspicion and Despair, all the Love in the world will not wholly take away that knowledge; though it may turn darkened eyes for a while to the light and teach Faith where no Faith was.

HYPL

This has nothing to do with the story.—
It's just a case of Greek meeting Greek.

"If you make me do that" said Black Sheep very quietly, I shall burn this house down and perhaps I'll kill you. I don't know whether I can kill you—you're so bony—but I'll try."

Aunty Rosa stitched it between his shoulders and bade him go for a walk.

Love in the world will not wholly take away
that knowledge; though it may turn darkened
eyes for a while to the light and ~~the teach~~
teach Faith where no Faith was.

His steps led him now not to the beach, but to the Cemetery
of Rockington, amid the potatofields. For hours the grey man
would sit on a tombstone, while Black Sheep read epitaphs,
and then with a sigh would stump home again.

"Antirosa"

... a boy of twelve,
black-haired and
oily in appearance.

"Uncle Harri"

The Same

"MY FIRST BOOK"

(*The Idler* [London], 2 [December 1892], 475–82;
collected in Sussex Edition, xxx
[London, Macmillan, 1938])

EDITOR'S NOTE

"My First Book" was written for a series of articles published in *The Idler*, a new magazine edited by Jerome K. Jerome and by Kipling's friend, the Canadian journalist Robert Barr. Other authors contributing to the series included Walter Besant, Hall Caine, Conan Doyle, Rider Haggard, Bret Harte, and Robert Louis Stevenson. Their articles were all collected and published in book form, with an introduction by Jerome, in 1894.

When Kipling's contribution to the series was published in *The Idler* it was prefaced by the poem now called "In the Neolithic Age" but then entitled "Primum Tempus." The poem has not since been included in any reprinting of "My First Book," but I include it here as Kipling's implicit comment on his first book.

The book that Kipling identifies as his "first" (curiously enough, he never names it in the article) is *Departmental Ditties and Other Verses* (Lahore, 1886). It was not, strictly speaking, his first: that would be *Schoolboy Lyrics*, printed by his parents without Kipling's knowledge, in Lahore, 1881; his second book, *Echoes* (Lahore, 1884), was a collection of parodies in collaboration with his sister; his third, *Quartette* (Lahore, 1885), was the work of all four Kiplings, father, mother, sister, brother. *Departmental Ditties* is thus the fourth of Kipling's books, but the first to be both wholly his own and published on his own initiative.

The text of this reprint, including the prefatory poem, is that in *The Idler*, corrected in one or two details from the Sussex Edition.

My First Book

PRIMUM TEMPUS

In the Neolithic Age savage warfare did I wage
   For Fame and food and two-toed horse's pelt;
I was poet to my clan in that dim red Dawn of Man,
   And I sang of all we fought, and feared, and felt.

Yea, I sang, as now I sing, when the Prehistoric Spring
   Made the piled Biscayan ice-pack split and shove;
And the troll, and gnome, and dwerg, and the Gods of Cliff and Berg,
   Were about me and beneath me and above.

Then a rival (of Solutré) told the tribe my style was outré:
   'Neath a hammer, grooved, of dolomite, he fell;
And I left my views of Art, barbed and tanged, beneath the heart
   Of a mammothistic poet at Grenelle.

So I stripped them scalp from scull, and my hunting-dogs fed full,
   And their teeth I threaded neatly on a thong,
And I wiped my mouth and said: 'It is well that they are dead,
   For I know my work is right, and theirs was wrong!'

But my Totem saw the shame—from his ridge-pole shrine he came,
   And he told me in a vision of the night:
'There are nine and sixty ways of constructing tribal lays,
   And every single one of them is right.'

     .   .   .   .   .

As there is only one man in charge of a steamer, so there is but one
man in charge of a newspaper, and he is the Editor. My chief[1] taught
me this on an Indian journal, and he further explained that an order
was an order, to be obeyed at a run, not a walk, and that any notion
or notions as to the fitness or unfitness of any particular kind of work
for the young had better be held over till the last page was locked up
to press. He was breaking me into harness, and I owe him a deep

debt of gratitude, which I did not discharge at the time. The path of virtue was very steep, whereas the writing of verses allowed a certain play to the mind, and, unlike the filling in of reading matter, could be done as the spirit served. Now a sub-editor is not hired to write verses. He is paid to sub-edit. At the time, this discovery shocked me greatly; but, some years later, when I came to be an editor in charge, Providence dealt me for my subordinate one saturated with Elia.[2] He wrote very pretty, Lamblike essays, but he wrote them when he should have been sub-editing. Then I saw a little what my chief must have suffered on my account. There is a moral here for the ambitious and aspiring who are oppressed by their superiors.

This is a digression, as all my verses were digressions from office work. They came without invitation, unmanneredly, in the nature of things; but they had to come, and the writing out of them kept me healthy and amused. To the best of my remembrance, no one then discovered their grievous cynicism, or their pessimistic tendency, and I was far too busy, and too happy, to take thought about these things.

So they arrived merrily, being born out of the life about me, and they were very bad indeed, and the joy of doing them was payment a thousand times their worth. Some, of course, came and ran away again, and the dear sorrow of going in search of these (out of office hours, and catching them) was almost better than writing them clear. Bad as they were, I burned twice as many as were published, and of the survivors at least two-thirds were cut down at the last moment. Nothing can be wholly beautiful that is not useful, and therefore my verses were made to ease off the perpetual strife between the manager extending his advertisements and my chief fighting for his reading-matter. They were born to be sacrificed. Rukn-Din, the foreman of our side, approved of them immensely, for he was a Muslim of culture. He would say: 'Your potery is very good, sir; just coming proper length today. You giving more soon? One-third column just proper. Always can take on third page.'

Mahmoud, who set them up, had an unpleasant way of referring to a new lyric as '*Ek aur chiz*'—one more thing—which I never liked. The job side, too, were unsympathetic, because I used to raid into their type for private proofs with old English and Gothic headlines.

Even a Hindoo does not like to find the serifs of his f's cut away to make long s's.

And in this manner, week by week, my verses came to be printed in the paper. I was in very good company, for there is always an undercurrent of song, a little bitter for the most part, running through the Indian papers. The bulk of it is much better than mine, being more graceful, and is done by those less than Sir Alfred Lyall[3]—to whom I would apologise for mentioning his name in this gallery—'Pekin,' 'Latakia,' 'Cigarette,' 'O.,' 'T.W.,' 'Foresight,' and others, whose names come up with the stars out of the Indian Ocean going eastward.

Sometimes a man in Bangalore would be moved to song, and a man on the Bombay side would answer him, and a man in Bengal would echo back, till at last we would all be crowing together like cocks before daybreak, when it is too dark to see your fellow. And, occasionally, some unhappy Chaaszee, away in the China Ports, would lift up his voice among the tea-chests, and the queer-smelling yellow papers of the Far East brought us his sorrows. The newspaper files showed that, forty years ago, the men sang of just the same subjects as we did—of heat, loneliness, love, lack of promotion, poverty, sport, and war. Further back still, at the end of the Eighteenth Century, Hickey's *Bengal Gazette*,[4] a very wicked little sheet in Calcutta, published the songs of the young factors, ensigns, and writers to the East India Company. They, too, wrote of the same things, but in those days men were strong enough to buy a bullock's heart for dinner, cook it with their own hands because they could not afford a servant, and make a rhymed jest of all the squalor and poverty. Lives were not worth two monsoons' purchase, and perhaps the knowledge of this a little coloured the rhymes when they sang:

> 'In a very short time you're released from all cares—
> If the Padri's asleep, Mr. Oldham reads prayers!'

The note of physical discomfort that runs through so much Anglo-Indian poetry had been struck then. You will find it most fully suggested in 'The Long, Long Indian Day,' a comparatively modern affair; but there is a set of verses called 'Scanty Ninety-five,' dated about Warren Hastings' time, which gives a lively idea of what our seniors in the service had to put up with. One of the most interesting poems I ever found was written at Meerut, three or four days before the Mutiny broke out there. The author complained that he could not get his clothes washed nicely that week, and was very facetious over his worries.

My verses had the good fortune to last a little longer than some others, which were more true to facts and certainly better workmanship. Men in the Army, and the Civil Service, and the Railway, wrote to me saying that the rhymes might be made into a book. Some of them had been sung to the banjoes round camp fires, and some had run as far downcoast as Rangoon and Moulmein, and up to Mandalay. A real book was out of the question, but I knew that Rukn-Din and the office plant were at my disposal at a price, if I did not use the office time. Also, I had handled in the previous year a couple of small books,[5] of which I was part owner, and had lost nothing. So there was built a sort of a book, a lean oblong docket, wire-stitched, to imitate a D.O. Government envelope, printed on one side only, bound in brown paper, and secured with red tape. It was addressed to all heads of departments and all Government officials, and among a pile of papers would have deceived a clerk of twenty years' service. Of these 'books' we made some hundreds, and as there was no necessity for advertising, my public being to my hand, I took reply-postcards, printed the news of the birth of the book on one side, the blank order-form on the other, and posted them up and down the Empire from Aden to Singapore, and from Quetta to Colombo. There was no trade discount, no reckoning twelves as thirteens, no commission, and no credit of any kind whatever. The money came back in poor but honest rupees, and was transferred from the publisher, the left-hand pocket, direct to the author, the right-hand pocket. Every copy sold in a few weeks, and the ratio of expenses to profits, as I remember it, has since prevented my injuring my health by sympathising with publishers who talk of their risks and advertisements. The down-country papers complained of the form of the thing. The wire binding cut the pages, and the red tape tore the covers. This was not intentional, but Heaven helps those who help themselves. Consequently, there arose a demand for a new edition, and this time I exchanged the pleasure of taking in money over the counter for that of seeing a real publisher's imprint on the title-page.[6] More verses were taken out and put in, and some of that edition travelled as far as Hong-Kong on the map, and each edition grew a little fatter, and, at last, the book came to London[7] with a gilt top and a stiff back, and was advertised in the publishers' poetry department.

But I loved it best when it was a little brown baby with a pink string round its stomach; a child's child, ignorant that it was afflicted with all the most modern ailments; and before people had learned, beyond doubt, how its author lay awake of nights in India, plotting and scheming to write something that should 'take' with the English public.

"AN ENGLISH SCHOOL"

(*Youth's Companion*, October 19, 1893,
pp. 506–7; collected in *Land and Sea Tales
For Scouts and Guides* [London, Macmillan, 1923])

EDITOR'S NOTE

Kipling's school was the United Services College, at Westward Ho!, North Devon, founded in 1874, only four years before Kipling entered it as pupil number 264 in January of 1878; he remained there until the spring of 1882. It is "The School Before its Time," described in Chapter 2 of *Something of Myself*, and it is the school transformed into the setting of *Stalky & Co*. It was here, at school, that Kipling left behind the miseries of his childhood in the House of Desolation and took on an identity as a man of words, a writer. He never failed in gratitude to his old school as the place of his metamorphosis.

The occasion of this article accounts for something of its character. The United Services College, never in good financial health, was almost wholly dependent upon its ability to provide a cheap entrance into the army for the sons of army officers by prepping them for the Army Examination. The school was reasonably prosperous in Kipling's time there, but, after he left, the decline in the exchange value of the rupee made it difficult for army men in India to send their sons back to England; at the same time, increased competition from other schools in the business of preparing students for the Army Examination hurt the school. By 1888 it was in trouble.

Kipling's aim in writing the article was to do a good turn for the school at a time when it needed all the help it could get. He had promised an article to Cormell Price as early as July 1890, when he wrote, after a visit to Westward Ho!: "I'll try to run out a school revisited and send it along as soon as may be" (MS, Library of Congress). There is no reference to such an article again until more than two years later, in the hectic time when, following the death of Wolcott Balestier, Kipling rushed back to England from India in record time, took out a special license, and, before his friends knew what was happening, married Caroline Balestier. On the day before his wedding he wrote to Price to say that "I am writing what is no less than a flagrant puff" of the school (January 17, 1892: MS, Library of Congress).

The distractions in Kipling's life following his marriage were enough to delay the completion of the article. It was, however, complete by January of 1893, when Kipling wrote to Cormell Price describing what he had done:

> The 'Youth's Companion,' a young man's paper with about 1,000,000 readers has got from me an article on my school. You can guess that I have just done my best to describe the old Coll. Indeed, I wouldn't have taken the work except for the sake of the school . . . We shall have the thing read in every country in the world and I want to make a good clean job of it.
>
> (*January 14, 1893: MS, Library of Congress*)

Two years later, something of the same mood persists in the description of schooldays in the story called "The Brushwood Boy." George Cottar, the Brushwood Boy, enjoys the happiness of captaining the First Fifteen, and is otherwise indulged with all the forms of schoolboy success as Kipling describes them in "An English School" (in reprinting "The Brushwood Boy" in volume form Kipling omitted most of the detailed references to George's school life: apparently he thought them too close to what he had already published in "An English School"). Other echoes from the article sound through the stories of *Stalky & Co*. "An English School" may be, as Kipling said, a "flagrant puff"; but he continued to imagine his school in just such terms: what Kipling wrote in 1893 is no more enthusiastic than what he wrote of the United Services College forty years later in *Something of Myself*.

"An English School" is printed here from the text in *The Youth's Companion*. In reprinting the article thirty years later in *Land and Sea Tales* (1923) Kipling made a number of deletions, a few revisions, and some additions. Without providing a complete collation, I indicate the major omissions and print the substantial additions and revisions in the notes.

An English School

So Eton may keep her prime ministers,
   And Rugby her preachers so fine;
I'll follow my father before me,
   And go for a sub of the line,
     The line.
   And pass for a sub of the line.
School Song.[1]

Of all things in the world there is nothing, always excepting a good mother, so worthy of honor as a good school. Our School was made for the sons of officers in the army and navy, and filled with boys who meant to follow their fathers' calling.

It stood within two miles of Amyas Leigh's house at Northam, overlooking the Burroughs and the Pebble-ridge, and the mouth of the Torridge whence the *Rose* sailed in search of Don Guzman. From the front dormitory windows, across the long rollers of the Atlantic, you could see Lundy Island and the Shutter Rock, where the *Santa Catherina* galleon cheated Amyas out of his vengeance by going ashore. If you know Kingsley's 'Westward Ho!' you will remember how all these things happened.[2]

Inland lay the rich Devonshire lanes and the fat orchards, and to the west the gorse and the turf rose and fell along the tops of the cliffs in combe after combe till you came to Clovelly and the Hobby and Gallantry Bower, and the homes of the Carews and the Pinecoffins and the Devonshire people that were old when the Armada was new.

The Burroughs, lying between the School and the sea, was a waste of bent and rush and grass running out into hundreds of acres of sand-hills, called the Bunkers, where people played golf. In the early days of the School there was a small club-house for golfers close to the Pebble-ridge, but one wild winter night the sea got up and drove the Pebble-ridge through the club basement and the walls fell out, and we rejoiced, for even then the golfers wore red coats and did not like us to use the links.[3]

Now there is a new club-house, and a carriage to take the red men to and from their game; but we were there first, long before golf became a fashion, and we turned out the champion amateur golfer of all England.[4]

It was a good place for a school, and that School considered itself the finest in the world, excepting perhaps Haileybury, because it was modelled on Haileybury lines;[5] and there was a legend that, in the old days when the School was new, half the boys had been Haileyburians.

Our Head-master had been head of the modern side at Haileybury, and talking it over with boys from other public schools afterward, I think that one secret of his great hold over us was that he was not a clergyman, as so many head-masters are. As soon as a boy begins to think in the misty way boys do, he gets suspicious of a man who punishes him one day and preaches at him the next. But the Head was different, and we loved him.

In all of five years I never saw him lose his temper, nor among two hundred boys did any one at any time say that he had his favorites. If you went to him with any trouble you were heard out to the end, and answered without being talked at or about, but always *to*. We trusted him absolutely, and when it came to the choice of the various ways of entering the army, what he said was so.

He knew boys naturally better than their fathers knew them, and considerably better than they knew themselves. So when the time came to read for the Final Examinations, he knew the temper and powers of each boy, the amount of training each would stand and the stimulus or restraint that each needed, and handled them accordingly till they had come through the big race that leads into Her Majesty's Army. Looking back on it all, one can see the perfect judgment, knowledge of boys, patience, and above all, power, that the Head must have had.

Some of the masters, particularly on the classic side, vowed that army examinations were making education no more than mark-hunting; but there are a great many kinds of education, and I think the Head knew it, for he taught us hosts of things that we never found out we knew till afterward. And surely it must be better to turn out men who do real work than men who write about what they think or what other people have done.

A scholar may, as the Latin masters said, get more pleasure out of his life than an army officer, but only little children believe that a man's life is given him to decorate with pretty little things, as though it were a girl's room or a picture screen. Besides, scholars are apt, all their lives, to judge from one point of view only, and by the time that an army officer has knocked about the world for a few years he comes to look at men and things by and large, as the sailors say. No books in the world will reach that knack.

So we trusted the Head at school, and afterward we trusted him more.

There was a boy in the Canada Mounted Police,[6] I think, who stumbled into a fortune,—he was the only one of us who ever did,—and as he had never drawn more than seven shillings a day he very properly wrote to the Head from his wilds and explained his trouble, proposing that the Head should look after all his wealth till he came back.[7] The Head was worth trusting—he saved a boy's life from diphtheria[8] once at much greater risk than being shot at, and nobody knew anything about it till years afterward.

But I come back to the School that he made and put his mark upon. The boys said that those with whom Cheltenham could do nothing, whom Sherbourne found too tough, and whom even Marlborough had politely asked to go, had been sent to the School at the beginning of things and turned into men.

'All our men,' said the School, 'go into the army, and there hasn't been a war for ten years where some of our fellows haven't played up. There are ninety of us in the Service now.' There are over two hundred now.[9]

The School motto was, 'Fear God, Honour the King;' and so the men she made went out to Boerland and Zululand and India and Burma and Cyprus and Hongkong, and lived or died as gentlemen and officers.

Even the most notorious bully, for whom an awful ending was prophesied, went to Canada and was mixed up in Riel's rebellion, and came out of it with a fascinating reputation of having led a forlorn hope and behaved like a hero.[10] The first officer killed in the last Burma war was one of our boys, and the School was well pleased to think it should be so.[11]

All these matters were noted by the older boys, and when their fathers, the gray-whiskered colonels and generals, came down to see them, or the directors, who were K.C.B.'s and had been desperate hard-fighting men in their time, made a tour of inspection, it was reported that the School-tone was 'healthy.' This meant that the boys were straining on their leashes, and that there was a steady clatter of singlesticks and clinking of foils in the gymnasium at the far end of the corridor, where the drill sergeant was barking out the regulation cuts and guards.[12]

Sometimes an old boy who had blossomed into a Subaltern of the Queen would come down for a last few words with the Head-master, before sailing with the regiment for foreign parts; and the lower-school boys were distracted with envy, and the prefects of the sixth form pretended not to be proud when he walked with one of their number and talked about 'my men, you know,' till life became unendurable.

There was an unwritten law by which an old boy, when he came back to pay his respects to the School, was entitled to a night in his old dormitory. The boys expected it and sat up half the night listening to the tales of a subaltern that the boy brought with him— stories about riots in Ireland and camps at Aldershot, and all his first steps in the wonderful world.

Sometimes news came in that a boy had died with his men fighting, and the School said 'Killed in action, of course,' as though that were an honor reserved for it alone, and wondered when its own chance would arrive.

It was a singularly quiet School in many ways. When a boy was fourteen or fifteen he was generally taken in hand for the Army Preliminary Examination, and when that was past he was put down to 'grind' for the entrance into Sandhurst or Woolwich; for it was our pride that we passed direct from the School to the army, without troubling the 'crammers.' We spoke of 'the Shop,' which means Woolwich, as though we owned it. Sandhurst was our private preserve; and the old boys came back from foreign parts and told us that India was Westward Ho! spread thin.

On account of this incessant getting ready for examinations there was hardly time for us to gather the beautiful Devonshire apples, or to ferret rabbits in the sand-hills by the golf-links, and saloon-pistols[13] were forbidden because boys got to fighting-parties with dust-shot, and were careless about guarding their eyes.

Nor were we allowed to lower each other over the cliffs with a box-rope and take the young hawks and jackdaws from their nests above the sea. Once a rope broke, or else the boys above grew tired of holding it, and a boy dropped thirty feet to the boulders below; but as he fell on his head nothing happened.[14]

In summer there was almost unlimited bathing from the Pebble-ridge, a whalebacked bank four miles long of rounded gray boulders, where you were taught to ride on the rollers as they came in, to avoid the undertow and to watch your time for getting back to the beach.

There was a big sea bath, too, in which all boys had to qualify for open bathing by swimming a quarter of a mile, at least; and it was a matter of honor among the schoolhouses not to let the summer end with a single boy who could not 'do his quarter,' at any rate.

Boating was impossible off that coast, but sometimes a fishing-boat would be wrecked on Braunton Bar, and we could see the life-boat and the rocket at work; and once just after chapel there was a cry that the herring were in. The School ran down to the beach in its Sunday clothes and fished them out with umbrellas.[15]

But the game of the School, setting aside golf, which every one could play if he had patience, was foot-ball. Both cricket and foot-ball were compulsory. That is to say, unless a boy could show a doctor's certificate that he was physically unfit to stand up to the wicket or go into the scrimmage, he had to play a certain number of afternoons every week at the game of the season.

If he had engagements elsewhere—we called it 'shirking'—he was reasonably sure of three cuts with a ground-ash from the Captain of the Games.[16] A good player, of course, could get leave off on any fair excuse, but it was a beautiful rule for fat boys and loafers.[17]

Curiously enough, the one thing that the School did not understand was an attempt to drill it in companies with rifles, by way of making a volunteer cadet-corps. We took our lickings for not attending *that* cheerfully, because we considered it 'playing at soldiers,' and boys reading for the army are apt to be very particular on these points.

We were weak in cricket, but our foot-ball team at its best devastated the country from Blundell's—we always respected Blundell's, because 'Great John Ridd' had been educated there[18]—to Exeter, whose team were grown men. Yet we, who had been taught to play together, drove them back over the November mud, back to their own goal-posts, till the ball was hacked through and touched down, and you could hear the long-drawn yell of 'Schoo-*ool*! Schoo- *ool*!' as far as Appledore.

When the enemy would not come to us our team went to the enemy, and if victorious, would return late at night in a three-horse brake,[19] chanting:

> It's a way we have in the Army,
> It's a way we have in the Navy,
> It's a way that we have in the Public Schools,
> Which nobody can deny![20]

Then the boys would flock to the dormitory windows, and wave towels and join in the 'Hip-hip-hip-hurrah!' of the chorus, and the winning team would swagger through the dormitories and show the beautiful blue marks on their shins, and the little boys would be allowed to get sponges and hot water.

Very few things that the world can offer make up for having missed a place in the First Fifteen, with its black jersey and white—snow-white—knickerbockers, and the velvet skullcap with the gold tassel—the cap that you leave out in the rain accidentally and casually step upon to make it look old and as if you had been in the First Fifteen for years.

The other outward sign of the First Fifteen that the happy boy generally wore through a hard season was the 'jersey-mark'—a raw, red scrape on ear and jaw bone where the skin had been fretted by the rough jerseys on either side in the steady drive of many scrimmages. We were trained to put our heads down, pack in the shape of a wedge and shove, and it was in that shape that we stood up to a team of trained men for two and twenty counted, steaming minutes. We got the ball through in the end.

At the close of the winter term, when there were no more foot-ball teams to squander and the Christmas holidays were coming, the School set itself to the regular yearly theatricals—farce and three-act play all complete. Sometimes it was 'The Rivals,'[21] or sometimes an attempt at a Shakespeare play; but the farces were the most popular.

All ended with the School-Saga, the '*Vive la compagnie*,' in which the senior boy of the School chanted the story of the School for the past twelve months.[22] It was very long and very difficult to make up, though all the poets of all the forms had been at work on it for weeks; and the School gave the chorus at the top of its voice.

On the last Sunday of the term the last hymn in chapel was 'Onward, Christian Soldiers.' We did not know what it meant then, and we did not care, but we stood up and sang it till the music was swamped in the rush. The big verse, like the 'tug-of-war' verse in Mrs. Ewing's 'Story of a Short Life,'[23] was:

> We are not divided,
> All one body we,
> One in faith and doctrine,
> One in charity.

Then the organ would give a hurricane of joyful roars, and try to get us in hand before we broke into the refrain. Later on, meeting our men all the world over, the meaning of that hymn became much too plain.

Except for this outbreak we were not very pious. There was a boy who had to tell stories in the Dormitory night after night, and when his stock ran out he fell back on a book called 'Eric, or Little by Little,'[24] as comic literature, and read it till the gas was turned off. The boys laughed abominably, and there was some attempt to give selections from it at the meetings of the Reading Society. That was quashed by authority because it was against discipline.

There were no public-houses near us except tap-rooms that sold cider; and raw Devonshire cider can only be drunk after a long and hot paper chase. We hardly ever saw, and certainly never spoke to, anything in the nature of a woman from one year's end to the other; for our masters were all unmarried. Later on, quite a little colony of mothers came down to live near the School, and their sons were day-boys who couldn't do this and mustn't do that, and there was a great deal too much dressing up on week-days and going out to tea, and meeting girls, and nonsense of that kind which is not in the least good for boys.[25]

Our masters, luckily, were never gushing. They did not call us Dickie or Johnnie or Tommy, but Smith or Thompson; and when we were undoubtedly bad we were actually and painfully beaten with an indubitable cane on a veritable back till we wept unfeigned tears. Nobody seemed to think that it brutalized our finer feelings, but everybody was relieved when the trouble was over.

Canes, especially when brought down with a drawing stroke, sting like hornets; but they were invented for certain offences, and a cut or two, given with no malice, but as a reminder, can correct and keep corrected a false quantity more completely than any amount of explanation.

There was one boy, however, to whom every quantity[26] was an arbitrary mystery, and he wound up his crimes by suggesting that he could do better if Latin verses rhymed as decent verse should. He was given an afternoon's reflection to purge himself of his contempt; and feeling certain that he was in for something very warm, he turned '*Donec gratus eram*' into pure Devonshire dialect, rhymed, and showed it up as his contribution to the study of Horace.[27]

He was let off, and his master gave him the run of a big library, where he found as much verse and prose as he wanted; but that ruined his Latin verses and made him write verses of his own. There he found all the English poets from Chaucer to Matthew Arnold, and a book called 'Imaginary Conversations'[28] which he did not understand, but it seemed to be a good thing to imitate. So he imitated and was handed up to the Head, who said that he had better learn Russian under his own eye, so that if he were ever sent to

Siberia for lampooning the authorities he might be able to ask for things.

That meant the run of another library—English Dramatists this time; hundreds of old plays; Marco Polo and Mandeville,[29] as well as thick brown books of voyages told in language like the ringing of big bells. And the Head would sometimes tell him about the manners and customs of the Russians, who are rather more your particular friends than ours, and sometimes about his own early days at college, when Morris and Swinburne and Rossetti, and other people who afterward became great and glorious, were all young, and the Head was young with them, and they wrote wonderful things in college magazines.[30]

It was beautiful and cheap—dirt cheap, at the price of a permanent load of impositions.

The School started a Natural History Society, which took the birds and plants of North Devon under its charge, reporting first flowerings and first arrivals and new discoveries to learned societies in London, and naturally attracting to itself every boy in the School who had the poaching instinct.

Some of us made membership an excuse for hooking apples and pheasant eggs and geese from farmers' orchards and gentlemen's estates, and we were turned out with disgrace. So we spoke scornfully of the society ever afterward. All the same, some of us had our first introduction to gunpowder in the shape of a charge of salt fired at our legs by angry keepers.

The institution that caused some more excitement was the School paper. Three of the boys, who had moved up the School side by side for four years and were allies in all things, started the notion[31] as soon as they came to the dignity of a study of their own with a door that would lock. The other two told the third boy what to write, and held the staircase against invaders.

It was a real printed paper of eight pages, and at first the printer was more thoroughly ignorant of type-setting, and the Editor was more completely ignorant of proof-reading, than any printer and any Editor that ever was. It was printed off by a gas engine; and even the engine despised its work, for one day it went through the floor of the shop and crashed—still working furiously—into the cellar.

The paper came out at times and seasons,[32] but every time it came out there was sure to be trouble, because the Editor was learning for the first time how sweet and good and profitable it is—and how nice it looks on the page—to make fun of people in actual print.

For instance, there was friction among the study-fags once, and the Editor wrote a descriptive account of the Lower School,—the classes whence the fags were drawn,—their manners and customs, their ways of cooking half-plucked sparrows and imperfectly cleaned blackbirds at the gas-jets on a rusty nib, and their fights over sloe-jam made in a gallipot. It was an absolutely truthful article, but the Lower School knew nothing about truth, and would not even consider it as literature.[33]

It is less safe to write a study of an entire class than to discuss individuals one by one; but apart from the fact that boys throw books and inkpots very straight indeed, there is surprisingly little difference between the abuse of grown-up people and the abuse of children.

In those days the Editor had not learned this; so when the study below the Editorial study threw coal at the Editorial legs and kicked in the panels of the door, because of personal paragraphs in the last number, the Editorial Staff—and there never was so loyal and hard-fighting a staff—fried fat bacon till there was half an inch of grease in the pan, and let the greasy chunks down at the end of a string to bob against and defile the lower study windows.

When the lower study—and there never was a public so low and unsympathetic as that lower study—looked out to see what was frosting their window-panes, the Editorial Staff emptied the hot fat on their heads, and it stayed there for days and days, wearing shiny to the very last.[34]

The boy who suggested this sort of warfare was then reading a sort of magazine, called *Fors Clavigera*,[35] which he did not in the least understand,—it was not exactly a boys' paper,—and when the lower study had scraped some of the fat off their heads and were thundering with knobby pokers on the door-lock, this boy began to chant pieces of the *Fors* as a battle-song, and to show that his mind was free from low distractions.

He was an extraordinary Irishman,[36] and the only boy in the School who had a genuine contempt for his masters. There was no affectation in his quiet insolence. He honestly did despise them; and threats that made us all wince only caused him to put his head a little on one side and watch the master as a sort of natural curiosity.

The worst of this was that his allies had to take their share of his punishments, for they lived as communists and socialists hope to live some day, when everybody is good. They were bad, as bad as they dared to be, but their possessions were in common, absolutely. And when 'the Study' was out of funds they took the most respectable clothes in possession of the Syndicate, and leaving the owner one Sunday and one week-day suit, sold the rest in Bideford town.

Later, when there was another crisis, it was *not* the respectable one's watch that was taken by force for the good of the Study and pawned, and never redeemed.

Later still, money came into the Syndicate honestly, for a London paper that did not know with whom it was dealing, published and paid a whole guinea for some verses that one of the boys had written, and the Study caroused on chocolate and condensed milk and pilchards and Devonshire cream.[37]

So things went on very happily till the three were seriously warned that they must work in earnest, and stop giving amateur performances of 'Aladdin'[38] and writing librettoes of comic operas which never came off, and worrying their house-masters into gray hairs.

Then they all grew very good, and one of them got into the army; and another—the Irish one—became an engineer, and the third one found himself on a daily paper half a world away from the Pebble-ridge and the sea-beach. The three swore eternal friendship before they parted, and from time to time they still meet boys of their year in India, and magnify the honor of the old School.

The boys are scattered all over the world, one to each degree of land east and west, as their fathers were before them, doing much the same kind of work; and it is curious to notice how little the character of the man differs from that of the boy of sixteen or seventeen.

The general and commander-in-chief of the Study, he who suggested selling the clothes, never lost his head even when he and his army were hemmed round by the enemy—the drill sergeant—far out of bounds and learning to smoke under a hedge. He was sick and dizzy, but he rose to the occasion, took command of his forces, and by strategic manoeuvres along dry ditches and crawlings through tall grass, outflanked the enemy and got into safe ground without losing a man of the three.

Last year he was bitten by a mad dog in India, went to be treated by Pasteur, and came out again in the heart of the hot weather to find himself almost alone in charge of six hundred Sepoys, his Drill Havildar dead and his office clerk run away, leaving the regimental books in most ghastly confusion. Then we met; and when he was telling his story there was just the same happy look on his face as when he steered us down the lanes with the certainty of a beautiful thrashing if we were caught.[39]

And there were others who went abroad with their men, and when they got into a tight place behaved very much as they behaved in the scrimmage at foot-ball.

The boy who used to take flying jumps on to the ball and roll over and over with it, because he was big and fat and could not run, took a flying jump on to a Burmese dacoit[40] whom he had surprised in a stockade; but he had forgotten that he was much heavier than he had been at School, and by the time he rolled off his victim the little dacoit was dead.

And there was a boy who was always being led astray by bad advice, and begging off punishment on that account. He got into some little scrape when he grew up, and we who knew him knew before he was reprimanded by his commanding officer what his excuse would be. It came out almost word for word as he was used to whimper it at school. He was cured, though, afterward by being sent off on a little expedition alone where he would be responsible for any advice that was going, as well as for fifty soldiers.

And the best boy of all—he was really good, not book good—was shot in the thigh as he was leading his Sepoys up the ramp of a fortress; and all he said was, 'Put me up against a tree and take my men on;' and when his men came back he was dead.[41]

Ten or eleven years ago,[42] when the Queen was shot at by a man

in the street, the School paper made some verses about it that ended
like this:

> One school of many, made to make
>   Men who shall hold it dearest right
> To battle for their ruler's sake,
>   And stake their being in the fight,
>
> Sends greeting, humble and sincere,
>   Though verse be rude and poor and mean
> To you, the greatest as most dear,
>   Victoria, by God's Grace, our Queen!
>
> Such greeting as should come from those
>   Whose fathers faced the Sepoy hordes,
> Or served you in the Russian snows
>   And, dying, left their sons their swords.
>
> For we are bred to do your will
>   By land and sea, wherever flies
> The flag to fight and follow still,
>   And work your empire's destinies.
>
> And some of us have fought for you
>   Already in the Afghan Pass;
> Or where the scarce-seen smoke-puffs flew
>   From Boer marksmen in the grass.[43]
>
> Once more we greet you, though unseen
>   Our greeting be, and coming slow.
> Trust us, if need arise, O Queen!
>   We shall not tarry with the blow.

And I think that there are one or two waste places in the world
that can bear witness how we kept our word.[44]

RUDYARD KIPLING'S
DIARY, 1885

(MS, Harvard University)

EDITOR'S NOTE

Kipling's Diary for 1885 is largely the record of his work for the *Civil and Military Gazette* in that year, a year that saw his contributions to the newspaper greatly increased over those of the previous years. By the beginning of 1885 he had already spent more than two full years of work on the *CMG* under the repressive editorship of Stephen Wheeler, who disliked "creative" work and kept Kipling to a demanding routine of sub-editing: condensing and restating other men's contributions, abridging and paraphrasing documents, cutting and pasting items from other papers, translating, taking down wire-service items, and other such unrewarding exercises. Slowly, Kipling made his way into the confidence of his editor: early in 1884 he was sent on special assignment to Patiala to report the Viceroy's visit; about the same time, his first verses appeared in the paper, and he also began the series of local gossip called "A Week in Lahore." Later in 1884 the first of his short stories appeared in the *CMG*. These would remain infrequent until the middle of 1886, when Wheeler left the paper and a new regime welcomed Kipling's creative work. Still, by 1885 he had become a useful and frequent contributor to, as well as a sub-editor of, the *CMG*. The diary for 1885 documents his work for the paper in a detail that usefully supplements the information from other sources, especially in view of the fact that none of Kipling's letters from early in 1885 appears to have survived. "Scraps," to which so much reference is made, were the untitled comments and reports on topics of the day to which the front page of the *CMG* was given over.

The diary also gives us information about Kipling's life apart from the *CMG*, and particularly about his literary work—his labor on the early masterpiece "The Strange Ride of Morrowbie Jukes," for example, or the inspiration for his unfinished and unpublished "Mother Maturin," or his plans for a monthly magazine to be published at Calcutta. The diary records the work and the ambition of a writer who, though he could not yet know it, was just on the verge of finding himself and his audience.

Finally, apart from its record of a crucial stage in a great writer's career, the diary also gives us some vivid glimpses of a young man's life in British India: work, the Club, prickly heat, fever, dining out, picnics, evenings "going round" the Lahore bandstand, mild flirtations, and something more than flirtations, if one may guess about some of the cryptic entries. Kipling's status as a newspaperman eluded the categories of the rigidly classified social system in British India; he was neither civil nor military, and he was thus free to come and go as official India was not. His routine may often have been boring; it certainly was always demanding, but as a journalist he was in touch with many things beyond the usual English boundaries. The diary gives us some idea of this range: a visit to an exhibition at Jullundur, a prowl through Lahore at night, a stint as special correspondent on the borders of Afghanistan, a walk in the Himalayas, all mingled with the account of routine journalistic work and with the recorded moments of literary inspiration. It is an interesting mixture.

The preservation of the diary is owing to the fact that Kipling left it behind in the offices of the *CMG* when he was transferred from that paper to its sister paper, the *Pioneer* of Allahabad, in November 1887. A note on the diary says "Given me by Wilson manager of the C. & M. Gazette" and is signed by William John Dare, 1899. Dare was the manager of the *Pioneer* and figures without credit to his reputation for prophecy as the man who told Kipling on his departure from India: "you'll never be worth more than four hundred rupees a month to anyone" (see *Something of Myself*, p. 45). Evidently Dare was of a different mind by 1899, perhaps the peak year of Kipling's fame. The diary was acquired by the Houghton Library, Harvard University, in July 1942.

The volume, in small quarto form, was published by Letts, Son & Co., London, and has a title page reading *Letts's Rough Diary or Scribbling Journal for 1885*. After a number of pages containing advertisements and miscellaneous almanac information, each opening of the diary presents one page with printed headings for three or four days of a week and a facing page left blank for notes. There are 202 of these pages for the diary proper; Kipling has made entries for 142 days, regularly through January and February, irregularly through March, April, and May; there is nothing for June and only one entry for July. He resumes fairly regularly in August and continues through September. After three entries in October, the diary ceases to be kept. Other items in the diary, which are all transcribed here, are either by way of preliminary or appendix to the regular diary: the items that RK has written before the commencement of 1885, for example, are on two blank preliminary pages.

Unless it is specified otherwise, all of the articles by Kipling mentioned in the diary appeared in the *CMG* and are uncollected.

In transcribing the diary for publication I have kept the irregularities and inconsistencies of the original in spelling, punctuation, and other details.

R. Kipling
C & MG

8/12/84

Mem. To finish handsomely the 'Village of the dead'[1] which was taken in hand three days ago; and to settle Review of D'rozio's life[2]

A week in Lahore 9/12.

New Chief Court. Trees by [?] wh. obstruct view of cathedral.

Year's work. Published Echoes[3] for which secured right good reviews and the sale of the 1st edition of 150 copies. Wrote in the course of the year 230 columns matter = Rs2300 @ Rs.10 per col.

Pay to April 250	=	1000–
Pay from Ap Dec. 300	=	2700
		Rs 3700
		– Rs.2300
		Rs.1400

Dec. 31st. Written to hitch the old year on to the new. Dinner last night. Gordon Walker and Mrs. Walker, Miss and Master Roe, Lawrence, Vi Marshall and Drake.[4]

Today called professor Bernhardy Ruchwaldy[5] (a bitter cold morn) and he had on a great coat over dress clothes!) for whom I made bundobust for entertainment Friday and Monday next.

THURSDAY 1 JANUARY: New Year's Day. Wrote inane scrap on Capture of Bhamo as it affected future of Burma.[6] Left office 2. to attend Aitchisons[7] big Durbar on Maidan opposite fort. Went on business and stayed till 6. or thereabouts.

199

With Pater's help managed to spin out a watery sort of special[8] to close upon three columns. Kept me up till 1. of the night.

FRIDAY 2 JANUARY: Retouched added to and corrected proofs of special—good three cols—wrote up notes for a week in Lahore—The Vol. Ball. and new year note and gave in matter for tomorrow's rag. Go down tonight to Jullundur[9]—stay with Massey[10] and try to make something out of inferior sort of local exhibition of arts and manufactures there. Amusing biz.

SATURDAY 3 JANUARY: Jullundur; where went to the Exhibition. took notes but did nothing save eat walk about and enjoy myself. Weather blowing up for rain in those parts and stormy forbye.

SUNDAY 4 JANUARY: Left at mid-day. Got in 5.30 and wrote leaded col and 3/4 on the exhibition.

MONDAY 5 JANUARY: Busy day. Jul[lundur] Special[11] h.o and added to. Put in two cols of The Week in Lahore[12] and blocked out rough idea for special on the Lahore Serai.[13] Jul. Special goes in tomorrow. $2\frac{1}{2}$ cols solid—a good business. Saw very good review in Calcutta review of Echoes[14] wh pleased me highly.

TUESDAY 6 JANUARY: Jullundur special went in today. $2\frac{1}{2}$ solid. Also wrote skit about column long on Punjab police[15] for tomorrow. Otherwise did nowt. Sent Englishman set of verses on the Indian Associations memorial.[16]

WEDNESDAY 7 JANUARY: Wrote an extremely ordinary scrap on Francis' 'Monograph on Punjab Cotton'[17] about $\frac{1}{2}$ column, and attacked Growse's book of Bulandshahr.[18] Did nothing however, the weather being dark and damnable and I myself much out of sorts. Corrected proof of Twenty Years After—skit on Punjab Police. This must go in tomorrow. Ferel[19] of the Gaiety Co. called on Wheeler and has arranged to act here till the end of the week.

THURSDAY 8 JANUARY: Twenty years after—nearly 1. col went in today. Wrote obituary scrap from Men of the Times on

Jackson late bishp Lond. Also scrap on Bengal and Punjab Museums[20]——a few lines only. All three came to just under the 1 col. Total. 2. col. Don't feel half fit.

FRIDAY 9 JANUARY: An Idle day. Wrote $\frac{3}{4}$ col scrap on Burmese Arts,[21] and did very little else—received Bom. Gaz. and Times of India's guides to Bombay for Review but didn't do 'em. Scrap wasn't wanted for that day and attempts to write notes for the Week, spoiled by bad head-ache.

SATURDAY 10 JANUARY: Wrote three scraps—one on Blockade of formosa and other on Calcutta Municipality and third on Mad[ras] Ploughing Match[22] in all nearly one column long. And did also seriously take in hand—having a spare hour at three, my City of the Dead—wh. may be of some use eventually. Felt seedy all day.—Haven't anything in hand for notes of the week.

SUNDAY 11 JANUARY: Drake turned up after breakfast and we went to Lahore Serai—I to see if I could find anything to write on. Felt abominably seedy and queer in the head all day. Did nothing except most necessary work on the papers.

MONDAY 12 JANUARY: My 'On a recent Memorial—an unofficial reply' appeared in the Englishman of the 9th inst. Wrote scrap on O'Donovan Rossa[23] and did my d–dest with bad materials to make up something for tomorrow's notes of the week—wh. have been deferred one day. Feeling abominably seedy and queer in the head—very much worried all day.

TUESDAY 13 JANUARY: Fudged up Notes of the week[24] after a fashion expect it to come to about $1\frac{1}{2}$ cols. Worked hard at special on the Lahore serai, but did no scraps—which is a nuisance as I am behind my average slightly.

WEDNESDAY 14 JANUARY: Wednesday. Wrote Review about one col long on H.A.B. Piffard his poems,[25] and began to settle about 2nd Edition of Echoes[26] for which book there seems to be still some demand. Wrote no scraps,—and generally took things easily. A bad headache all the afternoon.

THURSDAY 15 JANUARY: A bad day and a worse headache. Tried scrap on Growse's Bulandshahr could make nothing of it. Luckily there was no special urgency. So fell back on the village of the Dead and Among the Houhnyms[27] and did something to each of them. Mem. Must work up notes of the week. Heard Padre Montgomery is fetched about scrap in notes of the week on Coffee Palace.[28]

FRIDAY 16 JANUARY: Wrote scrap on Bombay cholera Hospitals[29] and Growse's Bulandshahr book. A busy day in other respects. Did attack my village of the dead and considerably elaborate the plot thereof. Felt much better than have done for some time.

SATURDAY 17 JANUARY: Wrote scrap on attempted assassination of Munquldass Nathoobhoy, Messrs Cook and Sons latest venture, also notice of Times of India and Bombay Gazette directories and Lahore Burglary,[30] and a couple of notes for the week in Lahore. Also My Village of the dead.

SUNDAY 18 JANUARY: Did the papers and a note for the week in Lahore.

W.R.W.M.[31]

MONDAY 19 JANUARY: Wrote Jellalabad horse fair from notes; notice of the Gaiety Company, para on Luker's Press Guide for India (a good biz.) wrote notes for a week in Lahore. doctored scrap of the Paters on E. About,[32] and was generally very busy over small jobs.—Week in Lahore ought to come to 2. cols. good.

TUESDAY 20 JANUARY: Finished up notes of the week and laboured at Morrobie Jukes, C.E. Not at all a busy day as far as scraps went; but I fancy I've kept up my average.

WEDNESDAY 21 JANUARY: A busy day as far as the paper was concerned but nothing except one small para to show for it.[33] *Bad.*

THURSDAY 22 JANUARY: Got cheque one gold mohur Pioneer, Moon of other Days and Maxims of Hafiz[34] / did nothing except necessary work—a racking headache and feverishness.

FRIDAY 23 JANUARY: Wrote scrap. Bombay Club [?[35]] at Chandernagore, and demoralization in Thongwa district. Also explanatory scrap on some Australian annexations— This with the help of an Atlas.[36] Went on with the Strange ride of Morrowbie etc.

SATURDAY 24 JANUARY: A Busy day. Wrote scrap about half col on the Bombay attempt to send home weekly telegrams to India:[37] got week's work ended and worked at long translation from the *Journal de Saint Petersburg*[38] which took home to finish. Also did a lot to Morrowbie Jukes who is beginning to look well.

SUNDAY 25 JANUARY: Three hours hard work in the morning finished translation, proofs, papers and all the rest—Did nothing else all day.

MONDAY 26 JANUARY: Translation (as I had expected not wanted). Worked up notes of the week, which have to go in tomorrow. Wrote close upon a column of Drivel and did the ordinary work. A letter from T[hacker]. S[pink]. and Co with estimates for the 2nd Edition of Echoes, on sm. pica, crown octavo, good paper, 1000 copies @ 2/1 p. page; 750 @ 1/12. p. page. 500 @ 1/7 p. page and plain binding at /3. per copy. This seems fairly satisfactory.[39]

TUESDAY 27 JANUARY: A very busy day. Did notes of the week[40] which were but an inferior business at the best and had to be done in a hurry. Put on the day's work by reason of tonight's dinner to Burne,[41] and went ahead with Morrowby J. Have decided not to deal with T.S. and Co but to work Echoes in my own place as handsomely as may be—Russian translation[42] went in today.

WEDNESDAY 28 JANUARY: Scraps on Accidents on Indian Railways, The Dynamitard's attempts at Westminster and Hume's vegetarianism.[43] About one column altogether. An easy day as far as the paper was concerned; there being plenty of matter in hand and not much proofwork.

THURSDAY 29 JANUARY: Nothing much as was feeling seedy. Did the ordinary work of the paper only.

FRIDAY 30 JANUARY: Bad headache, sore throat, and slight fever. Did only what was absolutely necessary, and left lately [*sic*].

SATURDAY 31 JANUARY: Wrote scrap on Porter's speech at Madras[44]—and went to Gymkhana tiffin the paper being held back for the mail. Went to office 10.30 pm: got away, 11.30 Pm.

SUNDAY 1 FEBRUARY: The ordinary work on the paper only—wrote more fair copy of Morrowbie J.

MONDAY 2 FEBRUARY: Scrap on article in Novoe Vremya on relations between Germany and Russia, and two scraps on the Journal of Indian Art.[45]

TUESDAY 3 FEBRUARY: A Busy forenoon—The Week in Lahore done.[46] Should be about 2 cols.

WEDNESDAY 4 FEBRUARY: Scrap on O'Donovan Rossa, and two locals.[47]

THURSDAY 5 FEBRUARY: Scraps Dr. G. Le Bon, Rivers Thompson's speech and the Romance of Indian Crime[48]—Note from G[eorge]. W. A[llen].[49] today.

FRIDAY 6 FEBRUARY: One scrap on Volapuk or Universal Language which, by the way did not go in.[50] A bad headache all the afternoon. Mem. eris cum [?] Thursd. [?][51]—a bundobast. My tack to lie low and wait.

SATURDAY 7 FEBRUARY: Hiatus valde deflendus.[52]

SUNDAY 8 FEBRUARY: Cowbyres and filth for the sake of a special Typhoid at Home.[53]

MONDAY 9 FEBRUARY: At it the whole day without a break. Notes of the week, Cowbyre special and two cols translation from the Invalide Russe.[54] A good days work.

TUESDAY 10 FEBRUARY: Another full days work. Week in Lahore[55] three cols went in today, finished translation sent it in and also special typhoid at home.

WEDNESDAY 11 FEBRUARY: Scrap, Rangoon Chamber Commerce, Frauds on Calcutta Dist Charitable Society.[56] (Mem. To make the narrators of "At the Pit's mouth" tell their tale at a spiritualistic seance in the heart of Lahore

City.[57] Happy thought! Must go on with the Strange Ride etc.) Have done so.

THURSDAY 12 FEBRUARY: The ordinary work of the paper only; including a large allowance of proofs. W.R.W.M. [ ].[58]—a thoroughly satisfactory conclusion.

FRIDAY 13 FEBRUARY: Scrap. Musketry schools. Annotated Prejvalsky's explorations in Thibet—and rec'd bellew's Sanitary Report for notes of the week.[59] '*Typhoid at home*' went in today: Mem scrap on Rai Kanega Lall and design for town hall must be done tomorrow.[60]

SATURDAY 14 FEBRUARY: Prejvalsky's Explorations in Thibet went in today: also scrap on Novoe Vremya and the russian annexation of corea.[61] Went to Rosa Towers Comp[62] in the evening for business. Found them fairly good—with a couple of xxx women. w.

SUNDAY 15 FEBRUARY: The work of the papers only; and blocked out roughly critique on the Rosa Towers Company.

MONDAY 16 FEBRUARY: Wrote effusive critique on Company—and three notes of the week—also note on Colonel Olcott[63] and the work of the paper. W[heeler]. left at 3.15 to go to Miss Lawrie's marriage.[64]

TUESDAY 17 FEBRUARY: Notes of the week.[65] Two cols of [*sic*] thereabouts. Literally ran dry for want of scraps—

WEDNESDAY 18 FEBRUARY: Scrap on Books published in the Northwest.[66]

THURSDAY 19 FEBRUARY: Long critique on last nights rendering of 'drink' a bad play wh. I'm afraid I 'buttered' shamelessly.[67] More Morrowbie Jukes. Its getting on. Note that butter paid. Very nice woman. V.[68]

FRIDAY 20 FEBRUARY: Fudged critique on Hudson's Surprise party[69]—a good piece of work and went ahead considerably on Morrowbie Jukes. Must keep the average up to time.

SATURDAY 21 FEBRUARY: Hudson's party critique—local only. To Hudson again[70] in the even for my sins—Sent 'In my Indian Garden' to the Pioneer.[71] Fallon's Hindustani proverbs and journal de St Petersburgh.[72]

SUNDAY 22 FEBRUARY: The usual work of the Papers and arranging second edition Echoes—

MONDAY 23 FEBRUARY: Scraps on M. Blavatsky and J[ournal] de St Petersburgh. Also local hudson surprise on Saturday night. Notes of the week[73] about one col gone in—Must settle Fallon's Hindustani Proverbs tonight.

TUESDAY 24 FEBRUARY: Notes of the week. Two cols and a trifle over, which brings me rather below my average— Stung by an ant in the eye—Hurts.

WEDNESDAY 25 FEBRUARY: Sting of yesterday blinded me couldn't see. Went to hospital Lawrie[74] came over about mid day and looked at it. Attention more occupied by blain of my face. Must come to hospital tomorrow and see how cocaine works. Did not go to office.

THURSDAY 26 FEBRUARY: Eye all right. W[heeler]. said it wasnt and so lost my work for the day—served him right. Went to hospital [word illegible] cocaine and was impressed. To Cinderella in the evening and was impresseder.

FRIDAY 27 FEBRUARY: Scrap Fallons Hindustani Proverbs. Settling arrears of work—A busy day with not much to show for it. Wrote note for the 'Week in Lahore.'

SATURDAY 28 FEBRUARY: The Burmah Annexation Company scrap.[75] Also notes for a week in Lahore, which ought to be about three cols long this week.

SUNDAY 1 MARCH: Seven cols proofs and the paper Shadera Picnic[76] xxx [?] [?] rh.[77] Jam! on toast.

MONDAY 2 MARCH: Scrap on Communication from P.O. anent stamps,[78] also notes of the week, and as much advance work as I could manage.

TUESDAY 3 MARCH: Notes of the week[79] a healthy instalment thereof. Review of Echoes appeared in Times of India[80]— very sweet indeed. Notes of the week come to three cols good and so bring up my average.

WEDNESDAY 4 MARCH: A busy day on special on the Umballa

Conference 1869[81]—About two cols altogether. One col of my scraps went in today.

THURSDAY 5 MARCH: Verses of occasion. Dufferin's cloture[82] written by noon—on tel that came in at 10.40. Not bad.

FRIDAY 6 MARCH: News Paper work only; with an occasional note of the week.

SATURDAY 7 MARCH: The idea of 'Mother Maturin'[83] dawned on me today. Did not however work on it but contented myself with other things.

SUNDAY 8 MARCH: Shadera xxx[84] where found opportunity for another note.[85] There's something wrong there.

Here came in the Pindi Conference and my work thereat. Whereof I retain no remembrance.[86]

Also journey to Peshawur and Jumrood where I wrote the 'City of Evil Countenances'[87] and an average of two cols specials per diem

SATURDAY 21 MARCH: Pindi. Wrote 1st Special on Pindi camp.[88]

SUNDAY 22 MARCH: Peshawur. Where wrote second special of To Meet the Amir.[89] Crowded D.B.

MONDAY 23 MARCH: Telegrams.

TUESDAY 24 MARCH: [no entry]

WEDNESDAY 25 MARCH: Second special 'to meet the Amir':[90] knocking about all over the place and cursing Abdur Rahman.

THURSDAY 26 MARCH: [no entry]

FRIDAY 27 MARCH: Still at Peshawur. No chance of getting away. Third special to meet the Amir.[91] Heavy rain.

SATURDAY 28 MARCH: Wrote the City of Evil Countenances and saw that it was good.

SUNDAY 29 MARCH: Jumrood at Dawn. To meet the Amir three columns.[92]

MONDAY 30 MARCH: To meet the Amir[93]—Heavy rain. Off to Pindi tonight.

TUESDAY 31 MARCH: To Meet the Amir. Still Heavy rain. Reached Pindi. Awfully tired.

WEDNESDAY 1 APRIL: City of Evil Countenances appeared. A Big Durbar. Wrote yet another Special[94] am beginning to object to this rain and never seem to get to sleep.

THURSDAY 2 APRIL: Wild excitement for nothing. Knocking about all over the place and wrote another special.

FRIDAY 3 APRIL: Wrote another special. Certainly I haven't been to sleep for a week or so—wonder how much longer this is going to last. Camp in an awful condition. I myself not much better.

SATURDAY 4 APRIL: A blessed interval: Got a little sleep at mid-day. Feeling *oh* so tired.

SUNDAY 5 APRIL: Spent today over special two and a half cols long,[95] and rode about all over the place.

MONDAY 6 APRIL: [Bank Holiday] No bank holiday for me. Special of three columns on review.[96] Fine weather at last but I *must* shut up with a click before long. Too little sleep and too much seen.

TUESDAY 7 APRIL: Two column special today.[97] Review and phantasm of hundreds of thousands of legs all moving together have stopped my sleep altogether. Top of head hot and eyes are beginning to trouble me.

WEDNESDAY 8 APRIL: Two and a half columns about the big Durbar:[98] Luckily got a good sleep last night and am fit for anything. Pindi Club crammed. Nothing but cannon all day and half the night.

THURSDAY 9 APRIL–WEDNESDAY 29 APRIL:[99] [no entries]

THURSDAY 30 APRIL: Left Simla with S. De Brath ex-Engineer and wife on way to Kotgurh.[100] Both De B. and I sadly out of condition took five hours to do $8\frac{1}{2}$ miles which is bad enough. Feel as if hot irons were struck down my marrow bones.

FRIDAY 1 MAY: On the road to Kotgur. May day at Mahasu inexpressibly lovely. Lay on the grass and felt health coming back, again. De brath a delightful man. What a blessed luxury is idleness. Eagles and shot at bottles.

SATURDAY 2 MAY: Mahasu to Mattiani. Only we stopped at Theog. Lady of the Party in the Family way. Unmitigated delight. My legs getting used to ground. Covered about eleven miles. Glorious weather.

SUNDAY 3 MAY: Theog Mattiani. A heavenly march.

MONDAY 4 MAY: Mattiani to Narkunda. Cold but I'm fit to walk for myself. Looks as if you could pitch a stone on the snowy ranges.

TUESDAY 5 MAY: Down to Kotgurgh a three thousand foot drop from pines to poppy fields. Rented a villa there and saw the Pardre[101] [sic]. Absolutely one of the queerest little devils that was ever cast away forty miles from anywhere.

WEDNESDAY 6 MAY: Day of rest wherein we photoed the Mission school. Every girl piling on as much jewellery as she had got. Very pretty females. Small wonder that the Padre has a charge of fornication preferred against him by non-converts. Should like to be Padre in these parts.

THURSDAY 7 MAY: De Brath persuaded to avoid hot marches to Rampur and went Bagi. Devils own climb of fourteen miles up hill the whole way. Bleak and desolate spot where I doctored d[e].B[rath's]. Khit[matgar]'s child with quinine. Poor little beggar. Next rest house burnt and hedge broken. Back to Khotgur tomorrow. I branch off at Nackunda. Raining heavily.

FRIDAY 8 MAY: More rain. Noor Ali cut open coolies eye.[102] Devil of a row all round and thus in the thick of it parted with De Brath and his wife. Felt lonely very. Heavy rain. Coolies mutinous and general shindy all round. Like 'em for their spirit but cursed Noor Ali for bringing me into such a mess. Did more than curse him and he bore it quietly. Seven on the back hard.

SATURDAY 9 MAY: Nackunda to Theog. 22 miles all in pouring rain. Great Scot how I walked. Thunder and lightning and pine struck. Difficulty with coolies. Saw two bears. Thought of Elisha the Tishbite[103] and bolted like blazes. Hadn't seen a bear loose before.

SUNDAY 10 MAY: Theog. Simla 17 miles. Thank heaven. Got back to civilization but up at Rekcliff. Nothing to be done there.

MONDAY 11 MAY: Ibbetson's[104] mostly to see pix.[?] Hewed off beard and felt better. Loafed and began to count days to getting in collar.

TUESDAY 12 MAY: More loafing and a walk and ride. Nothing to be done in my line—at least not yet. Must wait like Micawber for something to turn up.

WEDNESDAY 13 May–SUNDAY 24 MAY:[105] [no entries]

MONDAY 25 MAY: Queens Day. Gt. House Ball. Went with scar on cheek[106] painted up to the Eyes. Felt an abject worm and think looked it.

TUESDAY 26 MAY–MONDAY 13 JULY:[107] [no entries]

TUESDAY 14 JULY: Damn Thacker Spink & Co![108]

WEDNESDAY 15 JULY–FRIDAY 31 JULY: [no entries]

SATURDAY 1 AUGUST: Went over to the Walkers.[109] Banjoe Hayes[110] of Dagshai and wife staying there. Settled for a month. Wish they wouldn't put married couple next door to me with one ½ plank between. Saps ones morality.

SUNDAY 2 AUGUST: Same complaint. This is really ghastly. Only drawback to delightful visit. His Excellency[111] an Angel of the first water.

MONDAY 3 AUGUST: 'Pop' at Benmore[112] with Mrs. Hogan and Banjoe Hayes who made us both laugh consumedly.

TUESDAY 4 AUGUST: My own affair entirely. A wet day but deuced satisfactory.

WEDNESDAY 5 AUGUST: Begin to think I've been a fool but aint certain. Out for a ride round Jakko.[113] Weather vile.

THURSDAY 6 AUGUST–FRIDAY 14 AUGUST: [no entries]

SATURDAY 15 AUGUST: Got to go down. W[heeler]. dekks [?] too much to make it comfortable for me. Confound the man. But I must go. Cheerful interchange of telegrams all day.

SUNDAY 16 AUGUST: On this day I left Simla for Lahore. It was a pleasant three and half months and taught me much.

MONDAY 17 AUGUST: In train from morn till dewy eve with one Gempertz[114] on his way to kill things in Kashmere. A nice person but more lecherous than is safe for those parts. May he return safe *and sound*.

TUESDAY 18 AUGUST: Hell! 94 in the verandah at four in the morning. Went to office wanting to kill someone. Dined with the Light feet.[115] *Sit.*

WEDNESDAY 19 AUGUST: Worse. A blazing day. Took up the reins and went ahead. Dined with the *Kers*.[116] Madame seedy but not much out of spirits.

THURSDAY 20 AUGUST: Too savage to swear. Not a soul worth looking at in the Station. Dined with Levett Yeats[117] and laughed. *Mem.* Must really make my diary a working one. Went home and thought a good deal.

FRIDAY 21 AUGUST: Dinner with Tarleton Young[118] at His chummery. Where met one LeMaistre[119] who is a womans mind small and mean featured. He may be decent enough for aught I know. Usual philander in Gardens. Home to count the risks of my resolution.

SATURDAY 22 AUGUST: A heavy day: concluding with dinner at the Wrenchs'[120]—or at least beginning. Then a fall into the mire.

SUNDAY 23 AUGUST: Drake to spend Sunday. We talked and laughed though I was slack and would have slept. Small wonder.

MONDAY 24 AUGUST: Club. work. anticipation.

TUESDAY 25 AUGUST: I wonder! Club. Work of sorts. ? and gardens

WEDNESDAY 26 AUGUST: Gardens and talk to T. Young. He is sanguine and hopeful. I also. More anticipation.

THURSDAY 27 AUGUST: First period probation over. Mind easier. Now to look about me.

FRIDAY 28 AUGUST: Band after dinner when I did look about. Went round with Mrs L. which did not fill me with delight.

SATURDAY 29 AUGUST: Office day only. Got indistinct notion of playing Devils Pool at Club till two.

SUNDAY 30 AUGUST: A Mother Maturin day which came to nothing.

MONDAY 31 AUGUST–WEDNESDAY 9 SEPTEMBER: [no entries]

THURSDAY 10 SEPTEMBER: Feeling bad. In for fever I know. Went to bed.

FRIDAY 11 SEPTEMBER: Got it. Hell. All alone in house in bed.

SATURDAY 12 SEPTEMBER: Better but awful shaky. Out of bed.

SUNDAY 13 SEPTEMBER: All square. Drake in to cheer me up, and a pleasant enough Sunday between us.

MONDAY 14 SEPTEMBER: Went to office this morn. Too seedy to do much except cuss feebly at the Punkah wallah.

TUESDAY 15 SEPTEMBER: Three small scraps[121] of sorts about half a column. felt seedy. But went ahead at Trial by Judge.[122]

WEDNESDAY 16 SEPTEMBER: Got Trial by Judge in today. Aint half bad I think.

THURSDAY 17 SEPTEMBER: [no entry]

FRIDAY 18 SEPTEMBER: Three scraps. Pinhey on biting of [f] the nose of one's mistress. A'n [sic] extraordinary petition to the Viceroy and a still rummer pamphlet written by some blatant egoist.[123] Band after dinner.

SATURDAY 19 SEPTEMBER: [no entry]

SUNDAY 20 SEPTEMBER: Dull day. No one turned up. Spread work as thin as I could. Smoked and thought more than was good for me.

MONDAY 21 SEPTEMBER: Dead slow. Forget what did but know it was nothing of much importance.

TUESDAY 22 SEPTEMBER: Nothing much. Usual [frivol?] at the Hall but this time with M.J. who has something in her. Whether good or bad or indifferent I don't know.

WEDNESDAY 23 SEPTEMBER: Mule Hunt at Poona and State of Bantam.[124] Drearily comic scraps. To the people at Simla as usual. House full of whitewashing coolies. I'm a bit seedy and queer in the head.

THURSDAY 24 SEPTEMBER: Evolved my idea for the Unlimited Draw of Tick Boileau,[125] and did some of it.

FRIDAY 25 SEPTEMBER: Half column of accidents on Indian Railways scrap.[126] Otherwise nothing. Got another proof of His Excellency, which really aint half bad. To the band afterwards where went round with Miss C. A dull enough business. Home late and found a bad attack of measles[127] on me before I knew. Groaned under it till two.

SATURDAY 26 SEPTEMBER: Three small scraps[128] up to one column sent in. Wrote to People again and received late at night enormous letter from Wop of Europe[129] acknowledging receipt of necklace. What a clever girl it is. Dined at Club, and went to conjuring entertainment at Theatre.

SUNDAY 27 SEPTEMBER: Drake to Breakfast. Thereafter long letter to Margot—didn't write to people.

MONDAY 28 SEPTEMBER: Half col on Country bred racing in the Punjab.[130] Easy day. Went to Hennicke's performance[131] with [word illegible] and held converse will [sic] professor and wife. Motherly old woman who ought not to be in tights and spangles. Gave me idea for 'Mummers wife.'[132] Found broken down gharri on road and gave a woman and four children lift home. Mem. Name Mrs. Todd[133] and separated from her husband.

TUESDAY 29 SEPTEMBER: Three quarter column scrap on Lahore Agricultural Gardens and effusive notice which he deserved of Professor Hennicke.[134] Work. An easy day. Round with M.J. in evening. Queer unwholesome character. Felt slack.

WEDNESDAY 30 SEPTEMBER: Scraps Punjab Notes and Queries and attempted Human Sacrifice in Cochin.[135] One column in all. Sent in today. Got fifth proof of His Excellency. Parker[136] turned up at Club from Kasauli and drove me home. With Mrs. L[evett]. Y[eats]. and M.J. this even. Painfully slow and not even sure.

THURSDAY 1 OCTOBER: Hot weather dead. Smelt cold breezes today. Slack[137] has sent [sic] up Phantom Rickshaw for Xmas venture. Wrote to the people as per usual. Eight quarto pages. Got new table in swept and varnished. Pavey[138] dropped in to brekh at forenoon. Evening long talk with Y.L. French[139] down from Simla. Dug up a couple of opium dens in the city. Queer night altogether. Suddhu is his name.[140]

FRIDAY 2 OCTOBER: Scraps. Prjevalski's exploration; Hybridization of wheats; Grey Wilsons marriage Record and the Case of Tulsi Ram Mohun.[141] About one and a half columns altogether. To the Hall in the Even. where I danced with Miss C. Also talked with M.J. on P.F. a queer notion enough. Paid club bill.

SATURDAY 3 OCTOBER: Lay off aisy. Having one column and a bittock to my own check. Went ahead on the Tick Boileau biz and wrote to the people as per usual. Mem. To make bundobust about gharri with Dinanath.

. . . . .

[The regular entries in the diary end with October 3. At the end of the volume are twelve page openings, one for each month, each one headed with a printed line that reads "Cash Account" followed by the name of the month, its position in the year, and the number of days, thus: "Cash Account—JANUARY—1st Month, 31 days." On the three for January, February, and March, RK has entered the following accounts of his work.]

JANUARY

2nd.	Scrap. Capture of Bhamo.	3.	8.
3rd.	special. Proclamation day at Lahore	32.	8.
6th.	special. Week in Lahore.	20.	0.
7th.	special. A mofussil Exhibition. For one week	26. 82	0. 0
9th.	special. Twenty years after + 3 scraps.	18.	0.
12th.	Scraps/Burmah Art, Calcutta Municipality, Madras Ploughing Match, Blockade of Formosa	18.	0. 0.
(12th.	Poem 'On a recent Memorial' appeared in the Englishman of 9th)		
13th.	Scrap. O Donovan Rossa.	2.	12.
14th.	Notes. The 'Week in Lahore.'	22. 60.	0. 0. 12
16th.	Review. Piffard's Poems	11.	0. 0.
17th	Scrap. Growse's Bulandshahr.	8.	8.

18th.	Scrap. Cooke and Sons and Munqul Dass N.	5.	8
20th.	Scrap. Nawab of Mamdote, E. About para-Indian Press guide and local Gaiety Co	12.	4.
21.	Notes—'A Week in Lahore'—My share	15.	8
24	four scraps.	6.	0.
26.	Scrap. Bombay Conference.	5.	8
28th.	The Russians in Central Asia and Notes of the Week. All mine this time.	31.	0.
29th.	Three scraps. Hume. Ry. Accidents, dynamite.	11.	0.
(29th.	Poem to the Unknown Goddess[142] appeared in Pioneer 28th.)		
	Total for January	249.	0.

Nineteen days out of 27—

FEBRUARY

		R.	A.	P.[143]
Feb. 2nd.	Scrap. Porter's Speech at Madras	3.	0.	0
3rd.	Novoe Vremya and Journal Indian Art	14	0.	0.
4.	A Week in Lahore.	13.	0.	0
5	ODonovan Rossa. 2 locals.	6.	0.	0
6	Dr. G. Le Bon. Indian Crime. Rivers Thompson.	7.	8	
		43.	8.	0
9.	'Volapuk'	3.	0.	0
11.	A Week in Lahore.	30.	0.	0
12	Rangoon Chamber Commerce	3.	0	0
13.	Frauds Calcutta Dist Association	6.	0.	0
14.	Typhoid at Home and Scrap.	33.	0.	0
	For 12 working days.	118.	8.	0
16	Prejvalsky's explorations in Thibet and scrap on annexation of Chorea.	33.	0.	0

17.	Criticism Rosa Towers Company	7. 0. 0
18.	A Week in Lahore.	25. 0 0
19	local[144]	2. 8
20	local and scraps	11. 0
21	local.	6. 8.
23	local.	2. 0
		206 8.
24	local and scrap.	6. 0
25.	A week in Lahore.	23. 0
		235. 8

Two days off work through eye
Nineteen day out of 24.

March

	Rs. a. p
Mar. 3rd. Scrap. Upper Burma Annexation Company	5. 0. 0
4th A week in Lahore	30. 0. 0
5. Scraps. Fallons Proverbs and Stamps	10. 0. 0.
6 The Umballa Conference, a retrospect. Lord Dufferins cloture.	25. 0. 0
11th. A week in Lahore.	20. 0. 0
	90. 0. 0.

[The three items following are written on three of the blank pages at the end of the diary.]

To be written down for reference.

A monthly magazine—40 pages long primer on paper equal to that used for the Indian Review— to be published at Calcutta @ monthly expense Rs 50.0.0. This would be best managed with syndicate of five members eached [*sic*] contributing Rs 100 down, and a further payment of Rs. 50. within six months from the date of first payment. This would give initial capital of Rs.500 and a deferred capital of Rs. 250—total   Rs 750. 0. 0.

From this it will be necessary to deduct printing expenses of
first number =   Rs.50. 0. 0
Postage of 150 copies to, 124 members of
civil service or well educated men and the
newspapers who would be likely to take an interest
in the matter @ annas 6 per copy   Rs.9. 6. 0.
Expenses of printing on bank paper circular to
accompany copy   Rs.15. 0. 0
Postage and sundries allow liberal
margin   Rs.20. 0. 0
Total loss   = Rs.94. 6. 0
Which leaves the Syndicate with a reserve fund of Rs.400 odd
and the further reserve capital of Rs.250. to be called up when
wanted.—Nota Bene. Mr. Kipling (sen) is of opinion that I
could neither get men to write nor read it!

A SUMMARY OF THE YEARS ODD WORK—

Dis Aliter Visum[145]
De Profundis.[146]
City of Dreadful Night[147]
East and West[148]
Trial by Judge—
Twenty years after
Typhoid at Home
City of Evil Countenances
Proclamation day in Lahore
Lord Dufferins cloture
The Bungalow ballads[149]
My rival—[150]
To the unknown Goddess
Moon of other days
An Indignant protest[151]

Thacker Spink and Co's Estimate[152]

copies	pages	p. page								
1000	130	2/1	+ binding at –/3a per copy						456.	10
750	"	1/12	+	"	"	"	"		368.	2
500.	"	1/7.	"	"	"	"	"		280.	10.
	thinner paper		"	"	"	"	"			
1000.	"	1/14	"	"	"	"	"		431.	4
750	"	1/10	"	"	"	"	"		351.	14.
500	"	1/6.	"	"	"	"	"		272.	8.

GLOSSARY OF ANGLO-INDIAN
WORDS AND PHRASES

ayah	nurse, maid
baba	child
Belait	England, or Europe
bundobast, bundobust	arrangement, agreement
Burra Sahib	great man
Burra Sahib Bahadur	very great man
Chaaszee	farmer, agriculturist
dacoit	robber, one of a gang
dali	complimentary offering of fruit, flowers and the like
durbar	court, public audience
gharri	cart, carriage; "broom-gharri" is a brougham
ghaut	landing place, quay
gymkhana	sports ground, or sports meeting, including horse racing
hamal	porter
hubshee, hubshi	a black
khitmatgar	servant, especially a table servant

maidan	open space, park, common
meeta	bearer
memsahib	the lady of the house
mofussil	the provinces, country districts
pagal	mad, foolish
punkah wallah	*punkah* is a large fixed fan; *wallah* signifies the agent or doer: in this case, the servant who pulls the punkah rope
put-put	spank-spank
ranee	Hindu queen
serai	inn for travellers, built around a courtyard
tiffin	lunch

NOTES

SOMETHING OF MYSELF

Chapter 1 A Very Young Person

1 **Give me ... the rest** Variously attributed, to Loyola specifically or to
the Jesuits generally, or to Pascal, or Cardinal Newman, or Lenin. I
have not found the version that RK quotes, but he no doubt had the
Jesuits in mind. See his remark in a letter to André Chevrillon: "I was
born in Bombay (1865) and there I lived till I was between five and six –
those terrible first years of which the Jesuits know the value" (October
22, 1919: *Etudes Anglaises*, 19 [1966], p. 407).

2 **Ayah** A glossary is provided on pp. 219–20 for Anglo-Indian words
and phrases.

3 **my sister** Alice Macdonald Kipling (1868–1948), always called
"Trix," RK's only sibling. She married Col. John Fleming.

4 **Meeta** The word *meeta* means "bearer."

5 **vernacular idiom ... dreamed in** Hindustani is meant. Punch, in
"Baa Baa, Black Sheep" soon forgets "the Hindustani once his second
speech," and in "The Potted Princess" Punch and Judy "always talked
Hindustani because they understood it better than English" (Sussex
Edition, xxx, p. 11).

6 **Lord Mayo** Richard Southwell Bourke (1822–72), sixth Earl of Mayo,
Governor-General of India, 1869–72; assassinated on February 8, 1872.

Since RK was then living with Mrs. Holloway in Southsea and his mother was in Bombay this memory is confused.

7 **my Father's School of Art** The Sir Jamsetjee Jejeebhoy School of Art and Industry, Bombay, where JLK was professor of architectural sculpture, 1865–75. The house where RK lived in Bombay was on the grounds of the school.

8 **'Terry Sahib'** Wilkins Terry; beyond the fact of his name and that he was JLK's assistant, I have found nothing about him. He had been at the school since its founding in 1857. It has been said that Terry hired JLK while on a visit to England, but the evidence is all against this.

9 **'hens of Bombay'** The limerick and the picture were drawn by JLK in a copy of Edward Lear's *Book of Nonsense*, now in the Kipling Papers at the University of Sussex.

10 **a time in a ship** Alice Kipling left India in February 1868 with her son, then just over two years old; she was expecting the birth of her second child and wished to have it in England. The child, Trix, was born in June, and mother and children left England to return to Bombay in November.

11 **P. & O. *Ripon*** The paddlewheel steamer *Ripon*, 1,500 tons, was in the P. & O.'s service, 1846–70.

12 **small girl . . . whose face stands out still** RK describes this moment in 1868 in "A Return to the East" (*Egypt of the Magicians*, 1913): "Such a town, for instance, as Zagazig, last seen by a very small boy who was lifted out of a railway-carriage and set down beneath a whitewashed wall under naked stars in an illimitable emptiness because, they told him, the train was on fire . . . So all his life, the word 'Zagazig' carried memories of a brick shed, the flicker of an oil-lamp's floating wick, a sky full of eyes, and an engine coughing in a desert at the world's end" (p. 225).

13 **Then came a new small house** RK has here collapsed his first two visits to England. The first, in 1868 (see note 10, above), was followed by a visit of the entire family in 1871: they left India in April and stayed with various relatives over the next eight months. In November 1871 the parents returned to Bombay, leaving the children in England.

14 **I lived in that house . . . six years** The house (which still stands) is Lorne Lodge, 4 Campbell Road, Southsea; the woman was a Mrs. Sarah Holloway, and her husband, Pryse Agar Holloway, once an officer in the merchant marine. It was the standard practice of the English in India to send their children back to England as early as possible, and Alice Kipling preferred that her children should not stay

with relatives: "it led to complications," she said (Edith Plowden, "Fond Memory": MS recollections, Baldwin Papers, University of Sussex). RK and Trix went to Lorne Lodge in October 1871; they left it in April 1877.

15 **Navarino** Where an allied fleet defeated the Turks in 1827.

16 *By Celia's Arbour* The novel (1878) by Besant and James Rice, describes the Portsmouth of Besant's childhood, before the middle of the century.

17 **Portsmouth Hard** The street outside the entrance to the Royal Dockyard.

18 *Alert* (**or** *Discovery*) The ships of the 1875–76 Arctic expedition commanded by Sir George Nares; they returned to Portsmouth in 1876. RK's memory of this sight is confused, since Holloway died in 1874.

19 **the old Captain died** Holloway died September 29, 1874.

20 **an only son** Henry Thomas Holloway. Trix remembered him as having "dark eyes, set near together, and black hair, plastered with pomatum" ("Some Childhood Memories of RK," *Chambers's Journal*, March 1939, p. 169).

21 *Six to Sixteen* *Aunt Judy's Magazine* for 1872; Mrs. Ewing's story is about Anglo-Indian children sent back to England for their education. The identification of this and of the other items of his early reading mentioned by RK is largely the work of Roger Lancelyn Green.

22 *Tales at Tea-time* E.H. Knatchbull-Hugesson, *Tales at Tea-Time*, 1872.

23 *The Old Shikarri* Major H.A. Leveson published a number of stories of hunting and adventure under the pseudonym of "The Old Shekarry," 1860–74. "Shekarry" or "Shikarri" means "sportsman" or "hunter" or "hunter's guide."

24 **an old magazine** RK identifies this in "Baa Baa, Black Sheep" as *Sharpe's Magazine*, i.e., vol. 1 (1845–46).

25 **'mighty Helvellyn'** Not Wordsworth but Scott, "Helvellyn": corrected in later printings of *Something of Myself*.

26 *The Hope of the Katzikopfs* F.E. Paget, *The Hope of the Katzekopfs*, 1844; RK's spelling is corrected in later printings.

27 **This bore fruit afterwards** The poem is Bishop Richard Corbet's "The Fairies' Farewell" (1648), which RK quotes in "Weland's Sword" (*Puck of Pook's Hill*) and which gave RK the title of his *Rewards and Fairies*.

28 **some wicked baboons** James Greenwood, *King Lion*, a story serialized in the *Boy's Own Paper*, 1864.

29 **One – blue and fat –** Menella Bute Smedley and Elizabeth Anna Hart, *Poems Written for a Child*, 1868.

30 **'the name of England . . . could not burn'** RK's recollection is confused: the savages in the poem "Heroes," when commanded to free their slaves, think that "the name of England / Is something that will burn."

31 **The other book – brown and fat** Elizabeth Anna Hart, *Child Nature*, 1869.

32 **'Cumnor Hall'** William Julius Mickle, "Cumnor Hall," 1784. Roger Lancelyn Green has pointed out that these lines are quoted in the last chapter of Scott's *Kenilworth* (Harbord, vii, p. 3363).

33 *Robinson Crusoe* RK's earliest extant letter, conjecturally dated December 1872, thanks his uncle Alfred Baldwin for a copy of *Robinson Crusoe* (Kipling Papers): perhaps he had more than one copy, or has confused the giver?

34 **the Provost of Oriel** Edward Hawkins (1789–1882), Provost of Oriel. Why and how RK was taken to see him remain unexplained, though, as Roger Lancelyn Green notes (Harbord, vii, p. 3363), the Holloway family came from Charlbury, near Oxford, and had a number of connections with the university. Hawkins left Oxford in 1874, so that RK's visit was not later than that year.

35 **an old gentleman . . . near Havant** Captain Holloway's brother, General Sir Thomas Holloway (1810–75), of West Lodge, Havant.

36 **Aunt Georgy . . . North End Road** Aunt Georgy ("Georgie" in later printings) was Georgiana Macdonald Burne-Jones (1840–1920), the second of the Macdonald sisters. In 1860 she married Edward (afterwards Sir Edward) Burne-Jones (1833–98), the painter. Their house, now destroyed, stood at the Kensington end of North End Road and had once belonged to the novelist Samuel Richardson, who wrote *Clarissa* and *Sir Charles Grandison* there. Burne-Jones moved there in 1867 and remained until his death in 1898.

37 **bell-pull . . . rang it** The bell-pull still hangs at the door of Bateman's.

38 **my two cousins** Margaret (1866–1953), afterwards Mrs. J.W. Mackail; and Philip (1861–1926), like his father a gifted painter but without his father's success.

39 **William Morris** (1834–96) The poet, painter, craftsman, socialist; an intimate friend of Burne-Jones from their university days. The decorating firm of Morris and Co. had been founded in 1861, so RK is mistaken in thinking that Morris was "just beginning" to fabricate such things as tables and chairs.

40 **'Browning'** Robert Browning (1812–89), the poet; perhaps the most powerful single literary influence on RK, who liked to think of himself as of the brotherhood of Fra Lippo Lippi: see pp. 11, 22, 25, 43, 83–84.

41 *The Pirate* By Sir Walter Scott, 1821.

42 **'Norna of the Fitful Head'** See *The Pirate*, ch. 21.

43 **Saga of Burnt Njal** Not the "Saga of Burnt Njal" but "The Story of the Ere-Dwellers (the Eyrbyggja Saga)," not published until 1892, in the *Saga Library*.

44 **Why . . . For admonition** Browning, "Fra Lippo Lippi," lines 124–26.

45 **terrible little day-school** Identified by Roger Lancelyn Green as "Hope House" in Green Street, Southsea, conducted by Thomas Henry Vickery (*Kipling and the Children* [London, Elek Books, 1965], pp. 44–45).

46 **placard 'Liar' between my shoulders** Since this episode has a literary precedent in Dickens's *David Copperfield*, and is used by RK in "Baa Baa, Black Sheep," it has sometimes been doubted. RK's sister affirmed it to be true (Lord Birkenhead, *Rudyard Kipling* [New York, Random House, 1978], p. 26).

47 **'Who . . . concern himself with glass?'** This has been attributed to the Koran but is not to be found there.

48 **the Mother returned from India** In April 1877. The news that had brought Alice Kipling to her son's rescue came from Aunt Georgie, who wrote at the beginning of 1877 to report that RK was evidently deeply unhappy.

49 **on the edge of Epping Forest** The farm, belonging to a Mr. Dally, was called Golding's Hill, near Loughton, Essex.

50 **A cousin** Stanley Baldwin (1867–1947), afterwards first Earl Baldwin. Prime minister, 1923–24, 1924–29, 1935–37. He was the only son of RK's aunt Louisa Macdonald Baldwin and Alfred Baldwin.

51 **Brompton Road** 227 Brompton Road, now part of the Harrod's site.

52 **South Kensington Museum** Now the Victoria and Albert Museum. Before his marriage, Kipling's father had worked on the decoration of the building, not completed for many years.

53 **divided the treasures child-fashion** According to his sister, they had an elaborate plan to rob the jewel gallery of the museum, a plan described in her "More Childhood Memories of Rudyard Kipling," *Chambers's Journal*, July 1939, pp. 510–11.

54 **my Father 'wrote things' also** Both Alice and Lockwood Kipling were regular contributors to the English-language newspapers in India,

especially to those in Bombay, Lahore, and Allahabad.

55 **Sidonia the Sorceress** Johann Wilhelm Meinhold, *Sidonia the Sorceress* (1847). The book was a great favorite among the Pre-Raphaelites.

CHAPTER II The School before its Time

1 **school at the far end of England** The United Services College at Westward Ho!, North Devon, founded in 1874 by a group of Indian Army officers to provide inexpensive schooling for their children in England. It occupied the "twelve bleak houses by the shore" ("Let Us Now Praise Famous Men") left over from an unsuccessful real-estate speculation and bought cheaply by the school's governors.

2 **Cormell Price, otherwise 'Uncle Crom'** Price (1835–1910) was a friend from school-days of Burne-Jones and of Henry Macdonald, both among RK's uncles. Like Burne-Jones, Price was much influenced by his acquaintance with William Morris at Oxford, and was introduced into the Pre-Raphaelite group. From 1863 to 1874 he was Master of the Modern Side at Haileybury; in 1874 he became the first head of the United Services College and directed it for twenty years.

3 **three dear ladies** They were the sisters Mary and Georgiana Craik, and their friend Miss Winnard, of 26 Warwick Gardens, Kensington. The Miss Craiks were the daughters of the literary scholar George Lillie Craik. Georgiana, later Mrs. May, was a prolific writer of novels. Alice Kipling did not return to India until late in 1880, more than three years after she had left to rescue her son in 1877. Trix appears to have stayed on with Mrs. Holloway for at least some of those years before joining the ladies of Warwick Gardens, with whom she remained until she returned to India in 1883.

4 **Mr. and Miss de Morgan** William De Morgan (1839–1917), who made decorative tiles at his Fulham pottery before turning novelist at the age of 67; in his work as a craftsman he was closely associated with William Morris. His sister Mary Augusta (1850–1907) assisted him in his tile-making and was herself a writer of fairy stories.

5 **Jean Ingelow** (1820–97) A poet of high reputation in her time.

6 **Christina Rossetti** (1830–94) Poet, the sister of Dante Gabriel Rossetti.

7 **Firmilian** By William Aytoun, 1854, a parody of the "Spasmodic School" of poetry.

8 **The Moonstone** and **The Woman in White** Both by Wilkie Collins, 1868 and 1860.

9 **Wellington's Indian Despatches, which fascinated me** As they did Wellington: on re-reading them in his old age, he exclaimed "Damned good! I don't know how the devil I ever managed to write 'em" (J. St. Loe Strachey, *The Adventure of Living* [London, Hodder and Stoughton, 1922], 23).

10 **Spring of '78** RK arrived at the United Services College in early January 1878.

11 **my first term, which was horrible** On January 24, 1878, in RK's second week at the school, Alice Kipling wrote to Price that "this morning I had no letter from Ruddy – yesterday I had four. It is the roughness of the lads he seems to feel most – he doesn't grumble to me – but he is lonely and down – I was his chum you know, and he hasn't found another yet. . . . The lad has a great deal that is feminine in his nature – and a little sympathy from any greater will reconcile him to his changed life more than anything" (MS, Baldwin Papers, University of Sussex). For the roughness of the school, see especially L.C. Dunsterville, *Stalky's Reminiscences* (London, Jonathan Cape, 1928), ch. 2.

12 **'all smiles stopped together'** Browning, "My Last Duchess," line 46.

13 **Indian Exhibits** This episode with his father began in June 1878; it was the first that he had seen of his father since the desolate parting at Southsea in 1871. The Paris visit is described in the opening pages of *Souvenirs of France*.

14 **Jules Verne** (1828–1905) Writer of tales of fantasy and adventure.

15 **I hold . . . in Paradise** A distant parody of the opening stanza of Tennyson, *In Memoriam*.

16 ***Souvenirs of France*** Published in 1933.

17 **Stalky, M'Turk, and Beetle** The names given to the schoolboy triumvirate in RK's *Stalky & Co.* Stalky was Lionel Charles Dunsterville (1865–1946), afterwards Major-General Dunsterville. He was one of the early pupils at the school, and spent, in all, eight years there. M'Turk was George Charles Beresford (1864–1938), of Drumlease, Dromahair, County Leitrim. He went out to India as an engineer but returned to study art and became a photographer and antiques dealer. Both Dunsterville and Beresford published accounts of their school days with RK: Dunsterville, *Stalky's Reminiscences*, 1928; and Beresford, *School Days with Kipling*, 1936.

18 **before we were thirteen** The first concrete evidence of this triple alliance is RK's poem "The Dusky Crew," written in 1879.

19 **never troubled us again** Beresford, "The Battle of One against Three," *Kipling Journal*, June 1937, pp. 40–43, gives a very different version of what may have been the same occasion.

20 **Ruskin** John Ruskin (1819–1900), the impassioned voice of artistic conscience in nineteenth-century England.

21 **'socialisation of educational opportunities'** I do not know the source of the quotation. The idea is that the three divided the work to be done: see "The Impressionists," *Stalky & Co.*, p. 103.

22 **Little Hartopp** Herbert Arthur Evans (1846–1923), called "Little Hartopp" in *Stalky & Co.* When asked years later whether he remembered RK as a student he replied "Kipling? Yes! Yes! Tiresome little boy!" (*Kipling Journal*, October 1945, p. 16).

23 *Adventures of Dunsterforce* 1920, an account of Dunsterville's adventures in command of an improvised force in North West Persia and the Caucasus, sent to reorganize Russian resistance to the Germans and Turks in 1918. "Dunsterforce" got as far as Baku, but, without support, was compelled to withdraw.

24 **'lived and loved to destroy illusions'** "The Propagation of Knowledge," in *Debits and Credits*, 1926, p. 279.

25 **C——** William Carr Crofts (1846–1912), RK's master in English and in classics, the model for King in *Stalky & Co.*

26 **my House-master** Matthew Henry Pugh (1852–1914), mathematics master, caricatured as Prout in *Stalky & Co.*

27 **Sandhurst or Woolwich Preliminary** Examination for The Royal Military College at Sandhurst and the Royal Military Academy at Woolwich, as they then were.

28 **'pi-jaw'** "To give moral advice to; admonish"; school and university slang from the 1880s (Eric Partridge, *A Dictionary of Slang and Unconventional English*, 8th edn. [New York, Macmillan, 1984]).

29 **Third Book** Book III, 27, of Horace's *Odes* does not refer to Cleopatra; I, 37, does.

30 *The City of Dreadful Night* By James Thomson ("B.V."), 1874.

31 *Parables from Nature* By Mrs. Margaret Gatty, published in five series, 1855–71.

32 *Hiawatha* By Henry Wadsworth Longfellow, 1855.

33 **'as rare things will'** Browning, "One Word More," line 31.

34 *Aurora Leigh* By Mrs. Browning, 1856; RK got his title "The Light that Failed" from this.

35 *Men and Women* By Robert Browning, 1855.

36 *Atalanta in Calydon* 1865: the lines quoted come from near the end of *Atalanta*.

37 **'Heathen Chinee'** 1870, originally titled "Plain Language from Truthful James"; RK parodies the poem in a letter to Andrew Lang in 1889 (Morton Cohen [ed.], *Rudyard Kipling to Rider Haggard* [London, Hutchinson, 1965], 25–27).

38 **not without intention** Something seems to have been deleted before the second paragraph, which refers to "injustices of this sort" without any injustices having been described.

39 **H——** F.W.C. Haslam (1848–1924), classics master at the United Services College, 1874–79, afterwards taught at Canterbury College, Christchurch, New Zealand.

40 *The Pink 'Un* *The Sporting Times*, printed on pink paper.

41 **New Zealand** This was at Christchurch, New Zealand, where RK called on November 3, 1891.

42 **School Paper** *The United Services College Chronicle*, defunct but revived expressly for RK to edit, which he did through seven numbers, June 1881–July 1882.

43 **I should learn Russian** After leaving Oxford and before taking up his teaching in England, Price had served as tutor in the family of Count Orloff-Davidoff in St. Petersburg.

44 **Vevey** A cigar made in the Swiss town of that name.

45 **Joaquin Miller** Pen name of Cincinnatus Hiner Miller (1841?–1913), slightly fraudulent American poet of the West, who owed much of his reputation to an English vogue for his work. "The Battle of Assaye" is collected in RK's *Early Verse*, 1900.

46 *Competition Wallah* By George Otto Trevelyan, 1864, a book of sketches evoking post-Mutiny English life in India.

47 **holiday house at Rottingdean** The Burne-Joneses bought North End House, on the village green of Rottingdean, Sussex, a few miles east of Brighton, in 1880. Rottingdean was thereafter a center for Kipling, his aunts, uncles, cousins, and friends.

48 **'The bodies . . . of Death and of Birth'** Swinburne, *Atalanta in Calydon*, second choric ode. RK moved to The Elms in 1897, shortly after the birth of his son John, and remained there until 1902.

CHAPTER III Seven Years' Hard

1 **I am . . . to my face** Browning, "Fra Lippo Lippi," opening lines.

2 **sixteen years and nine months** That is, on October 18, 1882, when RK arrived in Bombay on the *S.S. Brindisi*, which had sailed from London on September 20.

3 **Lahore School of Art and Museum** JLK had gone to Lahore, the capital of the Punjab, in 1875 to be the head of the new Mayo School of Art and curator of the Central Museum.

4 **my sister came out** Trix came out with her mother to Lahore in December 1883.

5 **one daily paper of the Punjab** RK was sub-editor of the *Civil and Military Gazette*. The appointment had been arranged through his father, who knew the proprietors and who was himself a regular contributor to the *CMG*.

6 **the great *Pioneer* . . . proprietorship** *The Pioneer* was the leading paper outside those of the Presidency cities of India – Calcutta, Bombay, and Madras – and regarded as the peer of those. The principal proprietors were Sir George Allen and Sir James Walker.

7 **My Chief** Stephen Wheeler (1854–1937) edited the *CMG* until his return to England in 1887.

8 **Our chief picnic rendezvous . . . mausoleum of ghosts** The chief picnic grounds were the Shalimar Gardens, east of the city, built by Shah Jahan; the tomb of Anarkali, one of the "desired dead women" mentioned by RK, was built by the Emperor Jahangir and used by the British for the storage of records. Runjit (or Ranjit) Singh (1780–1839) was the founder of the Sikh power in the Punjab; Fort Lahore was formerly his palace.

9 **hit the crowds on the feet with the gun-butt** In "The City of the Two Creeds," *CMG*, October 1, 1887, RK describes this method of quelling riot, though the soldiers in that account use "lance butts."

10 **described openings of big bridges . . . European community of Lahore** Most of these references can be documented: RK wrote about the openings of bridges in the *CMG*, March 2 and May 18, 1887; about floods on railways, August 6, 1887; about village festivals, March 30, 1886; about communal riots in Lahore, October 19 and 22, 1885; about visits of Viceroys to neighboring Princes, March 22, 1884; about Army reviews, February 18, 1887; about receptions of an Afghan potentate, March 24–April 14, 1885. No items about divorce or murder have been positively identified, though doubtless he wrote such things; nor has a story about lepers among the butchers of Lahore been found. He *did* do a sufficiently disgusting story about the milk supply of Lahore, February 14, 1885. Incidentally, at the time of his visit to the Khyber Pass (April 1885) he makes no mention of being shot at, either in his articles for the *CMG* or in his letters, though a letter of January 30, 1886, says that he

had been threatened by a native with a knife in the preceding April as he walked towards the Khyber Pass,

11 **Squeers' method of instruction** Dickens, *Nicholas Nickleby*, ch. 8: Wackford Squeers, the brutal schoolmaster, goes upon "the practical mode of teaching" by putting the boys to menial labor.

12 **a Native State** This was perhaps Patiala, where RK was sent to report the Viceroy's visit in March 1884.

13 **Kay Robinson** Edward Kay Robinson (1854–1928), edited the *CMG* 1887–95; returned to England where he continued to work as a journalist.

14 **Phil Robinson** (1847–1902) published *In My Indian Garden*, 1878.

15 ***Timeo ... dona ferentes*** *Aeneid*, II, 48: "I fear the Greeks, even when bringing gifts."

16 **Central Russian Khanates** This was in 1884; Alikhanoff (or Ali Khan) was a Moslem soldier in the service of the Russians.

17 ***sax-aul*** A shrub (*Anabasis ammodendron*) growing on the steppes of central Asia.

18 **I fell sick in New York** This is the only reference in *Something of Myself* to the tragic experience of 1899, when RK's daughter Josephine, aged seven, died of pneumonia and when RK himself nearly died of the same disease. The account of his delirious visions, dictated by RK, was published by Lord Birkenhead, *Rudyard Kipling* (New York, Random House, 1978), pp. 370–76.

19 **In 1885** Altered to "In the early 'Eighties" in later printings. The reference is to Gladstone's second ministry.

20 **Native Judges should try white women** The reference is to the so-called Ilbert Bill, named after its official sponsor, the Legal Member of Council, Sir Courteney Ilbert, and introduced in February 1883. In trying to remove certain anomalies from judicial practice, the bill incidentally allowed native judges the authority to try British subjects.

21 **Viceroy** George Frederick Samuel Robinson (1827–1909), first Marquess of Ripon, Viceroy of India, 1880–84. He was a Liberal, a Catholic convert, and a fat man, facts that partly account for RK's contemptuous language.

22 **Indian White Paper** Setting forth the government's plan for the administration of India and under discussion from the end of 1932. Despite strong opposition the plan passed into law in August 1935, three days after RK began *Something of Myself*. From RK's point of view the plan yielded far too much of British authority to the Indians.

23 **'Your dam' rag has ratted over the Bill'** The *CMG* announced editorially in its November 19, 1883, number that it thought the Ilbert Bill should pass, since further opposition was "unreasonable"; that was perhaps the occasion that RK describes here.

24 **when one is twenty** RK was not yet eighteen at the time.

25 **made him a Knight** Neither Allen nor Walker was knighted at this time: see the Introduction, p. xxiv.

26 **In '85** Not 1885, but April 1886, though he was, as he says, under age, since he would not be twenty-one until December 30, 1886.

27 **Araya and Brahmo Samaj** Reform Hindu movements.

28 **a Jew tyler** A tyler is the doorkeeper of a Masonic lodge.

29 **another world . . . which I needed** RK slightly exaggerates the mixed character of the Lodge: it certainly had four, and perhaps as many as six, non-Europeans, in RK's day, a respectable proportion in a membership of only about thirty (Harry Carr, "Kipling and the Craft," *Ars Quatuor Coronatorum*, 77 [1964], p. 221).

30 **accounts of these prowls** The best-known is perhaps the sketch "The City of Dreadful Night" in the *CMG*, September 10, 1885 (*Life's Handicap*).

31 **Fort Lahore and . . . Mian Mir Cantonments** Fort Lahore, part of the walled city of Lahore, was garrisoned from Mian Mir, the cantonments some three miles to the east of Lahore.

32 **2nd Fifth Fusiliers** The 2nd Battalion of the Royal Northumberland Fusiliers, 5th Foot; they were at Lahore, 1882-87.

33 **30th East Lancashire** The East Lancashire Regiment, 30th Foot.

34 **31st East Surrey** The 1st Battalion, The East Surrey Regiment, 31st Foot, stationed at Allahabad.

35 **turned out a Quarter-Guard of Her Majesty's troops** RK also refers to this episode in "Quo Fata Vocant" (1902): "the clatter of sleepy feet descending the brick steps of the Quarter-guard; and the disgraceful attempt of a civilian at 2 A.M. to personate Visiting Rounds" (Sussex Edition, xxx, 257).

36 **Lock Hospitals** Hospitals for venereal disease, after the London hospital of that name.

37 **Lord Roberts** Field Marshall Lord Roberts (1832-1914), Commander-in-Chief in India, and afterwards commander in the Boer War. He is celebrated in RK's "Bobs."

38 **a full Colonel** This was probably in the summer of 1888, after the stories collected in *Soldiers Three* had begun to appear.

39 **Simla** A resort 7,000 feet high in the foothills of the Himalayas, Simla

was the summer capital both for the supreme government of India, normally resident in Calcutta, and for the government of the Punjab, whose home was in Lahore. Simla sheltered a very special society of high officials and their families, brought together for a short time in dramatic isolation from the rest of India.

40 **Correspondent . . . a power in the land** Howard Hensman (?–1916), famous both as the correspondent of the *Pioneer* at government headquarters and as the best bridge-player in India. Remembered as "wiser than most on most matters" and "one of the kindest and best" (General Sir Ian Hamilton, *Listening for the Drums* [London, Faber and Faber, 1944], p. 51).

41 **Madame Blavatsky** Helena Petrovna Blavatsky (1831–91), founder of the Theosophical Society in 1875. She resided in India after 1879.

42 **Editor** Alfred Percy Sinnett (1840–1921), editor of the *Pioneer*, 1872–88; he was an ardent Theosophist and published widely on the occult.

43 **I was sent off for rest . . . and his wife** See, below, RK's diary for 1885.

44 **'all might . . . henceforth and for ever'** From the "ascription" used at the end of the Anglican service.

45 **developed** Thus in text: for "devolved"?

46 **hirpling** A Scottish dialect word, meaning "to move with a limp"; RK uses it several times in his writings.

47 **my twenty-fourth year** That is, the year in which he left India, 1889.

48 **Lawrie** Dr. E.B. Lawrie, surgeon and professor at the Lahore Medical School.

49 *All in a Garden Fair* 1883.

50 **seemed pleased** RK met Besant (1836–1901) shortly after RK's arrival in London in October 1889, and they got on well. Besant sponsored him for the Savile, introduced him to a literary agent, and brought him in as a member of the Authors' Society, of which Besant was the chief animating spirit.

51 **our paper changed its shape and type** With the issue of August 1, 1887. See RK's "Our Change. By Us," *CMG*, August 1, 1887 (Thomas Pinney, *Kipling's India* [London, Macmillan, 1986] pp. 243–46).

52 **One new feature . . . 'write short'** This somewhat elliptical passage may be elaborated: the London *Globe* (printed on pink paper) had a regular story that ran on to the first column of the next page. In order to complete the reading, then, the reader had to turn over the page; hence the term "turnover." Robinson had worked for the *Globe* before coming to India, which was no doubt a factor in the decision to imitate the

practice. The "turnover" space was largely filled by RK in its first months, and what he wrote for it – including most of the stories collected in *Plain Tales from the Hills* – was rigidly confined to the space allotted. He had thus to "write short."

53 **a General . . . in the Great War** Brigadier General Frederick Hugh Gordon Cunliffe (1861–1955), at USC 1876–79; commanded the Nigeria Regiment, 1914–18.

54 ***Quartette*** This was published as a Christmas supplement to the *CMG*, and was wholly the work of the Kipling family: three items were by JLK; four by Alice Kipling; one by Trix; and the remaining eight by RK, including "The Strange Ride of Morrowbie Jukes" and "The Phantom 'Rickshaw."

55 ***Plain Tales from the Hills*** The series of this title began not in 1885 but on November 2, 1886.

56 ***Indigo Planters' Gazette*** Nothing by RK is known in a periodical of this name, but "The Ballad of Ahmed Shah" appeared in *The Indian Planters' Gazette, c.* 1886–88.

57 **'too good to inquire'** Charles James Apperley ("Nimrod"), *The Chace, the Turf, and the Road*, 1837, p. 51, describing a fox hunt: "a report is flying about that one of the field is badly hurt, and something is heard of a collar-bone being broken, others say it is a leg; but the pace is *too good* to inquire."

58 **a man under me** RK had several times to take over the chief editorial duty in the absence or illness of his superior; if he was lucky, temporary help might be sent to him; perhaps he means one of these occasions. Or perhaps he refers to the weeks he spent serving as relief editor of the *CMG* after he had been transferred to the *Pioneer*.

59 **Elia-like 'turnovers'** That is, in the manner of Charles Lamb's *Essays of Elia*. RK refers to this again in "My First Book," below.

60 **a writer called Browning** This review has not been identified.

61 **In '87** The precise date is not known, but it is probable that RK left Lahore for Allahabad in November 1887.

62 **a most holy river** Allahabad is on the Ganges, at its junction with the Jumna.

63 **chief proprietor** George Allen; RK lived in his house on first going to Allahabad.

64 **Would I not?** The weekly paper, called *The Week's News*, began publication on January 7, 1888.

65 **'sight of means to do ill deeds'** Shakespeare, *King John*, IV, ii, 219.

66 **Bret Harte** A story by Bret Harte appeared in the first number of *The Week's News*.

67 **''Twas ask ... more's ready'** Browning, "Fra Lippo Lippi," lines 163–64.

68 **Daemon** The first occurrence of this term, which RK uses in its sense of an attendant genius, or of a spirit mediating between the human and the divine; the association is with ancient theories of inspiration, or, specifically, with the *daemon* of Socrates, an inward monitor.

69 **'Gyp'** Pseudonym of the Comtesse de Martel de Janville (1849–1932); her *Autour du Mariage* appeared in 1883.

70 *The Story of the Gadsbys* Most of *The Story of the Gadsbys* appeared serially in *The Week's News*, May 26–August 18, 1888.

71 **'A Wayside Comedy'** *The Week's News*, January 21, 1888; since this was only the third number of *The Week's News*, the story rejected by his mother cannot have long preceded it.

72 **key to its method** Neither the Frenchman nor the phrase has been identified.

73 **Chief Correspondent** Hensman: see above, note 40 of this chapter.

74 **Native State mines ... and the like** The assignments that produced the articles collected in *From Sea to Sea* (1900) as "Letters of Marque," "The City of Dreadful Night," "Among the Railway Folk," "The Giridih Coal-Fields," and "In an Opium Factory." Almost all were written in 1888.

75 **knighthood in due course** Allen was knighted in 1897.

76 **And if ... you be!** "A Job Lot," *Pioneer*, September 1, 1888 (Andrew Rutherford, *Early Verse by Rudyard Kipling* [Oxford, Clarendon Press, 1986], pp. 421–23).

77 **railway bookstall volumes** These were the volumes of the "Indian Railway Library" series, made up largely but not exclusively of stories already published in *The Week's News*: *Soldiers Three*, *The Story of the Gadsbys*, *In Black and White*, *Under the Deodars*, and *The Phantom 'Rickshaw* appeared in 1888; *Wee Willie Winkie* in 1889.

78 **man who ... railway bookstalls** Emile Moreau (1856–1937), senior partner in the Allahabad firm of A.H. Wheeler and Co.

79 **I sold him ... royalty** RK bought back the copyright of the "Indian Railway Library" volumes in 1894 for £1,200.

80 *Plain Tales ... Departmental Ditties* These two titles were owned not by the firm of Wheeler but the Calcutta publisher Thacker, Spink, and Co.

81 **I left India for England** RK's decision to try his fortunes in England had been firmly taken as early as May 1888. The narrative at this point makes a large jump, omitting as it does the eight months of RK's journey through the Orient and across the United States, and saying nothing of his travelling companions, Professor and Mrs. Hill (see Introduction, p. xii).

82 **managing director** His name was William J. Dare.

83 **publication and sale** The scramble to exploit RK's Indian work began when the firm of A.H. Wheeler published three volumes of collected sketches from the *CMG* and the *Pioneer*: *The City of Dreadful Night and Other Sketches*, 1890; *The Smith Administration*, 1891; and *Letters of Marque*, 1891. These RK succeeded in having "suppressed," but the damage, as he saw it, was done, and the material included in Wheeler's suppressed volumes has been public ever since.

84 **alone and unsponsored** This happened in 1935, not long before RK set to work on *Something of Myself*.

85 **weathered the storm** RK invested in the *CMG* in 1935, partly out of sentiment. The paper ceased publication in 1963; the office file of the newspaper was recently (1983) acquired by the National Library of Pakistan; another file is in the India Office Library, London.

86 **Try as he will . . . our hearts will be** "The Virginity," 1914 (*The Years Between*).

87 **here I 'worked'** The building in which RK worked has long since been demolished. The memorial tablet to RK (which may have survived more than one of the *CMG*'s changes of office) read: "Rudyard Kipling Worked Here 1882–1887" (Noel F. Cooke, "The 'Pioneer' of Kipling's Day," *Kipling Journal*, March 1964, p. 22).

CHAPTER IV The Interregnum

1 **The youth . . . Must travel** "Ode, Intimations of Immortality," lines 71–72.

2 **autumn of '89** RK arrived in Liverpool from New York on October 5, 1889, and was in London by October 7.

3 **Mary Kingsley** (1862–1900) ethnologist and traveller in Africa. RK published a brief memorial of her in the *Journal of the African Society*, October 25, 1932 (Sussex Edition, xxx). The meeting he refers to here could not have been in 1889; it must have been either in 1898–99 or 1899–1900: see John Shearman, "Mary Kingsley and Rudyard Kipling," *Kipling Journal*, December 1987, p. 20.

4 **Mowbray Morris** Morris (1847–1911) edited *Macmillan's Magazine* from 1885.

5 **an Indian tale and some verses** "The Incarnation of Krishna Mulvaney" and "The Ballad of the King's Mercy."

6 **'this is none of I'** "The Little Woman and the Pedlar": see the *Oxford Dictionary of Nursery Rhymes*, no. 535.

7 **editor of the St. James's Gazette** (Sir) Sidney Low (1857–1932); RK's first contribution to the *St. James's Gazette* was "The Comet of a Season," November 21, 1889 (uncollected). He continued to contribute to it until 1892.

8 **interview in a weekly paper** Probably the interview published in the *World*, April 2, 1890, as part of the series called "Celebrities at Home."

9 **Villiers Street, Strand** Embankment Chambers, Villiers Street, Strand, two rooms on the fifth floor. The building is now called Kipling House.

10 **Lion and Mammoth Comiques** As the leading male singers were called.

11 **'Mary, pity Women'** Published in February 1894 (*The Seven Seas*).

12 *Barrack-Room Ballads* The series, in the *Scots Observer*, began with "Danny Deever," February 22, 1890.

13 **Henley** William Ernest Henley (1849–1903), poet, critic, and editor, noted particularly for his encouragement of young authors. He edited several different periodicals in Scotland and England, notably the *Scots Observer*, renamed, after its migration from Edinburgh to London, the *National Observer* (1889–94). RK contributed to the *National Observer* and to the *New Review*, Henley's last editorial project, largely out of loyalty to Henley.

14 **restaurant off Leicester Square** Solferino's restaurant; others in the "happy company" included Charles Whibley, Herbert Stephen, and George Wyndham.

15 **tiny book of Essays and Reviews** Henley's *Views and Reviews . . . Literature*, 1890.

16 **Mr. Gladstone** William Ewart Gladstone (1809–98), the embodiment of the Liberal Party in the nineteenth century, four times prime minister between 1868 and 1894.

17 **whitewashed the whole crowd** A special commission of the House of Commons appointed to inquire into charges that Charles Stewart Parnell, the Irish leader, had been implicated in the assassination of

Lord Frederick Cavendish fully acquitted Parnell in a report of February 13, 1890.

18 **Mr. Frank Harris** Frank Harris (1856–1931), then editor of the *Fortnightly Review*, was an editor of ability, but notorious as a liar and lecher. Since RK had just published "One View of the Question" in the *Fortnightly*, it is likely that he had at least a slight acquaintance with Harris before the episode of "Cleared." According to Herbert Stephen, Harris had RK's "Cleared" set in type for publication but then backed out ("William Ernest Henley," *London Mercury*, February 1926, p. 391). Harris's own account of the episode is in his *Contemporary Portraits: Second Series* (New York, the author, 1919), pp. 48–50.

19 *The Times* **quoted them in full** I cannot find the verses in *The Times*.

20 **elected a Member of the Savile** Not until 1891, though RK was evidently free of the Club almost at once after his return to England. The Savile especially attracted literary men and artists. Its premises are now in Brook Street.

21 **Hardy** Thomas Hardy (1840–1928), novelist and poet.

22 **Authors' Society** The Society of Authors was organized by Besant in 1884; RK accepted office as a member of council in 1892 but finally resigned in disagreement with the Society in 1917.

23 **A.P. Watt** Alexander Pollock Watt (1835?–1914), the effective founder of literary agency in England. His son was Alexander S. Watt (d. 1948).

24 **Gosse** Edmund Gosse (1847–1928), critic and essayist, one of the central figures of the literary establishment of his day.

25 **Andrew Lang** (1844–1912) man of letters, whose interests ranged from folklore to the classics; he was one of the first to notice RK's work publicly.

26 **Eustace Balfour** (1854–1911) younger brother of Arthur Balfour, practiced as an architect.

27 **Herbert Stephen** (1857–1932) a barrister, son of Sir James Fitzjames Stephen, whom he succeeded as second baronet.

28 **Rider Haggard** Sir Henry Rider Haggard (1856–1925), popular novelist and countryman; one of RK's close friends.

29 **Saintsbury** George Saintsbury (1845–1933), at this time assistant editor of the *Saturday Review*, afterwards Regius Professor of English at the University of Edinburgh.

30 **Walter Pollock** (1850–1926) editor of the *Saturday Review*, whose editorial offices were in the Albany.

31 **'Proofs of Holy Writ'** Published in April 1934, in the year after Saintsbury's death.

32 **Queen's Doll's House** A gift from her family to Queen Mary, designed by Sir Edward Lutyens and exhibited at the Wembley Exhibition, 1924. It is now at Windsor Castle. Its furnishings, complete in every detail, were contributed by artists and experts. See *The Book of the Queen's Dolls' House*, ed. A.C. Benson and Lawrence Weaver (London, Methuen, 1924).

33 **I do not care to think!** The point of this lies partly in the fact that Saintsbury, in dedicating his famous *Notes on a Cellar-Book* (1920) to RK, added the remark that "by some cantrip of fortune" he had never had the chance to offer a bottle to RK; thus the moment, when it came, would be one of high expectation.

34 **ambulance** It figures in "Brugglesmith," published in October 1891 (*Many Inventions*).

35 **Lion Comique from Gatti's** Roger Lancelyn Green conjectures that this was James Fawn (Harbord, VII, 3384).

36 **kick-up** A dance.

37 **Royal Academy** John Collier's portrait of RK, 1891, now at Bateman's. It was not exhibited at the Royal Academy but at the New Gallery.

38 **'certain people of importance'** Cf. Browning's volume entitled *Parleyings with Certain People of Importance*, 1887.

39 **sense enough to countermand** This was perhaps "The Book of the Forty-Five Mornings," announced for publication in 1890 and repeatedly advertised but never in fact published. There is evidence that part of it, at least, was to have consisted of selections from RK's Indian journalism.

40 **flying visit** They came in May 1890 and returned to Lahore in 1891 – a "flying visit" of eighteen months. They took a house at 101 Earl's Court Road, and RK moved in with his parents there, though still retaining his Villiers Street rooms.

41 **Wesleyan Ministers** The Reverend Joseph Kipling (1805–62) and the Reverend George Browne Macdonald (1805–68).

42 **'The English Flag'** First published in the *National Observer*, April 4, 1891 (*Barrack-Room Ballads*).

43 **fourteen-footer** The poem is written in lines of fourteen metrical feet.

44 **"Unto them . . . the reeds"** Elizabeth Barrett Browning, "The Romance of the Swan's Nest," stanza 14.

45 **approval of the verses** See Hallam Tennyson, *Alfred Lord Tennyson* (London, Macmillan, 1897), II, 392.

46 **live very well indeed** It is neither possible nor necessary to identify precisely what individuals RK may have had in mind. J.W. Mackail, the husband of his cousin Margaret Burne-Jones, might do as an instance of the "Liberals"; for the more seriously "seditious" the rolls of the Fabian Society would supply many names.

47 *arriding* The italic *arriding* is corrected to roman letters in later printings. "Arride" means "to smile at" or "to gratify," but RK seems to intend the sense of "offend" here.

48 **J.K.S.** James K. Stephen (1859–92); the "stanzas" are "To R.K.," *Lapsus Calami*, 1891; originally published in the *Cambridge Review*, February 1891.

49 **my health cracked again** RK appears to have made one breakdown out of two here: he suffered a nervous collapse in January–February of 1890, associated partly with his engagement to Caroline Taylor; in October, after a bout of illness, he travelled to Italy by sea.

50 **Lord Dufferin** Frederick Temple Hamilton-Temple Blackwood, first Marquess of Dufferin and Ava, spent his life in diplomacy and administration. He was Governor-General of India, 1884–88; Ambassador to Italy, 1889–91, and to France, 1891–96.

51 **'The Song of the Women'** Published in the *Pioneer*, April 17, 1888, in aid of Lady Dufferin's Fund for the Medical Education of Native Women.

52 **Cook** The travel agency of Thomas Cook and Son, the son being John Mason Cook (1834–99), the great manager and developer of the business. Cook's visit to India on the question of travel to Mecca was made in 1885.

53 *The Moor* This is circumstantial, but the records show that RK sailed from Southampton on August 22, 1891, not on the *S.S. Moor* but on the *S.S. Mexican* for Cape Town.

54 **a Navy Captain** This was Captain E.H. Bayly: see p. 86.

55 **Cecil Rhodes** (1853–1902) financier, politician, and imperialist, the most powerful figure in South Africa at the end of the century.

56 *The Doric* RK left Cape Town on the *S.S. Doric* of the Shaw-Savill Line on September 25.

57 **Melbourne** RK's account of his travels from this point on is particularly confused and inaccurate. He says that his route was Cape Town–Melbourne–Sydney–Hobart–New Zealand. It was in fact just the reverse: Cape Town–Hobart–New Zealand–Melbourne–Sydney. He ar-

rived in Wellington, New Zealand, on October 18, and sailed from Adelaide for India on November 25: the travels described in this section took place between those two dates.

58 **Sydney** RK arrived in Sydney on November 14, and left on the 16th.

59 **Then to Hobart … sort of strength** RK makes three mistakes in this account: it was Sir George not Sir Edward, Grey; the meeting took place in Auckland, not in Hobart; and the troops that Grey diverted to India were destined for China, not Cape Colony. In later printings the passage reads: "Then to Hobart, in Tasmania, to pay my respects to Sir George Grey, who had been Governor at Cape Town in the days of the Mutiny. He was very old, very wise and foreseeing, with the gentleness that accompanies a certain sort of strength." Sir George Grey (1812–98) was twice Governor of New Zealand, 1845–53 and 1861–67; he was then prime minister, 1877–79.

60 **white-marked shark** Corrected to "dolphin" in later printings; his territory was not Wellington but French Pass, across the Cook Strait from Wellington (*Kipling Journal*, September 1937, p. 71).

61 **Wellington Harbour** RK was in Wellington October 18–22. His activity then is described in detail by J.B. Primrose, "Kipling's Visit to Australia and New Zealand," *Kipling Journal*, March 1963, pp. 12–14. For most of the particulars of this trip I am indebted to Primrose's article.

62 **Auckland** Leaving Wellington on October 22, RK travelled through Napier, Taupo, Wairakei, and Rotorua to Auckland, where he arrived on October 28 (Primrose, *Kipling Journal*, pp. 14–15).

63 **a rising river** The River Esk.

64 **apteryx** J.B. Primrose says that "opinion in New Zealand" is divided on the question of whether RK could have eaten an apteryx. "Some think that the locals were 'pulling his leg' about the kiwi. Others maintain that the kiwi, though its flesh is coarse in texture and tough, can be eaten" (*Kipling Journal*, p. 14).

65 **Robert Louis Stevenson** (1850–94) The poet and story-teller had resided in Samoa since 1890; his letter of praise to RK on the Mulvaney stories appears in Stevenson's *Letters*, ed. Sidney Colvin (New York, Scribners, 1905), II, 257.

66 *The Wrong Box* 1889, in collaboration with Lloyd Osbourne.

67 **spluttering over my meal** "I have got R.L. Stevenson's 'In the Wrong Box' and laughed over it dementedly when I read it. That man has only one lung but he makes you laugh with all your whole inside" (RK to Edmonia Hill, Boston, September 17, 1889: Kipling Papers).

68 **back to India** In fact, RK found that the regular steamer connections were such as to make a trip to Samoa impossible on his schedule (Primrose, *Kipling Journal*, p. 13).

69 **'Mrs. Bathurst'** Published in March 1904 (*Traffics and Discoveries*).

70 **increasing seas** RK returned to Wellington from Auckland and sailed on the *S.S. Talune* for the South Island and Australia on November 2.

71 **Invercargill** In fact, RK's ship sailed from Bluff, at the southernmost extremity of the South Island.

72 **General Booth** William Booth (1829–1912), founder of the Salvation Army: he boarded the ship at Dunedin, not Invercargill.

73 **Atlantic** Corrected to "Pacific" in later printings: more strictly, the Tasman Sea is meant.

74 **Adelaide** RK sailed from Adelaide for Colombo on the *S.S. Valetta*, November 25, 1891.

75 **'if by … save some'** Cf. 1 Corinthians 9:22: "that I might by all means save some."

76 **native-fashion among natives** The Salvationist movement in India, which began in the year that RK returned to India from England, stressed the importance of living in native style for the missionaries.

77 **Degrees were being conferred** In 1907, when RK, Booth, and Mark Twain were awarded honorary degrees on the nomination of Lord Curzon, the new chancellor of the university.

78 **only real home I had yet known** This is somewhat misleading: there were no plans at this time for Kipling's parents to come home, and RK himself had every intention of revisiting India.

Chapter v The Committee of Ways and Means

1 **January '92** RK's plans were upset shortly after he arrived in Lahore; there he learned of the death of Wolcott Balestier in Germany on December 6. On receiving this news RK made emergency arrangements to return to England, a journey he managed in the extraordinary time of fourteen days. On his arrival in London he at once took out a special license and married Balestier's sister, Caroline, on January 18. This event, however long it may have been privately in preparation, took all his friends and family by surprise. Almost nothing before this time is known of the relation between RK and the woman he married.

2 **The plague … Manchuria** The so-called third Pandemic began in 1894 at Canton; in the period 1898–1928 some 13 million deaths,

mostly in the East, have been attributed to the plague. I do not know on what grounds RK connects it with a 'flu epidemic in London in 1892.

3 **Langham Place** All Souls Church, now in the shadow of the BBC building.

4 **Henry James** (1843–1916) the American novelist; he and RK were acquainted through the Savile Club, and James had written a "critical introduction" to the American edition of RK's *Mine Own People*, 1891. In addition to those named by RK, there were also present at the wedding Gosse's wife, daughter, and son, and William Heinemann, the publisher, who had been an associate of Wolcott Balestier.

5 **Ambrose Poynter** (1867–1923) RK's cousin, the son of Agnes Macdonald and Sir Edward Poynter, P.R.A. Ambrose practiced as an architect. He succeeded his father as second baronet in 1919.

6 **Canada deep in snow** RK here skips the first stage of their wedding journey, which was spent in New York City and in Brattleboro, Vermont. They left Liverpool on the *S.S. Teutonic* on February 3, and did not reach Vancouver until April 3, more than two months after their wedding.

7 **real estate** RK bought land in Vancouver in 1889 when he first visited the city, and this he sold many years later. If the story about "Steve" is true, it must refer to land he bought in 1892.

8 **no shadow of any claim** This was an Englishman named H.J. Hunt, the representative of a firm of London importers; he and his wife travelled with RK and CK on the *S.S. Empress of India* from Vancouver to Yokohama (see Catharine Morris Wright, "How 'St. Nicholas' Got Rudyard Kipling," *Princeton University Library Quarterly*, 35 [1974], 265–66).

9 **an earthquake** CK reports two earthquakes in her diary, one on May 11, and a "severe" one on June 3.

10 **suspended payment** The New Oriental Banking Corporation of London suspended payment on June 9; RK eventually recovered all of his money but in the meantime was left with $100 in a New York bank (CK diary, June 9).

11 **Back again, then** They left Yokohama on June 27.

12 **his home . . . many years before** Joseph Balestier (1814–80), a native of Martinique but an American from infancy; the town is Brattleboro, Vermont. RK's suggestion that his wife's family were long-time residents is incorrect. CK's grandparents, who had originally visited Brattleboro for its then-famous water cure, had bought

land for a summer house near the town in 1872, only twenty years earlier; they kept a house in New York City. CK's own family were residents of Rochester, New York, and only summer visitors to Brattleboro. By 1892, however, both CK's brother, Beatty, and her mother had become permanent residents of Brattleboro.

13 **Bliss Cottage** They learned on July 22 that Bliss Cottage was available and moved in on August 10. The cottage still stands, but has been moved from its original site on the Bliss farm.

14 **her grandmother** Caroline Starr Balestier (1818–1901) lived in the house called "Beechwood," built by her husband north of Brattleboro.

15 **buy back ... India in '89** RK had sold the copyright of his Indian Railway Library titles in March 1889, just before leaving India (see p. 45): he bought them back in July 1894. The copyright of *Departmental Ditties* and *Plain Tales* belonged to the firm of Thacker, Spink and Co.; RK bought that of *Departmental Ditties* in 1899, and perhaps he bought that of *Plain Tales* at the same time, though I have no record of the transaction. In any case, he had long left Bliss Cottage before these events.

16 **a stranger** He has been identified as Linn Taylor of Brattleboro, who sold RK a policy for $10,000 from the National Life Insurance Co. of Montpelier in 1894 (undated clipping from *Vermont Phoenix* in Howard Rice papers, Notebook 17, Marlboro College).

17 **Adjutant of Volunteers at Lahore** See p. 32.

18 **Leuconoë ... as possible** That is, Mrs. Kipling agreeing with Mr. Kipling: Horace, *Odes*, I, xi: "Ask not, Leuconoë (we cannot know), what end the gods have set for me, for thee ... Reap the harvest of to-day, putting as little trust as may be in the morrow!"

19 **'get the story'** CK's diary for October 14, 1892, records that their day was "wrecked by two reporters from Boston"; their articles appear in the *Boston Herald* and the *Boston Globe*, October 23, 1892. RK is reported as saying, among other things, "Why do I refuse to be interviewed? Because it is immoral! It is a crime, just as much a crime as an offence against my person, as an assault, and just as much merits punishment. It is cowardly and vile. No respectable man would ask it, much less give it."

20 **boy ... brought up by wolves** "In the Rukh," finished before January 26, 1893 (*Many Inventions*).

21 ***Nada the Lily*** Serialized in January–May 1892 and published in book form in May. The passage in question is identified by RK in a letter to Haggard, October 20, 1895: "You remember in your tale

where the wolves leaped up at the feet of a dead man sitting on a rock? Somewhere on that page I got the notion [of *The Jungle Books*]" (Morton Cohen [ed.], *Rudyard Kipling to Rider Haggard* [London, Hutchinson, 1965], pp. 31–32). The reference is to p. 103 of *Nada the Lily*.

22 **My first child and daughter** Josephine Kipling (1892–99).

23 **Dr. Conland** James Conland (1851–1903), a sailor and a fisherman before qualifying as a doctor; he practiced in Brattleboro from 1880 until his death, served in the state legislature, was a trustee of the local library, and a student of Vermont history.

24 **'considered a field and bought it'** Cf. Proverbs 31:16: "She considereth a field, and buyeth it." In fact, RK had bought a field for a house site barely a week after his first arriving in Vermont. Plans for a house were begun early in March 1892, and work on the site began before the end of the year.

25 **Jean Pigeon** RK quoted Jean Pigeon in a speech to the Canadian Authors' Association on July 12, 1933: "Everyt'ing which ze tree 'ave experience' in ze forest 'e take wiz 'im into ze 'ouse" (*The Times*, July 13, 1933).

26 **'Naulakha'** So called to commemorate the friendship between RK and Wolcott Balestier, his wife's brother, with whom RK wrote the novel called *The Naulahka* before Balestier's sudden death at the end of 1891. The word means "nine *lakhs*" (900,000), shorthand for anything extremely valuable (note that the title of the novel is a mis-spelling, an extraordinary oversight in a writer so scrupulous as RK). The house still stands essentially unaltered since RK built it.

27 **'A Walking Delegate'** First published in *The Century Magazine*, December 1894: collected in *The Day's Work*.

28 **burnt it severely** This was in January 1895, their second winter in Naulakha.

29 **a 'Dry' State** Vermont introduced state prohibition in 1852, and after abandoning that continued to maintain local prohibition.

30 **pledget** The usual sense of this obscure word is "compress for applying over wound." RK means it figuratively and ironically.

31 **John Hay** (1838–1905) made his reputation as secretary to Abraham Lincoln; he afterwards combined literature, diplomacy, and politics. He was Ambassador to Great Britain, 1897–98, and Secretary of State, 1898–1905. RK visited Hay at his summer home in Newbury, New Hampshire, in September 1895 (William Roscoe Thayer, *Life and Letters of John Hay* [Boston, Houghton, Mifflin, 1915], II, p. 126).

32 **Washington in '96** Corrected to 95 in later printings. RK and CK were in Washington, D.C., from February 26 to April 6, 1895.

33 **Theodore Roosevelt** (1858–1919) was a member of the circle of John Hay and Henry Adams in Washington; RK is mistaken in saying that Roosevelt was then Under-Secretary of the Navy; he was a Civil Service Commissioner. Later in 1895 he became president of the New York City Board of Police Commissioners. He was Assistant Secretary of the Navy, 1897–98, before going on active service in the Spanish–American War. In 1900 he was elected vice-president of the United States, and he took office as president on the assassination of McKinley in 1901.

34 **the Upper** John Davis Long (1838–1915).

35 **conforming-Dopper** A rigid sect among the Boers of the Transvaal.

36 **grizzlies that he had met** In his days in the American west in the 1880s.

37 **to keep her busy** RK refers to the growing crisis in South Africa after the Jameson raid at the end of 1895.

38 **Hannibal Chollops** Dickens, *Martin Chuzzlewit*, ch. 33: Hannibal Chollop "always introduced himself to strangers as a worshipper of Freedom; [and] was the consistent advocate of Lynch law, and slavery."

39 **spouse 'twisting the Lion's tail'** One may guess that Henry Cabot Lodge (1850–1924), senator from Massachusetts and one of the Hay–Adams–Roosevelt circle, is meant.

40 **New York Police Court Judge** In a communist-led riot at the New York pier of the German liner *S.S. Bremen* on July 27 the ship's flag, with the Nazi swastika, had been torn down and thrown into the Hudson. When some of the rioters were brought before Magistrate Louis B. Brodsky on September 6, Brodsky dismissed the charges, comparing the swastika to "the black flag of piracy" (*New York Times*, September 7, 1935). In response to German protest, Secretary of State Cordell Hull "expressed his regret" for Brodsky's remarks (*New York Times*, September 15).

41 **Professor Langley** Samuel Pierpont Langley (1834–1906), secretary of the Smithsonian Institution from 1887, a distinguished research scientist and a productive inventor. His experiments with power-driven aircraft in 1896 produced the first successful free flight of a power-driven heavier-than-air machine. RK has perhaps confused memories of Langley's 1896 experiments with his failure in 1903 with a full-size, man-carrying machine.

42 **The next time I met him** RK has confused the chronology of things here. His last meeting with Roosevelt was in 1910, when Roosevelt came to England to deliver the Romanes Lectures at Oxford: this was twelve years after the annexation of the Philippines. Roosevelt also gave a speech at the Guildhall in May on this visit: his topic there was Egypt.

43 **'Pithecanthropoid'** In 1903 Roosevelt exploited a revolution in Colombia to separate Panama from that country, under the administration of President J.M. Marroquin.

44 **delightful sons** Quentin (1897–1918) and Kermit (1889–1943).

45 **Sam Maclure** Corrected to "McClure" in later printings. Samuel Sidney McClure (1867–1949), American editor and magazine publisher, made his first success by developing a literary syndicate supplying newspapers around the world with stories and features. He was indefatigable in pursuing authors to write for his syndicate, and by his energy and generosity had great success in the pursuit. *McClure's Magazine*, begun in 1893, was famous as the magazine of the "Muckrakers." McClure was briefly in partnership with F.N. Doubleday, RK's American publisher.

46 *The Wrecker* By Stevenson and Lloyd Osbourne, 1892.

47 **Frank Doubleday** Doubleday (1862–1934), founder of the firm of Doubleday, publishers, in 1897, and RK's American publisher from 1898; he worked for the firm of Charles Scribner until starting on his own, and it was Scribner who published the "Outward Bound" edition of RK's works, a "collected edition" undertaken when its author was barely more than thirty years old. Doubleday's first visit to RK was on November 30, 1895.

48 **his wife** Doubleday's first wife, Neltje de Graff (1865–1918).

49 **stuff I had never written** RK has especially in mind a collection of his work called "The Brushwood Edition" assembled in 1898–99 by the New York publisher and bookseller, G.H. Putnam. RK brought suit against Putnam, and lost it after long and expensive proceedings. The episode also cost RK much public sympathy. Putnam was a reputable publisher and a champion of international copyright; the case against him was obviously a weak one; and RK commenced his action almost before he had recovered from his near-fatal illness in New York, when the American public had indulged in a frenzy of excited sympathy for the great writer. His attack on Putnam thus appeared both unseemly and ungrateful.

50 **cheaper and cheaper editions** E.g., the "Swastika Edition," 1899,

of 20,000 fifteen-volume sets at $15 the set.

51 **a pillar of the Copyright League** George Haven Putnam (1844–1930), head of G.P. Putnam and Son from 1872 to 1930. He was a leading figure in the cause of international copyright. See note 49, above.

52 **the Father was much amazed** JLK, just retired from India, arrived in Vermont in June; he and RK went to Quebec in early August, and called on Norton in early September.

53 **Charles Eliot Norton** Norton (1827–1908), Professor of the History of Art at Harvard. He had lived and travelled extensively in Europe as a young man, and was an intimate of the Rossetti circle and of Ruskin. His daughters Sarah (Sally) and Lily were life-long friends of RK and his family.

54 **Boston Brahmins** As the privileged caste of wealth and high culture in Boston were known.

55 **Shady Hill** Norton's house in Cambridge, Massachusetts.

56 **Emerson** Ralph Waldo Emerson (1803–82), poet and essayist, whose correspondence with Carlyle Norton edited, 1883.

57 **Wendell Holmes** Oliver Wendell Holmes (1809–94), poet, essayist, and Professor of Anatomy at Harvard.

58 **Longfellow** Henry Wadsworth Longfellow (1807–82), poet and Professor of Modern Languages at Harvard. Norton published *Henry Wadsworth Longfellow: A Sketch of His Life*, in 1907.

59 **the Alcotts** Bronson (1799–1888) and his daughter Louisa May Alcott (1832–88); the father was an educational reformer and the friend of Hawthorne, Emerson, and Thoreau; the daughter is famous as the author of *Little Women*, 1868.

60 **Continental supplanters** Cf. the remark of Mrs. Burton in "The Edge of the Evening" (1913): Lincoln, she says, "had wasted the heritage of his land by blood and fire, and had surrendered the remnant to aliens" (*A Diversity of Creatures*, p. 281). Mrs. Burton is a Southerner.

61 **Wiltshire** RK and his family visited England in the summers of 1894 and 1895. His parents had settled at Tisbury, Wiltshire, where they remained until their deaths. See p. 81

62 **hairdresser's waxen model** In Stevenson and Osbourne's *The Wrong Box*, ch. 7, Pitman, the artist, on contemplating the model in a hairdresser's shop, exclaims that "there's a something – there's a haughty, indefinable something about that figure."

63 **strove after that eye** See RK's two drawings illustrating "How the Whale Got Its Throat" (*Just So Stories*).

64 **Gloucester, Mass.** RK visited Gloucester in September 1894 and June 1895 (CK diary).

65 **Boston Harbour** RK made a one-day visit to Boston to "look at ships" on February 25, 1896, and he and Conland made two brief visits to Gloucester in May and August 1896: there is no further record of their visiting Boston together in CK's diary.

66 **Pocahontas coal** After the Pocahontas coal-field in West Virginia.

67 **San Francisco** Not San Francisco, but San Diego.

68 **schedule** The "railway magnate" was F.N. Finney (1832–1916), who had been an official of the Soo Line and then of the M.K.T. In a letter of March 10, 1896, he worked out the route that RK used in '*Captains Courageous*' (MS, Dalhousie University).

69 **real live railway magnate** Finney himself (Carrington, p. 231 n.).

70 **Super-film Magnate** Perhaps Irving Thalberg (1899–1936), head of production at Metro-Goldwyn-Mayer; he called on RK to discuss '*Captains Courageous*' on July 8, 1931 (A.S. Watt to CK, July 7, 1931; to RK, July 9, 1931: Berg Collection, New York Public Library).

71 **So we loosed hold** To anyone acquainted with the outline of RK's life in Vermont, this account is bound to seem quite disingenuous. At the time he left the United States, September 1, 1896, he showed no wish at all to watch developments in England. However important the general hostility that he imagined around him may have seemed in his later memory, two much more distinct events appear to have put him into motion at the time. The first was the wave of anti-English feeling that the press stirred up during the crisis over Venezuela at the end of 1895; more immediate and urgent was his quarrel with and his disastrous legal action against his unruly brother-in-law, Beatty Balestier (see Introduction). When RK left Vermont in 1896 for England it was by no means clear to him that he would not return.

72 **another small daughter** Elsie (1896–1976), born on February 2; she married George Bambridge in 1924.

73 **Woulds't thou . . . wrote the bill** "Suum Cuique," lines 1–2.

74 **spring of '96** Not spring but fall; they moved into Rock House, St. Marychurch, Maidencombe, Torquay, on September 10, 1896.

75 **Despondency within the open, lit rooms** Their experience in the house gave RK the suggestion for his story "The House Surgeon," 1909 (*Actions and Reactions*).

76 **'Two and a half' – Army biscuits** This measure is supposed to equal one pound of bread.

77 **fourteen years back** In fact, fifteen.

78 **in '96** That is, 1897.

79 **daughter of the Ridsdales** Stanley Baldwin married Lucy Ridsdale on September 12, 1892.

80 **my son John** John Kipling (1897–1915) was born on August 17, 1897, at North End House; he died in the Battle of Loos, in 1915, so that the omens attending his birth were falsified.

81 **house opposite the church on the green** See the end of ch. 2. The house, called The Elms, still stands on Rottingdean Green. RK rented it for three guineas a week, and lived there from September 1897 to September 1902. He tried but failed to buy it.

82 **little affair at Yokohama** The failure of their bank and their temporary embarrassment for money in 1892. But RK was by this time a wealthy man, by any standards.

83 **'Sussex'** First published in *The Five Nations*, 1903.

84 **fat bathers ... wallowing in the surf** Burne-Jones's comic sketches of "fat bathers" and others survive in many collections, e.g., The Royal College of Surgeons, London.

85 **Irish boy ... mixed up with native life** RK was at work on *Kim* as early as October 1892 (to Mary Mapes Dodge, October 15, 1892: MS, Princeton).

86 **Mr. Micawber** In Dickens, *David Copperfield*: see the end of ch. 36.

87 **left India for good** In 1893.

88 **Arthur Morrison** Corrected to Alfred Morrison in later printings. Morrison (1821–97), a wealthy collector, possessed every sort of precious object: porcelains, gems, gold work, miniatures, glass, engravings, portraits, and manuscripts.

89 **the Wyndhams** The Hon. Percy Scawen Wyndham (1835–1911), son of the first Lord Leconfield. JLK died at his house, "Clouds," East Knoyle, Wiltshire.

90 **'Backward . . . Time in thy flight'** Elizabeth Akers Allen, "Rock Me to Sleep, Mother" (1860), stanza 1.

91 *Kim* **came back to me** Perhaps the autumn of 1898, when CK's diary records that RK was working on *Kim* with JLK; but he had probably been at work on it in the preceding year too.

92 **good enough for Cervantes was good enough for him** RK means the form of the episodic narrative of the road, common to *Don Quixote* and to *Kim*.

93 **Grand Trunk Road at eventide** *Kim*, ch. 4.

94 **Deputy Curator for six weeks** On his first arriving in Lahore in 1882. Before taking up his work on the *Civil and Military Gazette*, RK assisted his father in the Lahore Museum, of which JLK was curator, in addition to his work in the School of Art. "Six weeks" is probably longer than RK actually spent in the Museum.

95 **Jatakas** Stories about one or another of the previous births of the Buddha.

96 **the Father attended to *Kim*** RK's statement requires some correction. JLK's illustrations in relief for *Kim* were made for the regular trade edition of 1901. They were then used when *Kim* was added to the Outward Bound edition in 1902, the edition that RK presumably means by "illustrated edition of my works." JLK had been making illustrations for that since 1897, and by the same method.

97 **'If you get . . . God invents'** Browning, "Fra Lippo Lippi," lines 217–18.

98 **High Cannibalism** "Higher Cannibalism" in later printings (see also pp. 111–12, below). In a letter to Sydney Cockerell, October 6, 1932, explaining why he could not undertake to write a memoir of Lady Burne-Jones, as Cockerell had urged him to do, RK wrote that "This here biography and 'reminiscence' business that is going on nowadays, is a bit too near the 'Higher Cannibalism' to please me. Ancestor-worship is all right but serving them up filletted or spiced, 'high' (which last is very popular) has put me off" (MS, Morgan Library).

99 **the Athenaeum** The London club founded in 1824 and distinguished by a membership of notables ever since. RK was not thirty-three but still in his thirty-first year at the time of his election, being then "the youngest member by 20 years," as his wife proudly put it (CK to F.N. Finney, June 9, 1897: Parke-Bernet catalogue, December 10, 1941).

100 **an old General** Major General John Barton Sterling (1840–1926), served in the navy but joined the Coldstream Guards, 1861. After commanding the regiment, he retired in 1901. A member of the Athenaeum and the Royal Yacht Squadron, Cowes.

101 **Parsons** Sir Charles Algernon Parsons (1854–1931), engineer and manufacturer of turbines; his experimental ship, *Turbinia*, 1897.

102 **Hercules Ross** Corrected to Hercules Read in later printings. Sir Charles Hercules Read (1857–1929), Keeper of British and Medieval Antiquities and Ethnography, British Museum.

103 **my spiritual comfort** RK perhaps means that his clubs were im-

portant to him because he had no London residence. But other interpretations are possible.

104 **Carlton** A Conservative club, in RK's days in Pall Mall.

105 **Beefsteak** A social club dating back to 1876.

106 **Villiers Street** That is, 1889–91.

107 **'no letters in the grave'** Boswell, *Life of Johnson*, December 1784 (Hill-Powell edn. [Oxford, Clarendon Press, 1934] IV, 413).

CHAPTER VI South Africa

1 **Jameson Raid** The abortive raid on the Transvaal in 1895, intended to set off a rising of the English against the Boers, and led by Rhodes's lieutenant, Dr. Leander Starr Jameson.

2 **'a sound of a going . . . mulberry trees'** 2 Samuel 5:24.

3 **Great Queen's Diamond Jubilee** 1897.

4 *The Times* **in '97** July 17, 1897.

5 **Captain Bagley** Corrected to "Captain E.H. Bayly" in later printings. Captain Edward Henry Bayly (1849–1904), whom RK had met in 1891 on the voyage to Cape Town (see p. 57). In 1897 and 1898, as captain of the *Pelorus*, he took RK on manoeuvres with the Channel Fleet.

6 **Joseph Chamberlain** (1836–1914) Colonial Minister, and the political force behind the English commitment to the Boer War.

7 **South African Verse in** *The Times* Altogether, RK published some nineteen poems in *The Times*, including those on Joseph Chamberlain ("Things and the Man," August 1, 1904), on Rhodes ("The Burial," April 9, 1902), and Milner ("The Pro-Consuls," July 22, 1905).

8 **winter of '97** 1898, not 1897: they left Southampton on January 8, and arrived back in England on April 30, 1898 (CK diary).

9 **Wynberg** The Vineyard Hotel, in the Cape Town suburb of Newlands, a district of Wynberg, near the Rhodes estate.

10 **Rhodes** They arrived in Cape Town on January 25, and had lunch with Rhodes on the next day (CK diary).

11 **Jameson** Dr. (afterwards Sir) Leander Starr Jameson (1853–1917). Rhodes's closest associate and the main agent in the creation of Rhodesia; leader of the notorious Jameson Raid. In consequence of the raid he was imprisoned in England, but returned to the Cape, led the Progressive Party after Rhodes's death, and was prime minister, 1904–8. RK says (p. 111) that "If" was "drawn from Jamesons' character."

12 **paper charged itself with the rest** The *Daily Mail*, at the beginning of the Boer War in October 1899, undertook to raise a "Soldiers'

Families Fund." For this, RK wrote his "Absent-Minded Beggar," exhorting the public to "pay – pay – pay!" The poem was reprinted, sung, recited, and reproduced in a myriad forms, with a part of the proceeds from performance and sales going to the *Daily Mail*'s fund. RK writes as though some, at least, of the fund was spent on the soldiers rather than on their families, and perhaps it was.

13 **Sir Arthur Sullivan** Sullivan (1842–1900), the composer now remembered for his comic operas written with Sir W.S. Gilbert.

14 **R.E.** Royal Engineers.

15 **Bloemfontein just after its capture** RK left Cape Town for Bloemfontein, the capital of the Orange Free State, on March 19, 1900, a week after the fall of the city to Lord Roberts's troops.

16 **Kadir Buksh** RK's body servant in India, referred to in several of his stories (sometimes as Kadir Baksh).

17 **H.A. Gwynne** Gwynne (1865–1950), after service as a Reuters correspondent, became editor of the London *Standard*, and, in 1911, of the *Morning Post*.

18 **Perceval Landon** Landon (1869–1927) was special correspondent for *The Times* in the Boer War; he afterwards served as special correspondent on many assignments, including the British expedition to Tibet, for *The Times*, the *Daily Mail*, and the *Daily Telegraph*.

19 **'You've got ... for the troops'** Roberts, who appreciated the value of public relations, had ordered the correspondents accompanying his army to produce a paper for the troops at Bloemfontein. The local English-language paper, called the *Friend of the Free State*, was commandeered and put at the service of Gwynne, Landon, RK, and others. RK contributed to fourteen numbers of the *Friend*, greatly enjoying himself but not distinguishing himself by the quality or the quantity of his work for the paper.

20 **Julian Ralph** (1853–1903) American journalist on the staff of the *New York Sun* for many years; he represented the London *Daily Mail* in South Africa. Ralph's *War's Brighter Side*, 1901, is the fullest account of the Bloemfontein *Friend* and of RK's part in it.

21 **a grown son** Lester Ralph (1876–1927), who accompanied the army as an illustrator.

22 **a fringe** Artificial hair worn as a fringe on the forehead. The alcohol would be used as a solvent for the adhesive holding the fringe in place.

23 **typhoid in Bloemfontein** This is close to the official estimates. See the term "Bloeming-typhoidtein" in RK's "The Parting of the Columns" (*The Five Nations*).

24 **'dead to the wide'** "Utterly drunk" in Eric Partridge, *Dictionary of Slang*, 8th edn. (New York, Macmillan, 1984); the same authority gives the meaning "utterly exhausted" for "done to the wide." Two phrases so close would presumably change places.

25 **raw Modder-River** RK had travelled *via* hospital train to the battle site of the Modder River in late February 1900. This is the episode just after Paardeberg referred to in the next paragraph.

26 **Mauser-wound** The Mauser, of German manufacture, was the standard rifle of the Boers.

27 **Paardeberg** Boer position along the Modder River where General Cronje was compelled to surrender to Roberts, February 27, 1900. The battle that produced the casualties took place on February 18.

28 **unknown Philip Sidney's name** "Thy need is greater than mine," as the dying Sidney is supposed to have said in the now-discredited familiar story.

29 **'Sanna's Post'** East of Bloemfontein, on March 31, when General Broadwood was ambushed by General De Wet.

30 **donga** A steep ravine or watercourse.

31 **'bill-stickin' expeditions'** That is, expeditions sent out to proclaim Roberts's offer of amnesty to the Boers if they would surrender.

32 **Lord Stanley, now Derby** Edward George Villiers Stanley (1865–1948) succeeded as 17th Earl of Derby in 1908. He was Roberts's private secretary in South Africa, and as such served as press officer.

33 **Battle of Kari Siding** Kari (or Karee) Siding is about twelve miles north of Bloemfontein; the battle took place on March 28.

34 **well-known war-correspondent** Bennet Burleigh (?–1914), was correspondent of the *Daily Telegraph* from 1882 and had travelled the world in his profession. His account of RK at the battle of Karee Siding appears in Lincoln Springfield, *Some Piquant People* (London, Unwin, 1924), p. 205.

35 **Krupp** The great firm of German steel and armament manufacturers.

36 **pom-poms** A new word in 1899: echoic coinage used to identify the Maxim automatic quick-firing gun.

37 **Pretoria** That is, capture and imprisonment: Pretoria, the capital of the Transvaal, was a center for prisoners of war.

38 **Le Gallais** Lt. Colonel P.W.J. LeGallais, commanding the mounted infantry. The official history has him out on the right flank of the British forces.

39 **hangar** Usually *hanger*, "a wood."

40 **'*Maffeesh*'** "Dead," "useless" (Arabic).

41 **French** John Denton Pinkstone French (1852–1925), afterwards Field Marshal and first Earl of Ypres, commanded the cavalry under Roberts. French was the commander at the Battle of Loos in 1915 in which RK's son, John, was killed.

42 **General commanding the cavalry** French himself.

43 **Tantie Sannie** The Boer woman in Olive Schreiner's *Story of an African Farm* (1883).

44 **shot them down as they ran** Among the Kipling Papers at Sussex is a clipping from *La Tribune de Genève*, January 18, 1901, reporting the story that RK must mean in this passage. In the newspaper account, RK and a group of officers are shot at as they pass a Boer farmhouse. The officers enter to find only women and children in the place; but on searching they discover a young man hiding under a bed. Without further inquiry, they make him mount a horse and ride for his life; then, at a distance of three hundred meters, they bring him down with their carbines.

45 **concentration-camps** As part of his drastic scorched-earth policy, introduced in 1901, Lord Kitchener swept the Boer women and children into "concentration camps." There some 26,000 died.

46 **Miss Hobhouse** Emily Hobhouse (1860–1926), representing a London relief committee, visited South Africa in 1901; her report on the conditions in concentration camps caused a furor in England and led to her deportation from South Africa. There is a monument to her in Bloemfontein.

47 **'Woolsack'** The Woolsack is a modified Cape-style cottage built in 1900 by Rhodes to the designs of Sir Herbert Baker and intended for the use of artists, beginning with RK, to whom Rhodes offered it for as long as he wished to use it. The Woolsack, not far from Rhodes's house, Groote Schuur, is now within the grounds of the University of Cape Town.

48 **De Wet** Christian De Wet (1854–1922), commander of the Orange Free State forces, famous for his elusive, raiding tactics.

49 **Smuts** Jan Christian Smuts (1870–1950), a law graduate of Christ's College, Cambridge, was prime minister of South Africa, 1919–24 and 1939–48. In the Boer War he commanded the raid into Cape Colony. He was commissioned a general in the British Army during the First World War to command the forces in East Africa and was appointed to the British war cabinet.

50 **meeting Smuts . . . during the Great War** January 8, 1918.

51 **Mr. Balfour** Arthur James Balfour (1848–1930), statesman and

philosopher, first Earl of Balfour. Conservative prime minister, 1902–05; a member of the coalition government during the First World War.

52 **Our own casualties ... six times as many** Thomas Pakenham, *The Boer War* (London, Weidenfeld and Nicolson, 1979), p. 607, lists them thus: English dead, 22,000; Boer dead, more than 7,000. Of the British deaths, probably the greater part were from disease.

53 **Magersfontein** A British defeat, December 11, 1889.

54 **Lord Dundonald's** General Douglas Mackinnon Baillie Hamilton Gordon (1852–1935), twelfth Earl of Dundonald.

55 **we were all beating the air** Greatly disturbed by the ineffectiveness of British preparation in the Boer War, RK after the war took up the cause of national military training. He founded and largely paid for the rifle club at Rottingdean. But, as he recognizes here, such preparation was irrelevant to the conditions of the First World War.

56 **from 1900 to 1907** That is, from December of 1900, when their first occupation of the Woolsack began, to April 15, 1908, when they left it, never to return.

57 **Matabele Wars** 1893–94 and 1896, enabling the establishment of Rhodesia.

58 **'Little Foxes'** First published in March 1909 (*Actions and Reactions*). RK's source was Col. Thomas Edgecombe Hickman (1860–1930), Governor of Dongola, 1899–1900.

59 **once came home with us** Jameson twice travelled from South Africa to England with RK, in 1902 and 1908. For Jameson's criminal career, see ch. 6, note 11.

60 **skilly** Northern dialect for "skilled, skillful."

61 **the Strubens at Strubenheim** Henry William Struben (1840–1915), one of the Rand gold millionaires, lived at Strubenheim (or Strubenholm) with his four sons and four daughters.

62 **we met him at the foot of the garden** RK describes this animal's visit in a letter to Jameson, April 1903 (MS, Dalhousie University).

63 **ghosts that inhabited the 'Woolsack'** See RK's "My Personal Experience with a Lion," *Ladies' Home Journal*, January 1902 (collected only in *The Kipling Reader for Elementary Grades* [New York, D. Appleton, 1912]).

64 **Scholarships** The scholarships to Oxford, established by Rhodes's will, and open to students from the Commonwealth, the United States, and Germany. RK was a trustee of the scholarship fund from 1917 to 1925.

65 **Palaver done set** West African trade English: "that's enough of

that." See Mary Kingsley, *Travels in West Africa* (London, Macmillan, 1897), ch. 19, and RK's "The Army of a Dream," *Traffics and Discoveries*, p. 267.

Chapter vii The Very-Own House

1 ***The Fires*** RK's verses, first published as the introduction to *Collected Verse*, 1907.

2 **Mr. Harmsworth** Alfred Harmsworth (1865–1922), afterwards first Viscount Northcliffe, journalist, publisher, and newspaper proprietor, notorious for yellow journalism; founded the *Daily Mail*, 1896, and the *Daily Mirror*, 1903; chief proprietor of *The Times*, 1908; one of the great promoters of his age. RK's connection with him came through the "Absent-minded Beggar" business: see above, p. 88. Harmsworth's visit by motor car was in October 1899 (Carrington, p. 367).

3 **'Steam Tactics'** Published in December 1902; RK bought his Locomobile, an American steam-driven car, in 1901. All of his cars had names: this one's was "Coughing Jane."

4 **Lanchester** Acquired in 1902 and named "Amelia."

5 **The heads of the Lanchester firm** Frederick William Lanchester (1868–1946) and his brother George Herbert (1874–1970); their firm was founded in 1899.

6 **and so spouted home** See Meryl Macdonald, "Lordly of Leather, iii," *Kipling Journal*, March 1983, p. 36, where a story something like this about RK's Lanchester is told on the authority of Archie Millership, once a sales director for Lanchester.

7 **'Bateman's'** Their first visit to Bateman's was in fact by horse-drawn fly, August 14, 1900; so too was their second visit, May 26, 1902, their car being out of order (CK diary). Bateman's, Burwash, Sussex, was bought by RK for £9,300 on June 10, 1902; he spent the rest of his life there. The house is now a memorial to RK, the property of the National Trust.

8 **Jane Cakebread Lanchester** The name that RK sometimes gave to "Amelia," after a notorious prostitute who was constantly appearing in court. This dialogue perhaps belongs to June 11, 1902, only six days after RK's Lanchester had been delivered, when he went over to Bateman's (CK diary).

9 **my chauffeur** RK himself never drove, but depended on a chauffeur from the beginning.

10 **Sir William Willcocks** (1852–1932) after the Assouan dam, 1898–

1902, he went on to build irrigation works in Iraq.

11 **mill-sluit** A word RK picked up from South African Dutch: a form of *sluice.*

12 **Fellahîn Battalions** Egyptian peasants, such as Willcocks would have had at Assouan.

13 *Cocculus Indicus* The dried fruit of an Indian shrub, containing picrotoxin. In large doses it is poisonous; it was sometimes used by pub keepers to increase the effects of their beer.

14 **Lord Ashburnham's** Probably Bertram Ashburnham (1840–1913), fifth Earl, of Ashburnham Place, near Battle, Sussex.

15 **Trugs** A trug is a shallow wooden basket, whose manufacture is one of the specialities of Sussex.

16 **latten** A metal alloy, resembling brass.

17 **Christopher Sly affected** *The Taming of the Shrew*, Induction, II, 88–90. "Sealed" means carrying an official stamp certifying that the container is of legal size.

18 **'. . . companion to owls'** Job 30:29.

19 **adventuring on the brook** The *Midsummer Night's Dream* production, with a donkey's-head mask fetched from London, was held in October 1904; the birchbark canoe arrived from Canada on June 30, 1907 (CK diary).

20 **I went off at score** The earliest known reference to RK's work on the *Puck of Pook's Hill* stories is September 25, 1904, about two years after they had moved into Bateman's: "Rud at work on a fresh idea, a set of stories, the History of England told by Puck to children" (CK diary). His preparation for the Roman stories, though, goes back at least as far as 1897.

21 **Boswell** Cf. Boswell, *A Journal of a Tour to the Hebrides*, September 8, 1773 (Hill-Powell edn. [Oxford, Clarendon Press, 1934], V, 163).

22 **walked the other way** *Alice Through the Looking Glass*, ch. 2.

23 **'deeper than the plaster'** "The Wrong Thing," p. 64.

24 **such a well to light** See William R. Power, "Pevensey Castle and 'Puck,'" *Kipling Journal*, September 1935, pp. 85–86.

25 **perfectly genuine** The inscription to the Thirtieth Legion is now held to be a fake, by some hand unknown; see Harbord, VI, 2724–35.

26 **niello and grisaille** *Niello* is a method of decorating engraved silver or gold objects by filling in the lines with a special metal paste. *Grisaille* is painting executed wholly in shades of gray (to imitate relief sculpture).

27 **cryptogram . . . forgotten** What RK means has not yet been discovered.

28 **Chief Morticians to that trade** I do not know what the fancied link between the Puck stories and the "Higher Cannibalism" can be. The words following the phrase "awful charge" in this sentence were supplied by Mrs. Kipling in editing the MS. The change may have had something to do with a reference, also deleted, to Marie Stopes, the advocate of birth control, in the preceding paragraph (CK to H.A. Gwynne, 15 October 1936: MS, Dalhousie University).

29 **Colonel Wemyss Feilden** Henry Wemyss Feilden (1838–1921) lived in the house called "Rampyndene" on Burwash High Street. He had served in the Indian Mutiny and in China before selling out. From 1862 to 1865 he served in the Confederate Army in the American Civil War. In 1875–76 he was naturalist on the British Arctic Expedition (see p. 5); he served in the first Boer War of 1881 and in the second, 1900–01. He visited most of the northern regions of the world as a naturalist. In RK's Burwash years Feilden succeeded to the role of "admired older man" earlier played in RK's life by Cormell Price, by JLK, by Sir Walter Besant, and by Charles Eliot Norton. Feilden's wife Julia (d. 1920) he married in Virginia in 1864.

30 **Colonel Newcome** The model gentleman in Thackeray's *The Newcomes*.

31 *Cranford* Mrs. Gaskell's volume of sketches of early-Victorian country life, 1853.

32 **'little fellow called Roberts'** Lord Roberts, as he became; this was the exploit for which Roberts was awarded the Victoria Cross in 1858.

33 **one of Lee's aides-de-camp** General Robert E. Lee (1807–70), Confederate commander in the American Civil War.

34 **visit of strangers** Haggard's son was born May 23, 1881, in Natal; Feilden was in South Africa then during the first Boer War.

35 **'Imperial Preference'** Joseph Chamberlain's policy of special concessions for trade within the British Empire, eagerly supported by RK and opposed by the Liberal Party.

36 **Laurier** Sir Wilfrid Laurier (1841–1919), prime minister of Canada, 1896–1911, and leader of the Canadian Liberal Party.

37 **an ex-Governor of the Philippines** William Cameron Forbes (1870–1959), investment banker; appointed Governor-General of the Philippines in 1909, he was relieved of his post by President Wilson in 1913.

38 **late summer of '06** 1907, not 1906: RK and CK sailed on September 20, and landed again in England on November 2, 1907.

39 **Allen Liner** Corrected to "Allan" in later printings. RK has confused

his ships here. They crossed to Canada on the Canadian Pacific liner *S.S. Empress of Ireland*. Their return was on the Allan Liner *S.S. Virginian*. CK's diary for October 29 notes that RK spent "two hours investigating the turbines" on the ship that day.

40 **Sir William Van Horne** (1843–1915) an American naturalized as a Canadian citizen. At the time of RK's wedding journey Van Horne was already president of the Canadian Pacific.

41 **honorary degree ... McGill University at Montreal** This was in June 1899, *in absentia*. RK was prevented from going to Montreal to receive it by his near-fatal illness in New York that spring.

42 **a highly moral discourse** October 17, 1907: "Values in Life" (*A Book of Words*).

43 *Letters to the Family* Published serially in 1908 and collected in *Letters of Travel*, 1919.

44 **Nobel Prize of that year for Literature** RK received notification of the prize on November 12. They left for Stockholm on December 7, and King Oskar II died on December 9.

45 **the new King** Gustavus V (1858–1950).

46 **the Queen** Victoria of Baden (1862–1930).

CHAPTER VIII Working-Tools

1 **Working-Tools** Mrs. Kipling wrote that this chapter was to be called "Tools of My Trade" (CK to H.A. Gwynne, October 15, 1936: MS, Dalhousie University). Evidently she found reason to change it.

2 **House of the Dear Ladies** The Ladies of Warwick Gardens: see above, ch. 2, n. 3. the privately printed verses were *Schoolboy Lyrics*, Lahore, 1881, a work carried out without RK's knowledge. They have been substantially reprinted in *Early Verse*, 1900, but are not part of the "definitive" edition of RK's verse.

3 **'in they broke, those people of importance'** Browning, "One Word More," line 56.

4 **Philadelphia lawyers** RK has especially in mind the eminent collector, Ellis Ames Ballard (1861–1938), who was, in fact, a Philadelphia lawyer.

5 **a spectacled school-boy bringing up the rear** This sketch is in the Kipling papers at Sussex and has been published by Andrew Rutherford in his edition of RK's *Early Verse by Rudyard Kipling* (Oxford, Clarendon Press, 1986).

6 **a woman** Perhaps RK's friend, Edith Plowden, whom he thanks in a

letter of [July 22, 1925] for returning "verses" (MS, Kipling Papers). But several of RK's notebooks containing early verse survived, unburned, among his papers: See Andrew Rutherford (ed.), *Early Verse by Rudyard Kipling*, p. 23 and notes.

7 **'lesser breeds without the (Copyright) law'** Cf. "Recessional," line 22.

8 **a series of Anglo-Indian tales** That is, the *Plain Tales from the Hills.*

9 **the naming of the series** After this sentence RK wrote: "Here I began to feel my feet." CK deleted it in order to avoid a comic connection with the next sentence: "They were originally much longer . . ." (CK to H.A. Gwynne, November 13, 1936: MS, Dalhousie University).

10 **the chimaera ... secondary causes *in vacuo*** One of the books that Pantagruel discovers in the library of Saint Victor in Paris is titled *Quaestio subtilissima, utrium Chimera in vacuo bombinans possit comedere secundas intentiones, et fuit debatuta per decem hebdomadas in concilio Constantiensis* ("Most subtle question, whether the Chimera, buzzing in a vacuum, can eat its secondary causes, which was debated for ten weeks by the Council of Constance"): Rabelais, *Gargantua and Pantagruel*, II, vii.

11 **This is the doom . . . earnest or jest** evidently by RK.

12 **'The Phantom Rickshaw'** Published Christmas 1885 in *Quartette*, but written not later than October 1885 (*The Phantom 'Rickshaw*).

13 **'The Eye of Allah'** Published in September 1926 (*Debits and Credits*).

14 **'The Captive'** Published December 6, 1902 (*Traffics and Discoveries*).

15 **smarmed down** "To smooth down, as with pomade" (Eric Partridge, *Dictionary of Slang*, 8th edn. [New York, Macmillan, 1984]).

16 **C——** His schoolmaster, Crofts.

17 **'The Wish House'** Published October 1924 (*Debits and Credits*).

18 **his knowledge of Chaucer** The review, September 15, 1926, was by H.B. Charlton, Professor of English at the University of Manchester. Charlton blundered: it is not the wife of Bath but the Cook who has a "mormal" on his shin: see *Canterbury Tales*, General Prologue, lines 383–86.

19 **my worst slip is still underided** Many possibilities have been suggested, but none carries conviction. Like Milton's two-handed engine or Dr. Johnson's dried orange peel, RK's "worst slip" seems likely to remain an unsolved literary mystery.

20 **dentist ... near 'Naulakha'** This suggests that the episode belongs to 1893: RK had visited Canada with his father in August, and RK was frequently seeing a dentist in November 1893 (CK diary).

21 **summer ... of '13** June 28–July 1, 1913: he "had a wonderful time and next day begins a story of his experiences at the camp" (CK diary, July 1, 1913).

22 **Karroo** The semi-arid region of the western Cape Province.

23 **helio** Heliograph, an instrument for signalling by means of reflected light.

24 **'But Winnie ... poor dear!'** Not identified. "Winnie" presumably refers to Winston Churchill, captured by the Boers in 1899. He escaped shortly after his capture.

25 **Duke of Northumberland** Alan Ian Percy (1880–1930), 8th Duke of Northumberland, an officer in the Grenadier Guards. He did not succeed to the title until 1918.

26 **'psychic'** RK's sister Trix was "psychic," and he no doubt has her in mind in this passage about the "wreck of good minds." RK's protest that he is in no way "psychic" is bound to provoke skepticism in view of the element of the visionary or supernatural in his own work – in "They," or "The Wish House," or "A Madonna of the Trenches," to name no more. His struggle against the temptation of "psychic" vision is written out in the poem "En-Dor."

27 **'passed beyond the bounds of ordinance'** The phrase is attributed to William James, *The Principles of Psychology* (New York, Henry Holt, 1890), ch. 4, but probably comes from an earlier date.

28 **a ceremony at Westminster Abbey** July 19, 1922: RK had been a member of the War Graves Commission since its founding in 1917.

29 **Sir John Bland-Sutton** (1855–1936) President of the Royal College of Surgeons, 1923–26. He performed surgery on RK in 1922. In his autobiography, Bland-Sutton dates this episode on Boxing Day 1917; he says that it was RK who was "keen for a demonstration" that the gizzard could be heard at work (*The Story of A Surgeon* [London, Methuen, 1930], p. 146).

30 **glairy** "Viscid" or "slimy."

31 **what David did with the water ... battle** II Samuel 23: 15–17. He poured it out before the Lord, saying that it was "the blood of the men that went in jeopardy of their lives."

32 ***Tarzan of the Apes*** By Edgar Rice Burroughs, 1912, the first of some twenty-five volumes in the story of Tarzan.

33 **military go-as-you-pleases** I.e., off-duty occasions?

34 **'The Green Eye of the Little Yellow God'** By the monologuist J. Milton Hayes to music by Cuthbert Clarke, 1901.

35 **Mr. Oscar Wilde** (1854–1900) critic, playwright, poet, imprisoned for homosexual offenses in 1895.

36 **'... Richard Baxter'** The reference books uniformly attribute this to John Bradford (1510–55) rather than to Richard Baxter (1615–91).

37 **Mr. Dent Pitman** See p. 76.

38 **I repented ... but not too much** As a guess, one might venture that the plagiarist was E.K. Robinson (see p. 29), who founded and edited the magazine called *Country-Side* (1905–15) and who was in the business of writing "nature-studies."

39 **'Tupperism'** After the enormously popular *Proverbial Philosophy*, 1838, of the English poetaster, Martin Farquhar Tupper (1810–89).

40 **'East was East ... should meet'** "The Ballad of East and West," published in December 1889 (*Barrack-Room Ballads*).

41 **a political Calvinist** If this needs a commentary, RK must be referring to the Calvinistic doctrine of the depravity of human nature rather than to the doctrine of pre-destination; in politics, as in other forms of human behavior, there is no hope of regeneration.

42 **'Mandalay'** Published June 21, 1890 (*Barrack-Room Ballads*); it has had many musical settings.

43 **Irrawaddy Flotilla steamers** Referred to in "Mandalay" as "the old Flotilla."

44 **'The Islanders'** Published January 4, 1902 (*The Five Nations*).

45 **set of verses ... junior officers** "The Lesson," July 29, 1901 (*The Five Nations*).

46 **'And which it may subsequently transpire'** Line 24: "And which, it may subsequently transpire, will be worth as much as the Rand." Cf. "The Propagation of Knowledge," in which Beetle witholds "one or two promising 'subsequently transpireds'" for fear of distracting King" (*Debits and Credits*, p. 294).

47 **non-Aryan 'and German at that'** "The Islanders," *Punch*, January 15, 1902, p. 52. The article says in passing of "The Lesson" that it is Kipling's "worst." Roger Lancelyn Green (Harbord, VII, p. 3413) identifies the author as Rudolph Chambers Lehmann (1856–1919), on the staff of *Punch*, 1890–1919. Lehmann's father was Frederick, a native of Germany living in London and the good friend of G.H. Lewes and George Eliot. Rudolph Lehmann had been an active opponent of the Boer War.

48 **'... the abettors of disorder'** The Koran, Surah 2, verse 47, and Surah 5, verse 64.

49 **no dealings for a dozen years or so** RK had in fact published "The Irish Guards" in *The Times* on March 11, 1918, little more than two months before the episode he is about to describe.

50 **'The Old Volunteer'** Published over RK's name on May 27, 1918.

51 **in '17** 1918 not 1917.

52 **would retire from business** The prime suspect at first was Ian Colvin (1877–1938), a journalist and a friend of RK's. Colvin was interviewed by the private detective retained by *The Times*, but RK himself does not seem to have thought Colvin very likely. The documents in this episode are still among the archives of *The Times*.

53 **I shall never know** "My theory from the first was and is that the 'old Volunteer' was a Hun trick meant to discredit and annoy" (RK to Ian Colvin, July 2, 1918: MS, Syracuse University).

54 **a detective to my home** May 29, 1918: the detective was named H. Smale.

55 **Moberly Bell** Bell (1847–1911), manager of *The Times*. RK had come into conflict with him over *The Times*'s treatment of Cecil Rhodes in 1901, which is perhaps the crossing of bows alluded to. RK had been on familiar terms with Bell since 1894.

56 **Buckle** George Earle Buckle (1854–1935), editor of *The Times*, 1884–1912.

57 **a picture of the death of Manon Lescaut** By Pascal Dagnan-Bouveret, exhibited at the Salon of 1878 (see Carrington, 3rd edn, 1978, p. 614).

58 **'one book' of the Abbé Prévost** *Manon Lescaut*, 1731.

59 **_Roman Comique_** Paul Scarron, *Le Roman comique*, 1651–57.

60 **_The Light that Failed_** Published in 1891. For the relation of *Manon Lescaut* and *Le Roman comique* to *The Light that Failed* see the articles by Margaret Newsom in *Kipling Journal*, September 1975 and March 1976.

61 **metagrobolised** A word from Rabelais, where it means "to puzzle, to mystify." RK uses it with that sense in *Stalky & Co*. Here it seems to mean "transmogrified."

62 **a thing imposed from without** Cf. the comparison with Cervantes, p. 82. It is perhaps not necessary to note that RK is being elaborately ironic here.

63 **_The Cloister and the Hearth_** By Charles Reade, 1861. The extended metaphor of the novel as three-decker sailing ship goes back to RK's poem "The Three-Decker," 1894, on the rapidly-vanishing convention of the three-volume novel that dominated Victorian fiction. The gentle

mockery in that poem may perhaps be heard in this later variation of the same metaphor.

64 **mould-loft** The space in which a ship's hull is laid down.

65 **Waverley nib** A patented nib made by the firm of Macniven and Cameron since 1863.

66 **faded as a palimpsest** The ink-stand is still on RK's desk at Bateman's.

67 **'intolerable entrails'** Shakespeare, *Merry Wives of Windsor*, v, v, 162.

68 **Warren Hastings** (1732–1818) the great British pro-consul in India.

69 **fur seal . . . little fetishes** Some of these objects are still preserved at Bateman's. So are the globes mentioned below.

70 **a great airman** Sir (William) Geoffrey Hanson Salmond (1878–1933), a pioneer Army aviator, laid out the air route from Cairo to South Africa while commanding the Air Force in the Middle East.

"BAA BAA, BLACK SHEEP"

1 **"When I was . . . a better place"** Cf. Shakespeare, *As You Like It*, ii, iv, 17: "When I was at home, I was in a better place."

2 **Punch** RK uses "Punch and Judy" for himself and his sister again in "The Potted Princess," 1893, a story not collected until the Sussex Edition in 1938.

3 ***Surti*** A native of Surat.

4 **Nassick** A hill station about a hundred miles from Bombay; the Kipling family spent the hot months there during RK's childhood.

5 **Parel** A northern suburb of Bombay.

6 **Apollo Bunder** The chief dock in Bombay.

7 **"Sonny, my soul"** John Keble's "Evening Hymn," 1827, beginning "Sun of my soul."

8 **"Downe Lodge"** RK's close variant of the actual Lorne Lodge, 4 Campbell Road, Southsea, where he and his sister Trix were taken in 1871 and remained until 1877.

9 **a woman in black . . . oily in appearance** These three – Aunty Rosa, Uncle Harry, and Harry – are drawn from Mrs. Sarah Holloway, her husband Pryse Agar Holloway, and their son Harry: see *Something of Myself*, pp. 5–12.

10 **she's the *Brisk*** A ship called the *Brisk*, a sloop of ten guns, did take part in the battle of Navarino, 1827.

11 **a February morning to say Good-bye** RK and Trix were taken to Southsea in October 1871, but their parents did not leave for India until

mid-November (Hannah Macdonald's diary, Worcestershire and Herefordshire Record Office).

12 *The City of Dreadful Night* Not from James Thomson's *City of Dreadful Night* but from Arthur Hugh Clough's "Easter Day, Naples, 1849," lines 72–75, which read thus:

> Eat, drink, and die, for we are men deceived,
> Of all the creatures under heaven's wide cope
> We are most hopeless who had once most hope,
> We are most wretched that had most believed.

13 *Sharpe's Magazine* Identified by Roger Lancelyn Green as *Sharpe's London Magazine*, I (1845–46); the story of the griffin is a translation from La Motte Fouqué; the words "falchion," "ewe lamb," "base usurper," and "verdant mead" do not appear in it. See Harbord, I, 378.

14 *Frank Fairlegh* By Frank Smedley; it appeared in *Sharpe's Magazine* beginning in May 1846.

15 **contributed anonymously** Not "contributed" but simply reprinted; e.g., "The Owl," which goes back to the "Juvenilia" of Tennyson's *Poems*, 1830, is in *Sharpe's*, February 7, 1846.

16 **'62 Exhibition Catalogues** The International Exhibition of 1862, held at South Kensington.

17 *Cometh up as a Flower* Rhoda Broughton, *Cometh Up As a Flower*, 1867.

18 **"Our vanship…at Navarino"** This song, about which the story is so circumstantial, has not been identified.

19 **Uncle Harry is *dead*** "The circumstances of the kind old Captain's death are fictitious" (Alice Kipling Fleming, "Some Childhood Memories of Rudyard Kipling," *Chambers's Journal*, March 1939, p. 168).

20 **Journeys end … doth know** Shakespeare, *Twelfth Night*, II, iii, 44–45.

21 **a day-school** The "terrible little day-school" of *Something of Myself*, p. 45.

"MY FIRST BOOK"

1 **My chief** Stephen Wheeler: see *Something of Myself*, p. 26, above.

2 **saturated with Elia** See *Something of Myself*, above, p. 41.

3 **Sir Alfred Lyall** (1835–1911) Lieutenant Governor of the North West Provinces during RK's years in India. He published *Verses Written in India*, 1889.

4 **Hickey's *Bengal Gazette*** James Hicky published the first newspaper in India, *The Bengal Gazette*, 1780–82; it was suppressed by Warren Hastings.

5 **a couple of small books** *Echoes* and *Quartette*: see introductory note to this part.

6 **imprint on the title-page** The second edition was published by Thacker, Spink and Co., Calcutta, 1886.

7 **the book came to London** The first English edition was published by W. Thacker and Co. in 1890.

"AN ENGLISH SCHOOL"

1 ***School Song*** These verses are omitted from *Land and Sea Tales*.

2 **how all these things happened** Amyas Leigh is the hero of Charles Kingsley's historical novel of North Devon in Elizabethan days, *Westward Ho!* (1855); when the unsuccessful resort whose buildings later became the home of the United Services College was founded in 1863, its developers named it after Kingsley's novel, hoping that some of the glamor would rub off.

3 **the links** *Land and Sea Tales* (p. 256) adds "We played as a matter of course and thought nothing of it."

4 **champion amateur golfer of all England** Horace Gordon Hutchinson (1859–1932), English amateur champion in 1886 and 1887. He was at the College from 1874 to 1878.

5 **modelled on Haileybury lines** The text in *Land and Sea Tales* (p. 256) here adds "and our caps were Haileybury colours."

6 **a boy in the Canada Mounted Police** Harbord, 1, 416, conjectures that this was E.A. Braithwaite, who served in the Canadian Mounted Police and was afterwards a doctor.

7 **look after all his wealth till he came back** *Land and Sea Tales* (p. 259) reads: "look after all his wealth till he could attend to it; and was a little impatient when the Head pointed out that executors and trustees and that sort of bird wouldn't hand over the cash in that casual way."

8 **saved a boy's life from diphtheria** See "A Little Prep" in *Stalky & Co.* for this episode.

9 **'All our men' . . . two hundred now** This paragraph is omitted in *Land and Sea Tales* (pp. 259–60), and this passage substituted: "They were, perhaps, a shade rough sometimes. One very curious detail, which I have never seen or heard of in any school before or since, was that the Army Class, which meant the Prefects, and was generally made up of

boys from seventeen and a half to nineteen or thereabouts, was allowed to smoke pipes (cigarettes were then reckoned the direct invention of the Evil One) in the country outside the College. One result of this was that, though these great men talked a good deal about the grain of their pipes, the beauty of their pouches, and the flavour of their tobacco, they did not smoke to any ferocious extent. The other, which concerned me more directly, was that it went much harder with a junior whom they caught smoking than if he had been caught by a master, because the action was flagrant invasion of their privilege, and, therefore, rank insolence – to be punished as such. Years later, the Head admitted that he thought something of this kind would happen when he gave the permission. If any Head-master is anxious to put down smoking nowadays, he might do worse than give this scheme a trial."

10 **behaved like a hero** This was, according to Harbord, 1, 416, a boy named Frank Owen, at USC 1878–81. Louis Riel (1844–85) led a rebellion against the Canadian government in Saskatchewan in 1884–85; he was defeated and executed.

11 **The first officer . . . should be so** This sentence omitted in *Land and Sea Tales* (p. 260). The officer was Lt. Robert Dury, killed November 1885. Dury was at USC 1878–81.

12 **This meant . . . cuts and guards** This sentence omitted in *Land and Sea Tales* (p. 260).

13 **saloon-pistols** "Light firearms for firing at short range" (*Oxford English Dictionary*).

14 **nothing happened** "except punishment at the other end for all concerned" added, *Land and Sea Tales* (p. 262).

15 **fished them out with umbrellas** "They were cooked by hand afterwards in all the studies and form-rooms till you could have smelt us at Exeter" added, *Land and Sea Tales* (p. 263).

16 **three cuts . . . from the Captain of the Games** "delivered cold in the evening" added, *Land and Sea Tales* (p. 263).

17 **beautiful rule for fat boys and loafers** "The only unfairness was that a Master could load you with an imposition to be shown up at a certain hour, which, of course, prevented you from playing and so secured you a licking in addition to the imposition. But the head always told us that there was not much justice in the world, and that we had better accustom ourselves to the lack of it early" added, *Land and Sea Tales* (pp. 263–64).

18 **'Great John Ridd' had been educated there** Ridd, the hero of

R.D. Blackmore's *Lorna Doone* (1869), a story of Devon. Blundell's School at Tiverton was founded in 1604.

19 **three-horse brake** A brake, or break, is a large wagon.

20 **It's a way we have . . . Which nobody can deny!** These lines also appear at the end of "A Little Prep"; they are parodied in "The Flag of Their Country," and are referred to in "Slaves of the Lamp, Part I," all from *Stalky & Co.*

21 **'The Rivals'** In his last year at USC RK played Sir Anthony Absolute in Sheridan's *The Rivals*, December 20, 1881: see G.C. Beresford, *Schooldays with Kipling* (New York, Putnam, 1936), pp. 177–80.

22 **story of the School for the past twelve months** Beresford, *Schooldays with Kipling* (pp. 182–83), says that RK contributed this "school-saga" for 1881, but that "every line of this peerless but not deathless ode has perished."

23 **'Story of a Short Life'** Juliana Horatia Ewing, *The Story of a Short Life*, 1885; originally published in *Aunt Judy's Magazine*, 1882. The "tug-of-war" hymn, sung by the soldiers in church in the story, is Heber's "The Son of God Goes forth to War." See Harbord, I, 418.

24 **'Eric, or Little by Little'** Frederic William Farrar, *Eric, or Little by Little*, 1858; a school-story repeatedly made fun of in *Stalky & Co.*

25 **and meeting . . . good for boys** The end of the sentence revised in *Land and Sea Tales* (p. 267) to read "and things of that kind, which, whatever people say nowadays, are not helpful for boys at work."

26 **every quantity** "Latin quantity" in *Land and Sea Tales* (p. 268).

27 **his contribution to the study of Horace** RK's translation of Horace, *Odes*, III, ix, was first published in the *United Services College Chronicle*, July 24, 1882. See Andrew Rutherford, *Early Verse by Rudyard Kipling* (Oxford, Clarendon Press, 1986) pp. 160–61.

28 **'Imaginary Conversations'** By Walter Savage Landor, 1824–29.

29 **Marco Polo and Mandeville** omitted in *Land and Sea Tales* (p. 269).

30 **And the Head . . . college magazines** This sentence revised in *Land and Sea Tales* (p. 269), to read: "And the Head would sometimes tell him about the manners and customs of the Russians, and sometimes about his own early days at college, when several people who afterwards became great, were all young, and the Head was young with them, and they wrote wonderful things in college magazines."

31 **started the notion** The received account is that Cormell Price revived the school paper in order to give RK the experience of writing for it and editing it. See *Something of Myself*, p. 24.

32 **times and seasons** "odd times and seasons" in *Land and Sea Tales* (p. 270).

33 **consider it as literature** Possibly RK means "Life in the Corridor," *United Services College Chronicle*, June 30, 1881; but the passage is a better description of the account he would write in "Slaves of the Lamp, Part I" (*Stalky & Co.*).

34 **shiny to the very last** RK uses this episode in "The Satisfaction of a Gentleman," *Stalky & Co.*

35 ***Fors Clavigera*** The boy was Beresford (see pp. 18–19). *Fors Clavigera* is the series of pamphlets attacking capitalism published by John Ruskin from 1871 to 1884. See also "Slaves of the Lamp, Part I," in *Stalky & Co.*, where M'Turk is reported to be reading *Fors Clavigera*.

36 **Irishman** Altered to "person" in *Land and Sea Tales* (p. 272).

37 **and the Study . . . Devonshire cream** In *Land and Sea Tales* (p. 273), the sentence after "written" reads "and sent up under a *nom de plume*, and the Study caroused on chocolate and condensed milk and pilchards and Devonshire cream and voted poetry a much sounder business than it looks." The verses were RK's sonnet "Two Lives," published in *The World*, November 8, 1882 (Rutherford, *Early Verse by Rudyard Kipling*, p. 137). RK was already in India by the time the poem appeared in print, but perhaps he had been paid for it in time to spend the money at Westward Ho! before leaving school, about July 1882.

38 **'Aladdin'** A pantomime by H.J. Byron, 1861; it figures in "Slaves of the Lamp, Part I," and is described by Beresford, *Schooldays with Kipling* (pp. 103–8).

39 **Last year . . . if we were caught** The paragraph reads thus in *Land and Sea Tales* (p. 274): "A little later, when he was a subaltern in India, he was bitten by a mad dog, went to France to be treated by Pasteur, and came out again in the heart of the hot weather to find himself almost alone in charge of six hundred soldiers, and his Drill Sergeant dead and his office clerk run away, leaving the Regimental books in the most ghastly confusion. Then we happened to meet; and as he was telling his story there was just the same happy look on his face as when he steered us down the lanes with the certainty of a superior thrashing if we were caught." Dunsterville describes the mad dog incident in his *Stalky's Reminiscences* (London, Jonathan Cape, 1928), pp. 106–7.

40 **Burmese dacoit** A *dacoit* is one of a gang of robbers.

41 **And the best boy . . . he was dead** In *Land and Sea Tales* (p. 275) the paragraph reads "And the best boy of them all—who could have become anything—was wounded in the thigh as he was leading his men

up the ramp of a fortress. All he said was, 'Put me up against that tree and take my men on'; and when his men came back he was dead."

42 **Ten or eleven years ago, when the Queen** "Ages and ages ago, when Queen Victoria" in *Land and Sea Tales* (p. 276).

43 **And some of us . . . in the grass** This stanza omitted in *Land and Sea Tales*. RK's poem (only five of its seven stanzas appear in the *Youth's Companion* text of "An English School") first appeared in the *United Services College Chronicle*, March 20, 1882; the attempt on the Queen's life took place on March 2. Critics have never agreed about whether the verses are to be taken as "serious" or as a mere schoolboy exercise. The most interesting remark on "Ave Imperatrix" occurs in some MS notes that RK made for the use of André Chevrillon when the latter was preparing his study of RK in *Three Studies in English Literature* (London, Heinemann, 1923). Speaking of the "imperial" character of USC, RK writes: "how far that school's life impressed me you can judge from a set of verses written when I was sixteen and published in the school paper. It seems to set the key for the rest of my writings" (MS, n.d. [*c.* 1920?], Kipling Papers). Chevrillon adapts RK's remark thus in *Three Studies*: "Let us mark this word 'Empire' uttered by a school-boy. For the first time it is used in the sense it has retained on English lips since the appearance of Kipling's great popular poems. These verses were called *Ave Imperatrix*. Now that nearly forty years have passed the poet is convinced that there and then, under the influence of 'Westward Ho!' the general direction of his life-work was determined" (p. 13).

44 **And I think . . . we kept our word** "And there are one or two places in the world that can bear witness how the School kept its word" in *Land and Sea Tales* (p. 276).

RUDYARD KIPLING'S DIARY, 1885

1 **'Village of the dead'** The story that became "The Strange Ride of Morrowbie Jukes," published in *Quartette* at the end of 1885.

2 **D'rozio's life** Henry Derozio, of mixed Indian and Portuguese blood, was one of the earliest "native" poets in English in India: *Poems* (Calcutta, 1827). RK's review of his life, if published, has not been found. The other items in this entry are: "A Week in Lahore," *CMG*, December 9, 1884, p. 6ab, and an unidentified item.

3 **Echoes** The volume of verse parodies published by RK and his sister Trix in 1884.

4 **Gordon Walker . . . Drake** T. Gordon Walker, Registrar of the

Chief Court; Miss and Master Roe were perhaps children of (Sir) Charles Arthur Roe (1841-1927), a judge in the Chief Court of the Punjab. W.R. Lawrence was then in the office of the Lieutenant-Governor. Lawrence (1857-1940) rose to a high position in the Indian Civil Service and was created a baronet in 1906. He remained a good friend of RK's; his recollections, *The India We Served*, 1928, was written with RK's assistance and partly in response to RK's urging. Vi Marshall I have not identified; Drake is perhaps Lieutenant F.R. Drake, Royal Artillery, stationed at Lahore.

5 **Bernhardy Ruchwaldy** not identified.

6 **Capture of Bhamo . . . Burma** *CMG*, January 2, p. 1b.

7 **Aitchisons** Sir Charles Aitchison (1832-96) was Lieutenant-Governor of the Punjab, 1882-87.

8 **watery sort of special** RK's "special" on the durbar is "Proclamation Day in Lahore," *CMG*, January 3, p. 3ad. This is signed "E.M." for "Esau Mull," a pseudonym that RK had been using since early in 1884 ("Mull," short for "mulligatawny," is a nickname for residents of Madras).

9 **Jullundur** Seventy-five miles east and south of Lahore.

10 **Massey** Captain Charles Francis Massy, Deputy Commissioner and District Judge, Jullundur.

11 **Jul[lundur] Special** "A Mofussil Exhibition," *CMG*, January 7, p. 3ac.

12 **The Week in Lahore** "A Week in Lahore," January 6, pp. 5d-6a.

13 **Lahore Serai** RK seems not to have carried out the idea for this article, though he later published an account of a visit to the Sultan Serai in Lahore (*CMG*, January 19, 1886: Thomas Pinney, *Kipling's India* [London, Macmillan, 1986], pp. 141-46). A *serai* is an inn or resthouse for travellers and their animals built around a courtyard.

14 **Saw very good review in Calcutta review of Echoes** *Calcutta Review*, 80, iv-vii: "A most quaint, original and altogether charming little volume of Anglo-Indian verse. The two authors are, we believe, two children."

15 **skit . . . on Punjab police** "Twenty Years After, (Or What It May Come To)," January 9, p. 3d.

16 **verses on the Indian Associations memorial** "On a Recent Memorial," *Englishman*, January 9 (Andrew Rutherford [ed.], *Early Verse by Rudyard Kipling 1879-1889* [Oxford, Clarendon Press, 1986], pp. 263-64). The *Englishman* was a Calcutta paper.

17 **'Monograph on Punjab Cotton'** Untitled scrap, "An interesting

monograph on the cotton manufactures," *CMG*, January 9, p. 1d.

18 **Growse's book of Bulandshahr** Notice of F.S. Growse, *Bulandshahr, or Sketches of an Indian District, Political, Historical and Social* (Benares, 1884), *CMG*, January 17, p. 1d.

19 **Ferel** J.B. Ferrell and the Gaiety Theatre Company performed at the Railway Theatre, Lahore, January 8–17 (*CMG*, January 8–17).

20 **obituary scrap . . . Bengal and Punjab Museums** Untitled scrap, "Bishop Jackson, whose death," *CMG*, January 9, p. 1b; untitled scrap, "The population of Lahore," *CMG*, January 9, p. 1ab.

21 **Burmese Arts** Untitled scrap, "A paternal government," *CMG*, January 12, p. 1cd.

22 **Blockade of formosa . . . Ploughing Match** Untitled scrap, "Blockade-running," *CMG*, January 12, p. 1bc; untitled scrap, "Another disgraceful attempt," *CMG*, January 12, p. 1b; untitled scrap, "At a recent ploughing competition," *CMG*, January 12, p. 1b.

23 **scrap on O'Donovan Rossa** Untitled scrap, "When H.M.S. '*Dotterel*' was mysteriously blown up," *CMG*, January 13, p. 1c. Jeremiah O'Donovan Rossa (1831–1915), Fenian newspaper editor; after being jailed in Ireland for treason, went to the U.S. where he edited the *United Irishman*.

24 **Notes of the week** "A Week in Lahore," *CMG*, January 14, pp. 5d–6ab.

25 **H.A.B. Piffard his poems** Review of H.A.B. Piffard, *Poems* (Calcutta, 1885?), *CMG*, January 16, p. 3ab. RK calls the work "very commonplace."

26 **2nd Edition of Echoes** No second edition was published, though, as the diary shows, RK thought seriously of it.

27 **Among the Houhnyms** Nothing further is known of this item, at least under this title. RK published "Among the Houyhnhnms" as no. 14 of *Letters of Marque*, *Pioneer*, February 4, 1888, but that can have only the title in common with this item from 1885.

28 **Coffee Palace** RK wrote skeptically of the idea of a "coffee palace" in Lahore as a place of temperate refreshment for the soldiers; Thomas Atkins, RK added, called such places "tract-traps" (*CMG*, January 14, p. 6a). The Reverend F.J. Montgomery was chaplain to the troops at Lahore.

29 **Bombay cholera Hospitals** Perhaps the item under "Telegraphic Intelligence" regarding the location of a cholera hospital (*CMG*, January 16, 1885, p. 1a).

30 **Wrote scrap . . . Lahore Burglary** Untitled scrap, "On Wednesday

last, it was reported in Bombay," *CMG*, January 19, p. 1cd; untitled scrap, "Messrs. Thomas Cook and Son," *CMG*, January 19, p. 1b; notice of Bombay directories, *CMG*, January 19, p. 5c; "Burglary at the Lawrence Hall," *CMG*, January 19, p. 6a.

31 **W.R.W.M.** Not identified: see also February 12.

32 **Jellalabad horse fair ... E. About** Untitled scrap, "The young Nawab of Mamdot," *CMG*, January 20, p. 1b; "The Gaiety Company in Lahore," *CMG*, January 20, p. 6a; "An Indian Press Guide," *CMG*, January 20, p. 5a; "A Week in Lahore," *CMG*, January 21, pp. 5d–6ab; untitled scrap, "The death of Edmond About," *CMG*, January 20, p. 1c. Edmond About, the French writer, is praised for the variety of his accomplishments.

33 **one small para to show for it** Not identified.

34 **Moon of other Days and Maxims of Hafiz** "The Moon of Other Days," *Pioneer*, December 16, 1884 (*Departmental Ditties*); details of the publication of "Certain Maxims of Hafiz" in the *Pioneer* are not established; the "Maxims" are in *Departmental Ditties*. A gold mohur was worth 15 rupees – very modest payment.

35 **[?]** Three letters – SRH? – not quite legible.

36 **Bombay Club ... help of an Atlas** Untitled scrap, "The Bombay Club have outgrown," *CMG*, January 24, p. 1c; untitled scrap, "Their Royal Highnesses' visit to Chandernagore," *CMG*, January 24, p. 1c; untitled scrap, "Thongwa, British Burma," *CMG*, January 24, p. 1b; untitled scrap, "The Louisade Archipelago," *CMG*, January 24, p. 1b.

37 **weekly telegrams to India** Untitled scrap, "A conference of enlightened English," *CMG*, January 26, p. 1d.

38 *Journal de Saint Petersburg* An official Russian paper, published in French.

39 **fairly satisfactory** See the end of the diary: "Thacker Spink and Co's Estimate."

40 **notes of the week** "A Week in Lahore," *CMG*, January 28, pp. 5d–6a.

41 **Burne** D.E. Burne, manager of the Lahore branch of the Bengal Bank; the farewell dinner to be given to him on his transfer to Bombay is noted in RK's "A Week in Lahore," *CMG*, January 28, p. 6a.

42 **Russian translation** "The Russians in Central Asia," *CMG*, January 28, p. 3cd.

43 **Scraps on Accidents ... Hume's vegetarianism** Untitled scrap, "Accidents on Indian railways," *CMG*, January 29, p. 1a; untitled scrap, "The dynamitards have really begun," *CMG*, January 29, p. 1c;

untitled scrap, "Mr. A.O. Hume is at present in Bombay," *CMG*, January 29, p. 1c. Allan Octavian Hume (1829–1912) was the organizer of the Indian National Congress.

44 **Porter's speech at Madras** Untitled scrap, "They have a Mr. McNabb in Madras," *CMG*, February 2, p. 1c.

45 **article in Novoe Vremya . . . Journal of Indian Art** Untitled scrap, "The mania for fancy bazars has spread to St. Petersburg," *CMG*, February 3, p. 1c; untitled scraps, "The fourth number of the '*Journal of Indian Art*'," and "Rustic Ornamentation in the Punjab," *CMG*, February 3, p. 1cd.

46 **The Week in Lahore done** "A Week in Lahore," *CMG*, February 4, p. 6ab.

47 **O'Donovan Rossa and two locals** Untitled scrap, "The worthy O'Donovan Rossa," *CMG*, February 5, p. 1cd. A "local" is an item appearing in the "Lahore and Mian Mir" section, in the back pages of the *CMG*. One of the two that RK mentions must be the notice of "The Lahore Amateurs" at the Railway Theatre, *CMG*, February 5, 1885, p. 6a. Nothing else appears in the *CMG* around this date that can plausibly be attributed.

48 **Dr. G. Le Bon . . . Indian Crime** Untitled scrap, "Dr. Gustave Le Bon," *CMG*, February 6, p. 1b; untitled scrap, "Sir Rivers Thompson's speech," *CMG*, February 6, p. 1cd; untitled scrap, "An ex-superintendent of the Calcutta Detective Department," *CMG*, February 6, p. 1b.

49 **G[eorge] W. A[llen]** Chief proprietor of the *CMG* and of the *Pioneer*.

50 **did not go in** Untitled scrap, "The approaching 'Parliament of man and federation of the world'," *CMG*, February 9, p. 1c. *Volapuk* is a "universal" language propagated about 1879.

51 **Mem. eris cum [?] Thursd. [?]** The two bracketed question marks stand for two undecipherable signs made by RK, resembling capital "T"s combined with other lines. The Latin may be translated "Remember. You will be with [?]." Cf. Thursday, February 12.

52 **Hiatus valde deflendus** "A gap (or an interruption) greatly to be lamented."

53 **Typhoid at Home** "Typhoid at Home," *CMG*, February 14, pp. 2bd–3a (Pinney, *Kipling's India*, pp. 69–77); an account of the conditions under which Lahore got its milk.

54 **translation from the Invalide Russe** For the translation, see below, February 13.

55 **Week in Lahore** "A Week in Lahore," *CMG*, February 11, pp. 5d–6ac.

56 **Rangoon . . . Charitable Society** Untitled scrap, "We publish elsewhere, to-day, a letter," *CMG*, February 12, p. 1d; untitled scrap, "The frauds on the Calcutta District Charitable Society," *CMG*, February 13, p. 1cd.

57 **spiritualistic seance . . . Lahore City** This is not the story of the same title in *Wee Willie Winkie* but an unfinished story, the MS of which is now in the Berg Collection, New York Public Library. The MS is written in two parallel columns: the right-hand column is the journal, dated 1884, of a narrator tentatively called Duncan Parrenness (a name that RK had used before in a dream-story and evidently used now only until a better one should occur – the name as it stands at the head of the journal has been lined out); the left-hand column, headed "Incidental Digressions," is a complex series of comments on the events of the journal, some in the person of Parrenness, some in the person of his mistress, and some in the person of Kipling, or the writer. The main event of the journal is a dream in which Parrenness and his mistress, who are on the eve of running away together from her husband in Simla, are killed in a fall over a cliff. Their ghosts watch all the events that follow, and continue to behave just as they had before. Evidently RK's new idea was to have the ghosts give an account of themselves through a medium rather than through Parrenness's description of a dream.

58 **W.R.W.M [ ]** The final item in this list of unexplained initials seems related to the indecipherable sign used in February 6. "W.R.W.M." first occurs in January 18.

59 **Musketry schools . . . notes of the week** Untitled scrap, "Two musketry schools for the instruction," *CMG*, February 14, p. 1c; "Colonel Prejvalsky's Explorations in Thibet," *CMG*, February 16, p. 4ac; I do not find anything on Bellew's Sanitary Report. H.W. Bellew was Sanitary Commissioner of the Punjab.

60 **Rai Kanega Lall and design for town hall . . . tomorrow** The first is unidentified. The second is an untitled scrap, "It appears to have been decided," *CMG*, February 26, p. 1d.

61 **annexation of corea** Untitled scrap, "This week's mail brings us the news," *CMG*, February 16, p. 1d.

62 **Rosa Towers Comp** The Rosa Towers Company opened in *Lady Audley's Secret* and *Le Chalet* at the Railway Theatre, Lahore, on the 14th.

63 **critique on Company . . . Colonel Olcott** "The Rosa Towers Company," *CMG*, February 17, p. 6bc; untitled scrap, "Colonel

Olcott," *CMG*, February 19, p. 1b. Olcott was Madame Blavatsky's co-adjutor in the work of Theosophy in India.

64 **Miss Lawrie's marriage** Miss Lawrie, daughter of the Lahore surgeon, married W.O. Clark, Deputy-Commissioner, Lahore, on February 16 (*CMG*, February 18, p. 6b).

65 **Notes of the week** "A Week in Lahore," *CMG*, February 18, p. 6ac.

66 **published in the Northwest** Untitled scrap, "The character of the two hundred books," *CMG*, February 20, p. 1b.

67 **'buttered' shamelessly** "'Drink' at the Railway Theatre," *CMG*, February 20, p. 6a. The play is an adaptation of Zola's *L'Assommoir* by Charles Reade, and was a sensation in London in the late 1870s, where RK saw it as a schoolboy; his recreation of the climactic scene of *delirium tremens* is described by G.C. Beresford, *Schooldays with Kipling* (New York, Putnam, 1936), p. 104. The *CMG* review, while calling it "a thoroughly nasty and in every respect unworthy-of-being-acted-by-so-good-a-company-play," says of the two leading women, Miss Rosa and Miss Katie Towers, that they "were wicked, pathetic, proud and pitiful in turns with the most praiseworthy diligence and good taste."

68 **Note that butter paid. Very nice woman. V.** These words appear to have been added later.

69 **Hudson's Surprise party** "Hudson's Surprise Party," *CMG*, February 21, p. 6a. This was a variety show at the Railway Theatre.

70 **To Hudson again** Untitled notice, "The second night (Friday) of Mr. Hudson's Surprise Party," *CMG*, February 23, p. 6a.

71 **to the Pioneer** Published as "In the Spring Time," *Pioneer*, March 20, p. 7a (collected in *Departmental Ditties* as "In Spring Time").

72 **Fallon's Hindustani . . . St Petersburgh** Untitled scrap, "The second portion of the late Dr. Fallon's '*Dictionary of Hindu Proverbs*'," *CMG*, March 5, p. 1d. The other item is unidentified.

73 **M. Blavatsky . . . Notes of the week** Untitled scrap, "During her recent visit to Europe, Madame Blavatsky," *CMG*, February 24, p. 1c; untitled notice, "The third performance of Hudson's Surprise," *CMG*, February 24, p. 5d; "A Week in Lahore," *CMG*, February 25, p. 6ac.

74 **Lawrie** The Lahore surgeon.

75 **Burmah Annexation Company scrap** Untitled scrap, "Like the Scotch editor of old," *CMG*, March 3, p. 1cd.

76 **Shadera Picnic** Shahdera or Shahdara is a district of Lahore between the walled city and the river, where gardens surround the tomb of Jahangir.

77 **xxx [?] [?] rh** Indecipherable notation.

78 **anent stamps** Untitled scrap, "The Postmaster General is unburdening his mind," *CMG*, March 5, p. 1c.

79 **Notes of the week** "A Week in Lahore," *CMG*, March 4, p. 6ac.

80 **Times of India** "Anglo-Indian Verse," *Times of India* (Bombay), February 27, p. 4f. A laudatory notice that says the volume "has attracted a considerable amount of private interest among all who are acquainted with the artistic family from which it emanates."

81 **Umballa Conference 1869** "The Amballa Conference, a Retrospect," *CMG*, March 6, p. 3ac.

82 **Dufferin's cloture** "L--d D-ff-r-n's Cloture," *CMG*, March 6, p. 5c (Rutherford, *Early Verse*, pp. 264-65).

83 **'Mother Maturin'** The novel on which RK worked through the rest of his Indian days; it was never published, but is supposed to have furnished some part of *Kim*. In a letter of February 19, 1884, RK says that he is busy with a "novel of sorts" (Kipling Papers), but nothing more is known of this, and it is impossible to say whether it had any connection with "Mother Maturin."

84 **Shadera xxx** See the entry for March 1.

85 **another note** A paragraph in "A Week in Lahore" on the neglected graves of some British soldiers near the tomb of Jahangir. On his visit to Hong Kong in 1889 RK remembered these graves: "My mind went back to a neglected graveyard a stone's throw from Jehangir's tomb in the gardens of Shalimar [Shahdera], where the cattle and the cowherd look after the last resting-places of the troops who first occupied Lahore" (*From Sea to Sea*, Letter 9).

86 **Here came . . . no remembrance** These two and the next sentence are written in a large hand over two pages, covering the space for March 9 through 15. The spaces for March 16 through 20 are blank. RK's journey to Rawalpindi, Peshawar, and Jumrood, at the mouth of the Khyber Pass, was undertaken as a special correspondent for the *CMG* to report a meeting between Lord Dufferin, the Viceroy, and Abdur Rahman, Amir of Afghanistan, in which the British sought an alliance with the Amir against Russia. This was the most important occasion on which RK served as a "special," and occupied him from the end of March until the middle of April. He produced thirteen articles for the *CMG*, working under miserable conditions: it rained nearly every day, the Amir delayed coming, and both tempers and diplomatic arrangements began to spoil.

87 **'City of Evil Countenances'** An account of Peshawar, *CMG*, April 1 (Pinney, *Kipling's India*, pp. 81-85).

88 **1st Special on Pindi camp** "The Rawal Pindi Camp," *CMG*, March 24, p. 3c.

89 **second special of To Meet the Amir** "To Meet the Ameer," *CMG*, March 26, p. 3cd.

90 **Second special 'to meet the Amir'** "To Meet the Ameer," *CMG*, March 28, p. 2bd. RK here loses count of his specials: this is the third, not the second. See above, note 89.

91 **Third special to meet the Amir** "To Meet the Ameer," *CMG*, March 31, pp. 2cd-3a. This was the fourth, not the third.

92 **To meet the Amir three columns** "To Meet the Ameer," *CMG*, April 1, pp. 2d-3ab (Pinney, *Kipling's India*, pp. 85-91).

93 **To meet the Amir** "To Meet the Ameer," *CMG*, April 2, pp. 2cd-3a. This item carries the dateline of March 30-31 (Pinney, *Kipling's India*, pp. 91-95).

94 **Wrote yet another Special** "The Rawul Pindi Durbar," *CMG*, April 6, pp. 5ad-6a: dated April 1, 2, and 3.

95 **special two and a half cols long** "The Rawalpindi Durbar," *CMG*, April 7, p. 3bd (Pinney, *Kipling's India*, pp. 95-97).

96 **Special of three columns on review** "The Rawalpindi Durbar," *CMG*, April 8, pp. 3bd-4a (Pinney, *Kipling's India*, pp. 97-104).

97 **Two column special today** ["The Rawalpindi Durbar"], *CMG*, April 9, pp. 3d-4a.

98 **Two and a half columns about the big Durbar** "The Rawalpindi Durbar," *CMG*, April 10, p. 3bd.

99 Thursday 9 April-Wednesday 29 April RK was back in Lahore by April 15 in the wake of the Viceroy's visit to the city. He contributed an article to the *CMG* on the Viceroy's visit with the dateline of April 17, and must shortly thereafter have gone to Simla.

100 **Left Simla...to Kotgurh** This tour, RK says, was occasioned by his having been ill with dysentery: "I was sent off for rest along the Himalaya-Thibet road in the company of an invalid officer and his wife" (*Something of Myself*, p. 36). DeBrath was assistant engineer on the Rajputana-Malwa State Railway, Nasirabad. Their itinerary was east from Simla to Theog (about 15 miles), then north to Kotgarh, via Matiana and Narkanda, another 15 or 20 miles; from Kotgarh, instead of going on north-east to Rampur, they dropped off south-east to Bagi, and then doubled back. The route took them over 3,000 meters high.

101 **saw the Pardre** Not identified.

102 **Noor Ali cut open coolies eye** For RK's later summary of the events of May 8 and 9, see *Something of Myself*, pp. 36-37.

103 **Elisha the Tishbite** II Kings 2:24: "And there came forth two she bears out of the wood, and tare forty and two children of them." RK has confused Elijah the Tishbite with Elisha.

104 **Ibbetson's** (Sir) Denzil Ibbetson (1847–1908), the Director of Public Instruction, Lahore; afterwards Lieutenant-Governor of the Punjab.

105 Wednesday 13 May–Sunday 24 May RK resumed writing by May 12: his "Simla Notes" in the *CMG*, June 16, have that dateline. But he was obviously working under very low pressure when more than a month intervened between a dateline and publication.

106 **scar on cheek** RK was suffering from "Lahore sores" and regarded himself as "scarred for life" (to Edith Macdonald, July 30–August 1, 1885: MS, Library of Congress).

107 Tuesday 26 May–Monday 13 July RK was in Simla for all of this unrecorded period, sending only a few notes and reviews to the *CMG*.

108 **Damn Thacker Spink & Co!** RK and Thacker Spink quarrelled over *Echoes*: "I wound up my communications by a series of caricatures of a violent and personal kind. Then 'all smiles stopped together'" (to Cormell Price, September 19, 1885: MS, Library of Congress).

109 **the Walkers** (Sir) James Walker (1845–1927), a banker and a principal proprietor of the *CMG*. In saying that he "went over" to the Walkers, RK means that he took up his residence there. As he explains in a letter of July 30–[August 1] 1885, his father had just arrived in Simla and there was not room for all four of the family to work comfortably in their rented house (to Edith Macdonald: MS, Library of Congress). Walker's house in Simla, where RK had stayed in the summer of 1883, was called Kelvin Grove.

110 **Banjoe Hayes** A.E. Hayes, surgeon at Dagshai, a station only a few miles south of Simla.

111 **His Excellency** Erik Oakley Hogan, an infant of nine months, to whom RK's "His Excellency" is addressed (*CMG*, October 8, 1885): see September 25. The Hogans, who appear to have been staying with the Walkers, were presumably related to Mrs. Walker, who was born Lizzie Marion Hogan.

112 **'Pop' at Benmore** A hall of public assembly in Simla, with band concerts, a ballroom, and a skating rink.

113 **Jakko** The hill dominating Simla.

114 **Gempertz** Not identified.

115 **Light feet** J. Lightfoot, Chief Auditor, Sind, Punjab, and Delhi Railway, Lahore.

116 **the *Kers*** A.M. Ker was the Lahore agent of the Alliance Bank of

Simla, James Walker's bank.

117 **Levett Yeats** S.K. Levett-Yeats was Deputy-Examiner of Public Works Accounts in the government of the Punjab. He later acquired some reputation as a novelist. His wife was described by RK as the best of the company when she appeared as Helen of Troy at a Lahore costume ball (*CMG*, December 29, 1886).

118 **Tarleton Young** L. Tarleton Young, surgeon, and professor at the Lahore Medical College.

119 **LeMaistre** G.H. Lemaistre, Deputy-Examiner, Office of Audit and Account, Public Works Department, Lahore.

120 **the Wrenchs'** J.M. Wrench, personal assistant to the Chief Engineer, Lahore.

121 **Three small scraps** These have not been identified.

122 **Trial by Judge** Verses published in the *CMG*, September 16: Rutherford, *Early Verse*, pp. 286–92.

123 **Pinhey...blatant egoist** Untitled scrap, "Mr Justice Pinhey of the Bombay High Court," *CMG*, September 18, p. 1b; untitled scrap, "A 'confidential, private and very urgent address or memorial'," *CMG*, September 18, p. 1bc; untitled scrap, "The Indo-European Art Amateur," *CMG*, September 18, p. 1c.

124 **Mule Hunt at Poona and State of Bantam** Untitled scrap, "Poona seems to have been amused," *CMG*, September 23, p. 1c; untitled scrap, "Dahomey and its Amazons have taught," *CMG*, September 23, p. 1c.

125 **Unlimited Draw of Tick Boileau** Published at the end of the year in *Quartette*.

126 **Indian Railways scrap** Untitled scrap, "The returns of accidents on Indian railways," *CMG*, September 25, p. 1d.

127 **attack of measles** Perhaps RK means prickly heat.

128 **Three small scraps** These have not been identified.

129 **Wop of Europe** RK's cousin, Margaret Burne-Jones. "Wop" was a name they had used from childish days; after RK went to India, he became the "Wop of Asia" and she the "Wop of Albion," or, as here, the "Wop of Europe."

130 **Country bred racing in the Punjab** Untitled scrap, "A memorial is abroad for signature," *CMG*, September 29, p. 1bc.

131 **Hennicke's performance** See note 134.

132 **'Mummers wife'** George Moore's novel of that title had appeared in this year.

133 **Mrs. Todd** Not identified.

134 **Lahore Agricultural Gardens... Professor Hennicke** Untitled

scrap, "The annual report of the Lahore agri-horticultural gardens," *CMG*, September 30, p. 1cd; "Professor Hennicke in Lahore," *CMG*, September 30, p. 6a. Hennicke was an "illusionist" and conjurer.

135 **Punjab Notes and Queries . . . Sacrifice in Cochin** Untitled scrap, "The interest of '*Punjabi Notes and Queries*'," *CMG*, October 1, p. 1c; untitled scrap, "An interesting case of attempted human sacrifice," *CMG*, October 1, p. 1c.

136 **Parker** E.W. Parker, District Judge, and an officer of the Lahore Masonic Lodge to which RK later belonged.

137 **Slack** Not identified.

138 **Pavey** Not identified.

139 **French** Perhaps Edward Lee French, Assistant Superintendent of the Government Railway Police, Lahore.

140 **Suddhu is his name** Perhaps this was the germ of RK's "In the House of Suddhoo," originally published as "Section 420, I.P.C.," *CMG*, April 30, 1886 (*Plain tales from the Hills*).

141 **Prjevalski's exploration . . . Tulsi Ram Mohun** Untitled scrap, "The latest news which the Russian government," *CMG*, October 3, p. 1bc; untitled scrap, "A series of most interesting experiments," *CMG*, October 6, p. 1c; untitled scrap, "There flourish in England," *CMG*, October 6, p. 1c; untitled scrap, "In spite of a certain free and easy handling," *CMG*, October 6, p. 1cd.

142 **to the Unknown Goddess** Collected in *Departmental Ditties*.

143 **R.A.P.** Rupees, annas, pice.

144 **local** "A Murder in the City," *CMG*, February 19, p. 6a, on the revenge of a sepoy on his adulterous wife and her lover.

145 **Dis Aliter Visum** *Pioneer*, July 4, 1885 (uncollected).

146 **De Profundis** *CMG*, August 7, 1885 (Pinney, *Kipling's India*, pp. 118–24).

147 **City of Dreadful Night** *CMG*, September 10, 1885 (*Life's Handicap*).

148 **East and West** *CMG*, November 14, 1885 (reprinted in *United Services College Chronicle*, May 31, 1888).

149 **The Bungalow ballads** Published in the *Pioneer* in six numbers, August 15–September 5, 1885. Only two of the six were collected in *Departmental Ditties*.

150 **My rival** *Pioneer*, July 8, 1885 (*Departmental Ditties*).

151 **An Indignant protest** *CMG*, September 4, 1885 (Rutherford, *Early Verse*, pp. 281–82).

152 **Thacker Spink and Co's Estimate** For a second edition of *Echoes*: see the diary for January 14, 26, and 27.

INDEX

Page references should be understood to include related notes. Frequently, the name listed in the index will not appear on the page cited but will be found in one of the notes to that page (e.g., Stephen Wheeler, p. 173).

Kipling, Rudyard (*cont.*)
"'Drink' at the Railway Theatre," 205, 216
"Dymchurch Flit," 110
"East and West," 217
Echoes, 171, 176, 199, 200, 201, 203, 206
"The English Flag," 54
"The Eye of Allah," 122
"The Fires," 103
"Gunga Din," 127
"Hal o' the Draft," 110
"His Excellency," 212, 213
"Home," viii
"Hudson's Surprise Party," 205, 216
"If," 111
"An Indignant Protest," 217
"A Job Lot," 44
In Black and White, xi
"The Incarnation of Krishna Mulvaney," 48
"Indian Railway Library," 44–45, 66
"In Spring Time," 205–6
"In the Neolithic Age," 171
"In the Rukh," 67
"The Islanders," 129
Jungle Books, xiii, 7, 67–68, 122, 127
Just So Stories, 76
Kim, xiii, xxxii, 36, 81, 82–84, 111, 122, 132
Land and Sea Tales, 180
"The Lesson," 130
Letters of Marque, xi
Letters to the Family, 116
Life's Handicap, xiii
The Light that Failed, viii, ix, xiii, 132
"Little Foxes," 97
"L--d D-ff-r-n's Cloture," 207, 216, 217
"The Maltese Cat," xxxii
"Mandalay," 128–29
Many Inventions, xiii
"Mary, Pity Women!" 49
"A Mofussil Exhibition," 200, 214
"The Moon of Other Days," 202, 217

"Mother Maturin," 196, 207, 211
"Mrs. Bathurst," 60–61
"A Murder in the City," 216
"My Rival," 217
The Naulahka, xiii
"On a Recent Memorial," 200, 201, 214
The Phantom 'Rickshaw, xi, 122, 213
Plain Tales from the Hills, 41, 45, 66, 121, 133
"Primum Tempus," *see* "In the Neolithic Age"
"Proclamation Day in Lahore," 200, 214, 217
"The Pro-Consuls," 87
"Professor Hennicke in Lahore," 213
"Proofs of Holy Writ," xxx, 52
"The Propagation of Knowledge," 19
Puck of Pook's Hill, xviii, xxviii, xxix, xxxiii, materials for, 108–9; false starts, 109–10, 122
Quartette, 41, 122, 171, 176, 213
"Quo Fata Vocant," viii
"The Rawal Pindi Camp," 207
"The Rawalpindi Durbar," 208
"The Rawul Pindi Durbar," 208
"Recessional," 86, 121
Rewards and Fairies, xxix, xxxiii, 110, 111, 122
"The Rosa Towers Company," 205, 216
A School History of England, xiii n.
Schoolboy Lyrics, 120, 171
The Seven Seas, xiii
Soldiers Three, xi, xiii
"The Song of the Women," 56
"Souvenirs of France," viii, 17
The Smith Administration, xi
Stalky & Co., vii, xiii, xxxii, 18, 21, 79–80, 179, 180
"Steam Tactics," 104
The Story of the Gadsbys, xi, 43
"The Strange Ride of Morrowbie Jukes," 196, 199, 201, 202, 203, 204, 205
"Sussex," 81

Lincoln, Abraham, 76
Lion Comique, 49, 53
lions, on Rhodes estate, 98, 99–100
Lions, Masonic, *see* James Greenwood
Lock Hospitals, 34
Locomobile, 104
"Long, Long Indian Day," 175
Longfellow, Henry Wadsworth, 75;
    Hiawatha, 22
Lyall, Sir Alfred, 175

McClure, Samuel, 74, 79
McClure's Magazine, 74
McGill University, 116
Macmillan, xix
Macmillan's Magazine, 48
Madeira, 57
magazine, RK's plans for monthly,
    216
Magersfontein, 96
Mahmoud, *CMG* compositor, 174
Mammoth Comique, 49
Manchester Guardian, 123–24
Mandeville, Sir John, 189
Manon Lescaut, 132
Marco Polo, 189
Marcus Aurelius (horse), 69
Marlborough College, 183
Marshall, vi, 199
Martel de Janville, Comtesse de,
    "Gyp," *Autour du Mariage*, 43
Massy, Captain Charles, 200
Matabele Wars, 97, 101
Mauser, 91, 92
Mayo, Lord, 4
Meerut, 176
Meeta, 3, 4
Meinhold, Johann Wilhelm, *Sidonia the
    Sorceress*, 14
Melbourne, Victoria, 58
Melville, Sir James, *Memoirs*, xxxv
Mian Mir, cantonments, Lahore, 34
Mian Rukn Din, 26, 174, 176
Mickle, William Julius, "Cumnor
    Hall," 7
Miller, Joaquin, 24
Milner, Alfred, Lord, xv, 87
Montgomery, F.J. 202

Montesquieu, baron de, 75
Moor, S.S., 57, 58
Moore, George, *A Mummer's Wife*, 213
Moreau, Emile, 45
Morning Post (London), xix, xx
Morris, Mowbray, 48
Morris, William, 9, 10, 189
Morrison, Alfred, 82

Naples, 56
Napoleon, 12
National Observer, 49
Naulakha (RK's house in Vermont),
    68–69, 70, 74, 78, 124
Navarino, battle of, 5
New York City, xiv, 30
New York Times, xix
New Zealand, 23, 59–61
Newhaven, 80, 81
Newsom, Mrs. Margaret, xxxv
Nimrod, *see* Apperley
Nip and Tuck (Morgan horses), 69–70
Nobel Prize, xxvii, 117
Noor Ali, RK's servant, 209
North West Provinces Club,
    Allahabad, 42
Northumberland, Duke of, 125
Norton, Lily, 75
Norton, Charles Eliot, 75
Norton, Sarah, 75
Novoie Vremya (Moscow), 30, 204, 205

O'Donovan Rossa, Jeremiah, 201, 204
Olcott, Col. H.S., 205
Old Shikarri, *see* Leveson
"Old Volunteer, The," xxiv, 130–32
"Onward, Christian Soldiers," 187
Owen, Frank, 184
Oxford, 8; General Booth at, 62

Paardeberg, 91
P. & O. (Peninsular and Oriental
    Line), 5, 61, 139
Paget, F.E., *The Hope of the Katzekopfs*, 7
Panama, 73
Paris, 1878 Exhibition, 17, 132
Parker, E.W., 213
Parsees, 4